**Hassle-
Free
Homework**

Hassle-Free Homework

A six-week plan for parents and children

to take the pain out of homework

Faith Clark, Ph.D. Cecil Clark, Ph.D.

with Marta Vogel

Doubleday

New York Toronto London Sydney Auckland

Published by Doubleday, a division of
Bantam Doubleday Dell Publishing Group, Inc.
666 Fifth Avenue, New York, New York 10103

Doubleday and the portrayal of an anchor
with a dolphin are trademarks of
Doubleday, a division of Bantam Doubleday Dell Publishing Group, Inc.

Library of Congress Cataloging-in-Publication Data

Clark, Faith.
    Hassle-free homework : a six-week plan for parents and children to
take the pain out of homework / Faith Clark & Cecil Clark with Marta
Vogel. — 1st ed.
    p. cm.
    Bibliography: p.
    Includes index.
    1. Homework. 2. Study, Method of. 3. Education—Parent
participation. I. Clark, Cecil. II. Vogel, Marta. III. Title.
LB1048.C53 1989
371.3′028′12—dc19   89-1238
                                                CIP

ISBN 0-385-24684-6
ISBN 0-385-24685-4 (paperback)

Contents

Acknowledgments and Dedication

THIS BOOK IS like a much-desired first child whose birth was put off for too many years while the authors were making sure that they could provide the best for it. But the time has come to begin a family of writings. We, as the proud procreators, give full credit to the gene pool from which this volume sprang—the several thousand children and parents who have passed through our clinic and given us their trust. The validity of what we write is not based on theory alone; it lies in the families who have shared their personal struggles with us.

Thanks go to Pat McNees, the book's godmother, who helped prepare the original proposal. We thank our office staff, Karen Kneussl, Linda Tristano, and Sue Dolan for their hours of careful work nursing the infant through its neonatal period. We declare blanket appreciation to all others, including our worthy learning therapists, Winnie Conley, Gerry Mc-Whinney, Lori Harrington, Teri Hocking, and Donna Langford, who have added to the merit of this work by their critiques and anecdotes. Special thanks go to Winnie for her contribution to the initial development of the ideas in this book and for her constant encouragement and friendship. We are grateful to Gerry for his assistance with reviewing and selecting the computer programs recommended in this book.

Warm appreciation goes to our respective significant others, Dr. Robert Quinn and Cynthia Reid, for their support and understanding, especially on weekends, during the months of preparing the manuscript. We also thank our mothers, Marjorie Clark and Dell Thompson, for their encouragement and inspiration in teaching us how to learn.

THIS BOOK IS dedicated to Cameron and Jennifer Jones; Bo, Joel, Josh, and Jonathan Barrere; Ken and Jennifer Clark; and Anisa and Samira Ansari—all of whom enjoy Hassle-Free Homework almost all the time.

FAITH T. CLARK
CECIL N. CLARK

Bethesda, Maryland
January 1989

A Note

WHEN I FIRST heard about the Human Development Clinic, I had the normal amount of skepticism any good journalist has. "What do you mean when you say you can raise children's intelligence by changing the pictures in their minds?" I asked. I had been familiar with visualization and "rah-rah" motivation tapes—I had used a few myself. But on children? To help with school?

And homework. I couldn't think of a more lackluster topic. Sure, I thought, kids *should* do it (not knowing at the time how limiting that attitude was).

Then I saw the children, many of whom, when they first came here, were as lethargic and uninterested in school and learning as any I've seen. After they'd been here only a short time, I saw children happy to talk about the pictures and sounds and feelings in their minds. Children excited about "the planning calendar in my brain." Children helping other children learn in ways they thought of themselves. Children with a confidence in learning that they had not had before.

Many educators have talked about changes in education but no one I've seen has put them into practice the way the Clarks have. The learning-enthusiastic children at the Human Development Clinic are a testimony to that.

MARTA VOGEL

Introduction

WE OPENED the Human Development Clinic to work with children who had learning disabilities and as a result of those disabilities were failing in the school system. We soon realized that a large part of every learning disability is psychological (and chiefly a matter of low self-esteem), so we began to develop an approach called "learning therapy"—traditional psychotherapy combined with a thorough diagnosis of how people learn. We gathered the best learning materials and methods available and applied them to children's psychological and learning problems.

But even after we had helped children work through their psychological problems and learning disabilities, many children still had problems at school. They seemed to lack the necessary "tool kit" of organizational and thinking skills.

Parents were often part of the problem. They were playing the role of their child's educational manager, but had never had management training for this task. They were desperate for information.

They particularly found homework to be a source of stress. We found that parents viewed homework as the family headache, as busywork, as a punishment, as a reflection of the school's failure to do an adequate teaching job, as something children naturally dread. Even parents who were fairly confident about their parental role generally viewed homework with something between ambivalence and dislike.

We began to see homework as a mirror reflecting the psychological pattern of the child and his family. Were the parents nonchalant about homework? Did they keep a watchful eye, without letting the child be aware of it? Were they ever-fearful of mistakes, or did they see learning as an adventure which they looked forward to sharing? Were they overinvolved? Did they invest in each daily assignment all their hopes for the child graduating from Harvard Law School?

We also saw homework as an opportunity to help children become autonomous. Through homework we could improve the child's concentration and memory, help him and his parents understand his motivation for learning and thereby improve the parent-child relationship.

In 1976, we devised the Six-Week Plan to fortify the first part of the school year with skills that would apply all year long. The more we used the Six-Week Plan, the more children showed a marked increase in performance. Parents said the Six-Week Plan changed their attitude about how to help their children. They started off the new year feeling very upbeat. As one newly divorced mother said, "You really made me see homework as a learning opportunity, something I could get a handle on and get excited about." She set up work tables in the dining room, where she did her own work while her third-grade son worked on handwriting and her first-grade daughter on addition.

In 1981, in an attempt to answer the many questions from parents about managing homework, we offered an evening seminar, "Turning Homework Into Learning." Our clinic was jammed. When articles about our work appeared in the Washington *Post* and *Parents Magazine*, we received over five thousand letters and over four hundred phone calls—as many as our two-line phone system could handle. We continue to hear from parents, teachers, and principals of public, private, and religious schools. Clearly, we had struck a nerve.

In our practice we have only one homework assignment: Take charge of your own learning. Because of severe vision problems, both of us have had to do this from an early age. Cecil, born with insufficient eye pigmentation, could barely read the chalkboard, and Faith, as a result of Marfan Syndrome,* could see only two inches in front of her nose. While suffering the embarrassments of poor vision, we had to devise ways around the blackboards we couldn't see and the books we could barely read. It was our good fortune to have parents who helped us focus on our strengths and who encouraged our creative efforts to adapt to the regular classroom, an approach we later used to help children with similar learning handicaps. As a child, Faith learned to *hear* chemistry equations, to recognize the large body movements the teacher made for each letter of the alphabet (because she couldn't see them) and to recognize people by their voices

---

*Marfan Syndrome is a genetic disorder that affects the connective tissue of the eyes and the heart.

and objects by their feel. Cecil's method of adapting to the classroom was to turn everything into a moving picture—a movie he could later replay on the video screen in his brain.

When Faith was thirty-three years old, she had two miraculous eye operations, which gave her near perfect vision. She saw herself and a field of daisies for the first time in 1977. A wealth of wondrous new information flooded her brain, but it was, at the same time, uncomfortably unfamiliar. Seeing was not automatic—she had to learn to see. This new vision provided Faith with the energy and insight to investigate further the deep processes that unlock learning.

Neither a school nor an educational service, we are a clinical psychology practice dedicated to diagnosing and overcoming mental and emotional barriers to life achievement. In our work with over three thousand mostly middle-class families in suburban Maryland, we have seen astonishing improvements in many cases: thirteen-year-old Thomas, who saw no reason to go to school; fourteen-year-old Charles, who went to school but flunked because nobody had taught him how to study; eleven-year-old Sara, whom teachers called lazy, unmotivated and "not working up to potential"; "gifted" Sam, who did little schoolwork because he had problems with family relationships; David, who could memorize five hundred baseball cards, but had an emotional block to learning the multiplication tables; John, who was labeled hyperactive; Susan, who was said to be dyslexic; Jessica, who had attention-deficit disorder; and six-year-old Mary, who refused to go to school, had quickly learned to say of herself: "Oh, don't you know, I'm a Montessori dropout."

When a child comes to the center, we conduct an interview, first with the parents, and then with the child. We administer five to six hours of diagnostic testing, some traditional, such as the Wechsler Intelligence Scale for Children, and some not as traditional. For example, we videotape children to determine their learning and personality style.

If you walked into our clinic, you might find one of us at a computer playing a game which simulates real-life problems with a child, and another role-playing a robot who is unemotionally helping a child overcome math anxiety. Winifred Conley might begin a child's session by fencing with foam bats to calm the child's frustration over an F paper from school. Lori Harrington might be helping a child mindmap choices and goals. Gerry McWhinney might be doing a technique to help a child change his beliefs and to positively image his teachers and parents.

If a child is having trouble with math, we would never drill him on his multiplication tables—at least in no ordinary way. We might well help him picture a series of mental images, such as four groups of four knights on horseback. (Math has to do with the process of internal visualization —being able to see the problem in your mind—and when a student cultivates that process, math becomes something he can control and his frustration eases.) Or we might even focus on teaching the child to "speak math" using a strength he already has—language—as a bridge to his understanding of math.

Play therapy is the umbrella for our work with children. Instead of the traditional sandbox or dolls, we take advantage of advanced educational techniques based on the latest research as the medium of change in our face-to-face sessions with child clients. The goal is to give the child charge of his own mind, and the secondary outcome is an increase in abilities and learning.

When Michelangelo was asked why he was hammering on the block of marble that later became a famous statue, he said, "There is an angel in there trying to get out." On another occasion, the artist was asked to look at the gigantic nineteen-foot hunk of Ferraro marble in Florence out of which three other sculptors had attempted to carve David out of and failed because of a fissure in the marble. They could only see the flaw and said it couldn't be done. Michelangelo chipped away the flaw and there was David! We seek to uncover, in the same way that a sculptor chisels rock to reveal its underlying form, an approach, however traditional or unorthodox, that will "click" with a child—his own "aha" of learning. To paraphrase Michelangelo, inside every child there is a motivated learner trying to get out. The Six-Week Plan will help you to bring out that learner in your child.

This Book

• This book takes an unorthodox approach to learning. Its methods are not derived from the mainstream of education but from brain/mind research applied to the children we've seen in our clinic.

• This book addresses the processes inside the head. By breaking down thoughts into pictures, sounds, and feelings, we teach parents how to take unconscious thought and bring it into consciousness. Many adults may be uncomfortable contemplating these "inside" thoughts. But to children, talking about what is inside their head is very natural and taps into their largely unconscious world. Children who are aware of what is going on in their heads are better learners.

• This book will give you cues to your own learning style. If you prefer outlining to mindmapping, you may be auditory. If you prefer the exercises to the stories, you may be more kinesthetic. If you prefer the pictures and diagrams, you may be more visual. Observe your reaction to the things that don't naturally appeal to you.

• This book advocates bold steps. You may be confronting the educational bureaucracy head-on. More parents following these simple bold steps could revolutionize our educational system.

• This book is not for parents only. Share the book with teachers, principals, and members of the board of education.

• This book is not for learning-disabled children only. Our advice is equally useful for parents of normal or gifted students, particularly "underachievers," which includes most of the school population. In our clinic, we have applied the concepts to a wide range of people.

• This book presents a system. Try it long enough to adapt it to your child. Take what works from our system and then do it your way. One size does not fit all.

• This book does not require a masters degree in psychology. When you're relating to how the child feels, instead of fussing at him, you're already in the right ball park and some of what you communicate is that you care. Follow the spirit of the law rather than the letter of the law.

• This book is "should"-less. It does not take an authoritarian approach to a child.

• The best way to read this book is to read it through all the way, underlining or highlighting the techniques you think might work. Then go back and read and do the techniques in each week of the plan.

• This book is not about homework only. It's about getting yourself to do something in an organized fashion, whether in business or personal life.

• This book says "thumbs up" to computers for children. We believe that no one should graduate from high school without having a knowledge of word processing. We encourage computers in home and school.

• This book says homework assignments are not written in stone. Talk to the teacher about adjusting your child's assignments.

• This book is a sampling of the techniques we use. Use the Notes and the Recommended Reading as a springboard to finding out more about innovative approaches to learning.

• This book is a call for educational reform and for a commitment of time and energy from parents, teachers, and schools to begin applying these philosophies and techniques.

In life, homework
is the work we do
inside ourselves.

Part One

Homework:
Reframing
an Old
Subject

EVERY TIME WE talk about homework with Kevin, sixteen, he puts his hand over his cheek, opens one eye, and his shoulders sink slowly into the chair. He has learned to feel bad at the mention of the word.

"My life is ruined by my child's homework," says one mother. "It's a knock-down, drag-out fight from the minute he gets home until the minute he goes to bed."

When eleven-year-old Bill came in to work on his weekly vocabulary words, of which he usually has twenty, he only had ten. When we asked him about the reduced number, he replied, "We were good in class; the teacher told us we didn't have to do the other ten."

"It was a joke when I was in school, and it is even more absurd now," says one father. "My second grader brings home the most inane, routine, repetitious busywork I've ever seen."

Homework undoubtedly tops the list of "Things Most Distasteful to Kids." And not only children have learned to squirm at the mention of the word. Homework, a topic of disagreement since the 1800s, is the distasteful medicine of our society. The debate in recent decades has centered around how much of the bitter pill we need to swallow—one hour, two hours, three hours? Even well past our school years, we still use the word "homework" to mean a responsibility someone is expected to meet, as in "The President didn't do his homework." Not even homework "experts" consider the possibility of liking it. Frederic Levine and Kathleen Anesko, authors of *Winning the Homework War*, for example, note that "While homework will probably never become the child's favorite thing to do, trying hard will make it more fun."[1]

Much homework in its current form is rightfully criticized. We, too, refuse to defend the vague, senseless assignments that so often pass for homework: "Give me everything you can find on Venezuela," "Do the first forty problems" (of a boring math assignment, when ten would do), or "Write four pages on any topic you like."

We have seen blatant homework abuse, such as teachers saying, "You were bad in school, you get extra homework." Some teachers operate on an if-then approach to homework: If and when the child doesn't do his homework, then here's what we're going to do to him. Elizabeth's teacher had her draw a picture of herself staying in at recess, the punishment for the anticipated homework failure, despite the fact that she had done her homework.

Homework is sometimes set up as competition among parents. In one case, Steven, age twelve, was asked to do a family genealogy. The school he attended was in a wealthy neighborhood. The day it was due, limousines pulled up outside with drivers delivering professionally rendered family trees. Steven's, done in his own rather poor handwriting, received a D, while the professionally orchestrated projects were given top honors and displayed in the hallway.

We have seen homework that is not graded, graded homework that isn't corrected, and corrected homework that fails to teach the child what he might do differently next time.

But consider a world where homework is as popular as the Cabbage Patch Doll among young children, or the latest designer jeans or rock music among teens: a world where children say, "I can't wait to do my homework." When Faith taught third grade, she gave homework for a reward; children only got homework if they earned it, a treat many began to plead for. Our experience shows that through good homework assignments done in an interactive, stimulating manner, children can be united with their families and schools, become independent learners, and find intense enjoyment in learning.

Without this new homework, we may see more of the kind of situation we've encountered in some county school systems: The longer a child stays in that system, the lower his achievement and intelligence level fall. Given declining test scores, and increasing concern about what our children don't know, we believe that good homework assignments matched to the learning style of the child are a critical factor in saving our children "at risk."

But this world where homework is highly desirable will require major changes in how parents, teachers, and children view learning. Study after study (and experience after experience) shows that the best predictor of school success is parent-child interaction, including reading together and conversation. Parents need to lay to rest their own negative emotional connections to the old kind of homework and become actively engaged in a new type of homework with their children. Teachers need to become master assigners of new homework. Then children will become master operators of their own homework brains.

Fortunately, our knowledge of the human brain and how we learn have given us the means to do this.

Your Part

You are responsible for your child's education. This statement has incited controversy at PTA meetings where we've spoken. Some parents let their children grow up like weeds, assuming that all learning is automatic, that children will get what they need and that how they turn out is how they turn out. Some parents go to the other extreme and get overinvolved, so the child has no space for privacy and independent growth. Other parents run in from the sidelines as a kind of Kelly Girl problem solver.

One report indicates that school "amounts to only about thirteen percent of the student's waking hours in the first eighteen years of life, leaving eighty-seven percent of children's time under nominal control or influence by parents."[2] In addition, a recent report from the University of Illinois shows that as much as one-half the difference in student grades and test scores is attributable to parent participation in school-related activities at home.[3]

But parenting is predictably unpredictable. What works with one child may not work with another, and while a parent's love and enthusiastic attitude about learning are crucial, sometimes they just aren't enough.

One very well-educated couple, who read constantly and whose daughter loved school, was exasperated with their son Dexter, who hated "anything to do with paper and pencil." Despite his parents' educationally nurturing attitude, Dexter was simply not involved with homework. He loved to build things, he loved to cook, and he had such a well-trained nose that he could walk into a room and name the spice used in cooking. His senses were turned on everywhere except in school. And when we asked him, "If we knew some magic that could cause you to like school, would you be interested?", he said enthusiastically, "Yes, do the magic."

Loving your child is the best thing you can do, but helping the brain along sometimes requires a little "magic"—the magic we have learned about how the brain works, based on work by Michael Gazzaniga at Cornell University Medical Center, Robert Sternberg at Yale University, Paul MacLean at the National Institutes of Health, as well as Robert Sperry's split-brain research, Harvard's Howard Gardner and his theory of intelligences, and the writings of Joseph Chilton Pearce.

For the first time in history, through simple processes, we can access the brain, unlock its obstacles, and make use of its extraordinary capabilities. We see it happen every day. We now know, for example, that doing cross-lateral movements on a rebounder improves learning, that some brains learn better when they can see things, and that some brains almost shut down when the body they're attached to is made to "sit still."

Parents can learn this magic and use it to help their children become successful with homework.

This magic may be as simple as parents asking their children what type of learning they are doing: "Are you going to use memory or problem solving? What part of your brain are you going to use to do this?" Soon the child gets used to looking at an assignment and asking himself, "What skill am I going to use to do this?" Instead of thinking, "It's hard work and I can't do it," he thinks, "Well, I have two memory things to do, and one problem-solving thing to do, and after that I've got to go over it and do a mindmap so I can remember it."

This magic may mean not assuming that once material is presented a child will automatically learn it. Some children will, but others "get it" only after it's been through several different sensory loops—through the ears, the eyes, the nose, the hands.

Annie, eight, came to the clinic because she wasn't learning the multiplication tables. We tried everything: We sang the multiplication tables, we drew them, we jumped them (by twos, threes, and fours), we shouted them (two, four, six, EIGHT!), we did timed drills, used computer programs, but still nothing worked.

One day in desperation we said, "Let's make the sixes Gummi Bears." Suddenly, a light switched on in Annie's eyes. "Let's make the sevens those little gummy bottles," Faith continued, and Annie said excitedly, "Let's make the eights worms and the nines fish!"

Quickly, Annie became hooked on multiplication. Her mother all too happily bought the candy, and the next week Annie laid out Gummi Bears for the sixes: one set of six, two sets of six, three sets of six. . . . She had no intention of eating more than one piece of candy; she was excited by a concept she finally had grasped. When we took the Gummi Bears away, Annie could picture each set vividly in her mind. Nothing anybody had done in a year had gotten through to this little girl, but Gummi Bear math had inspired her and allowed her brain to accept multiplication.

"Oh, you're a psychologist; you can do things I couldn't get away with," parents will often say to us. We used to believe that it was easier for someone outside the family to have an effect than the parent, who, at times, may be too close to the problem. But our experience has since proven that, with training, parents can change how they relate to their child. A parent's close bond to the child can be an advantage rather than an obstacle.

Parents can also be instrumental in helping to improve the quality of homework assignments. "On Monday, copy each word three times; on Tuesday we will have a spelling pre-test; on Wednesday, make sentences with each word; on Thursday, do exercises F, G, H in the spelling book." With assignments like these, students learn to loathe spelling. A better approach to spelling might include helping the child do a crossword puzzle with words, helping him spell the word forward and backward (to see the word in his mind), or making a large chart and color-coding the sounds the child is studying—making all the "ou" sounds in green—and putting it on the wall in his room.

To learn geography and the capitals of the states, a good homework assignment might be to help the child use a computer detective game called *Where in the USA is Carmen Sandiego?* Using a map and atlas to "travel" from city to city, the child-turned-secret-agent searches for Carmen.

We can no longer afford to view homework as information to

be stuffed into a child. In the information glut of modern times, what's important is not memorizing information (though some of it is important to know), but knowing how to find information and what to do with it. We must focus on the process, not the content, and teach children to think and problem-solve as well as to read, write, and compute, three skills that are a means toward learning, not the end itself.

Your Child's Part

But even the most innovative process-oriented assignments will fail to penetrate a child's mind if that mind is closed to its own potential. Amy, thirteen, didn't do her homework, and was turned off to school because she didn't like her history teacher. When we asked her to picture what school would be like if she liked her teacher, she said, "I would be able to listen and I wouldn't have any trouble doing my homework. It would be really different."

Through visualization, Amy was able to change her mental image of school and to learn that, "even though the teacher annoys me, I can still listen and learn."

Thirteen-year-old Tom was also convinced that school and homework were a disaster. He couldn't take notes in class because he didn't *hear* the sounds in his head. When we said, "oceanography" to him, he could see pictures of fish and oceans, and so on, but he didn't hear the word "oceanography" in his mind. On the other hand, he brought in vibrant water-color and pen-and-ink drawings of animals and houses. He could draw anything. As soon as he learned how to translate the pictures into sounds, he lost interest in his regular "homework excuses" (playing with computer games and watching TV), and said, "I want to do my homework. Now I know how to do it."

We frequently ask children to draw pictures of themselves doing homework. They are inevitably small, colorless, static drawings like the "before" pictures on the opposite page. (The range of time between "before" and "after" pictures is six weeks to three months.)

Ten-year-old Carter's "before" picture shows how spatially disoriented he was. (He's the little darkened scribble in the middle of the page.) Both his bookbag and his bedroom at home were crammed with loose, unsorted papers from his short school career. Organi-

Before and After Six Week Plan

zation helped him feel more "grounded," as evidenced in the "after" picture where everything is labeled. In addition, the sterility of the "before" picture is now replaced with music, something he loved but which he had not previously associated with homework.

Twelve-year-old Patsy was very hyperactive and only succeeded in doing minimal homework by "gluing" herself to the chair. Like Carter, Patsy saw homework as a sterile, useless activity until she found that she could incorporate something she loved into it—in her case, drawing. With her drawings and her planning calendar on the wall, she loved homework.

Sixteen-year-old Martin's only concept of homework was lying on the couch; he hadn't even made it to a chair. He would do his assignments for four days in a row, then do nothing for weeks. His "before" drawing indicates how low his self-concept and motivation were. When he was on the couch, he toyed with the idea of doing drugs. We did not demand that he get off the couch and sit at a desk to do his homework. Surprisingly, the materials and structure we provided made him feel an importance he had never experienced. The Six-Week Plan made Martin an executive in charge of his own learning. He moved from nonacademic to high achiever.

Once children know that they can turn the negative pictures in their minds into positive, active, enjoyable ones, they become qualified as master brain operators and, hence, lovers of homework. The first step is to understand how the brain works.

The Homework Brain

• Jim, sixteen, can do any logic puzzle we give him. He's well read and he loves to talk about ideas, but often, he doesn't feel like doing anything. If he doesn't feel like going to school, he doesn't go; he's all locked up in his feelings and he says, "It's artificial to think." Jim operates almost entirely through what we call the "Feeling Brain."

• Fourteen-year-old Scott, on the other hand, operates primarily from the "Thinking Brain." He always has his nose stuck in a science book and he knows thousands of facts. But he's a bit like "Star Trek"'s Mr. Spock when it comes to feeling—he'd rather think than do anything else.

• Ten-year-old Pamela is in every afterschool activity possible. "Don't tell me about it, just do it" is her motto. She is upset by changes in her schedule and she likes to eat the same food for dinner each night. Pamela operates in the "Doing Brain."

Understanding how the brain develops in children and how it works is crucial to understanding how a child uses it to learn. And homework *is* learning. When you understand how the brain takes in and processes information, you understand why children have trouble with homework and why a more deliberate use of the brain will help. Notes Richard Bandler, "People spend more time learning how to use a food processor than they do learning how to use their

11

brains."[1] We offer a practical rather than an anatomical view of the brain, a kind of homework-brain user's guide.

The Three-Part Brain

Over the last thirty years, Paul MacLean, at the National Institutes of Mental Health, has developed a model called the "triune brain."[2] Joseph Chilton Pearce calls MacLean's work "easily the most important item in current brain research."[3]

For the sake of simplicity, we call the three parts of the triune brain the Doing, Feeling, and Thinking Brains. The *Doing Brain* is the seat of habit and it maintains the body processes (breathing, heart rate, blood pressure, et cetera). The *Feeling Brain* is sometimes called the "mammalian brain," because higher mammals have this part as well as the Doing Brain. The *Thinking Brain*, or neocortex, is divided into two hemispheres referred to as the right and left brain.

The three brains, MacLean notes, are "biological computers, each with its own special form of subjectivity and intelligence, its own sense of time and space and its own memory, motor, and other functions."[4]

Think of the three brains as a way to view the child's relationship to homework. Doing Brain children may do homework in an uncaring way just to get it over with, or use ritual to help them concentrate. Feeling Brain children may say, "I just don't feel like doing my homework," or become excited about the new things they're learning. Thinking Brain children may think of reasons not to do their work, or they may choose to see themselves as highly successful.

When one brain predominates, the other parts of the brain can't perform the homework processes as effectively. But when all three brains work together, homework and learning become satisfying, motivating, organized, and interesting whole-brain experiences.

If the child refuses ritual, she's looking for something to stimulate her Thinking Brain. However, if she's crying because she hates homework, she's saying, "I'm in my Feeling Brain" and you need to take care of the feelings first, before she can proceed to the Thinking Brain. The brain's "default value" is too often the Doing Brain or the Feeling Brain—a child does whatever she's done before

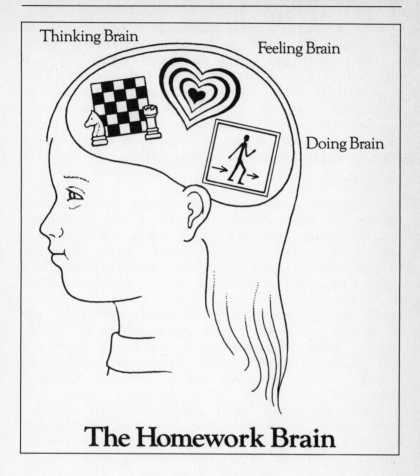

Thinking Brain

Feeling Brain

Doing Brain

The Homework Brain

(for example, no homework or just-getting-by homework) or what she feels like doing. But it's the Thinking Brain that allows a child to have a choice, to make a conscious decision to learn.

Learning processes differ in each brain. Repeating dance steps, exercises, or a physical game is a good ritualistic way to learn body movements in the Doing Brain, for example. But repeating spelling words in the Thinking Brain is not as effective as visualizing the words.

For years, advertisers hawking soda pop, fast cars, and blue jeans have used their highly refined skills to make changes in our brains.

Only recently have we come to understand that we, too, can teach children to initiate and create changes in their brains—changes that will benefit them. They can take something they don't think is important (homework) and change their perception of it. If we can elicit from the child what bothers her about homework or school, we can help her reframe the situation; shift the feelings; and change the negative pictures, images, and sounds in her brain. All of this incredible ability lies within the power of the Thinking Brain, in cooperation with the other two brains.

The Doing Brain

The Doing Brain is the sensory brain. It keeps the heart beating and the lungs breathing while the rest of the brain is thinking, "ninety-six divided by twelve is? . . ." or feeling, "I really like that boy next door." The Doing Brain's interest in survival makes it a "slave to precedent," notes MacLean, as evidenced by animals, who once having found a safe watering hole, avoid the risk of drinking elsewhere.[5]

The Doing Brain craves ritual—studying at the same place every day with the same pencils at the same time. It would be happy to eat peanut butter and jelly every day for a lifetime. Ritual provides a thread of continuity. Little Adam's ritual for saying goodbye to his mother is a run, jump, hug, and a kiss, without which he is despondent.

If your child has a *habit* of doing homework in front of the TV, that's a ritual, Doing Brain, problem. (Our experience shows that most children don't prefer TV; it's just that they don't have anything more interesting to do. They've established the ritual of television and not the ritual of studying or playing a game.)

Children (and adults) perceive ritual with mixed feelings: They can't live with it and they can't live without it. The activities of the Doing Brain ("Let's do this at four o'clock every afternoon") are sometimes stodgy and initially, at least, seem to abruptly interrupt more amusing activities. However, once begun, rituals are gladly embraced. One grandmother who took her four grandchildren to a mountain cottage quickly established her own rituals—hiking in the morning and reading after lunch. When she announced the plans on the first day, the children were disgruntled. But after lunch on the second day, they said eagerly, "Aren't we going to read now?"

A person who is *too* oriented to the Doing Brain may take habits such as eating or cleaning to the extreme. Also, children of parents who demand too much ritual may resist it themselves. When we helped Judy get organized for college with a new study notebook, file folders, and an alarm clock, she said, "Oh, that's too much like my father. My father has four alarm clocks so he's sure to get up." We pointed out that just because he overuses his Doing Brain doesn't mean she can't use her Doing Brain rituals effectively. As we will see in Week One, the rituals of the Doing Brain play an important part in homework.

The Feeling Brain

The Feeling Brain is used by mothers to take care of their young; it is also the one that many teens operate from. When a child says, "I freeze and I can't learn anything," her Feeling Brain has overtaken her Thinking Brain's auditory self-talk that says "Let's see, if there are four apples here at sixty cents each . . ."

The Feeling Brain houses the amygdala, which is the sensation-regulating device that accounts for a child's being excited or bored, and the hippocampus, which deals with memory.

Everything that goes to the Thinking Brain has to first go through the Feeling Brain. The history facts, the math problem, the Spanish words—all are filtered through the emotions first, which is why the relationship to the teacher is so important. If the child dislikes the teacher and *believes* that this causes her to stop learning, she does stop learning. "That which is 'boring' is boring," suggests educator Robin Beebe, "perhaps because it makes no emotional connection to us."[6] Making friends with the teacher and the other children is a big part of satisfying the Feeling Brain.

The Thinking Brain

The Thinking Brain is the executive control panel of the brain. The Feeling Brain and the Doing Brain are designed to be servants to the Thinking Brain, but more often than not, it's the other way around. When we say, "Her emotions rule" or "She's just a creature of habit," we're saying that the child's executive has lost control.

The Thinking Brain frees the child from compulsive ritual and gives her a "thinking cap" with which to figure out new solutions.[7] It allows her to control her own behavior by controlling the other

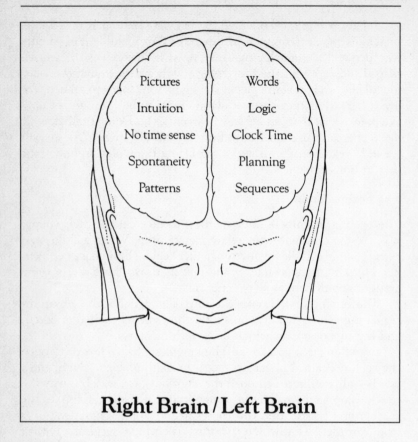

Pictures	Words
Intuition	Logic
No time sense	Clock Time
Spontaneity	Planning
Patterns	Sequences

Right Brain / Left Brain

brains, to choose to do homework, and to think of inventive ways to do it. The Thinking Brain allows a child to bring up pictures, sounds, words, and smells, and to use her "thinking cap" to modify those pictures. It is the planning calendar of the brain. (When we told Melinda, eight, about this she immediately thought of a big notebook, her planning notebook, in front of her brain.)

Left and Right Brain

When a child is born, the brain functions as a whole. Then, during the first years of life, connections begin to grow between the hemispheres and each side takes on its own specializations. In most children, the Thinking Brain is divided into left and right hemispheres by age four.

We use the idea of "left brain/right brain," as many psychologists have done, to distinguish opposite functions. The Thinking Brain, however, is not "one hemisphere completely idle and the other frantic with activity. . . . it is oversimplified and misleading, even wrong, to assume that the two hemispheres are separate systems, 'two brains,'" note Ornstein and Thompson.[8] Music, language, math, logic, and many other activities involve both sides of the Thinking Brain.

Nonetheless, looking at the hemispheres separately (and calling a child "left-brained" or "right-brained") is a useful way to examine the thought processes of the brain. Generally, the left brain deals with literal words, logic, clock time, planning, and sequencing. Generally, the right brain deals with pictures, intuition, timelessness, spontaneity, and patterns. The left brain, for example, interprets the literal or dictionary meaning of the word "cow" and the right brain interprets the connotative meaning of the word "cow," which to one person may be a funny cartoon character and to another a tasty roast beef. The right hemisphere has more neural connections to the Feeling Brain. Thus, right-brained people (at least as seen by left-brained people) are more emotional. All of us must use both brains, but in each of us one side may tend to be more active in certain situations.

Ornstein and Thompson report on a study comparing differences in brain activity while reading technical passages and while reading folktales. When subjects read the technical material, the left hemisphere was more active; for the folk stories, the right was more active. Technical material is almost exclusively logical (left brain), but stories involving images and feelings stimulate the right hemisphere.

A child's previous experience will also have an impact on hemisphere activity. A child untrained in music who listens to a song will show more activity in the right brain. A trained musician, on the other hand, while analyzing, evaluating, and classifying the music, will show more activity in the left.

Whole-Brain Homework

The best learning takes place when both sides of the brain are accessed equally, when both parts are singing in harmony from the same score. Notes University of Chicago biopsychologist Jerre Levey: "When a normal person hears the word 'dog,' he does not merely derive the dictionary definition, but also generates images of dogs in various postures and activities, recalls the sounds of barks and howling, and, probably, recreates the emotions that real dogs elicit. This rich and full meaning of 'dog' is derived by an intimate, collaborative integration of the processes of both sides of the brain."[9]

In our culture, however, school has traditionally been more organized around the left brain, while right-brain experiences are often considered "frills." The traditional skills of reading, writing, and arithmetic tend to educate one hemisphere at the expense of the other. Teachers and parents keep on with their "Buckle down, nose to the grindstone" approach when a right-brained approach— a song, a game, a cartoon character—might be the most effective way to learn about World War Two, the water cycle, or the amendments to the Constitution. If schools dealt effectively with right brain/left brain issues, they would make more visual and fewer verbal presentations, there would be more emphasis on problem finding and less on problem solving, and less emphasis on grading. Instead of having separate art, music, and physical education departments, each class would be filled with these right-brain experiences.

What the school system blindly cuts short may be a fuel for adult success. Many executives make top-level decisions in a right-brain mode, using intuition instead of logic.

We don't need to excuse the right brain; we can find a way to harness it to the system. "She is very right brained," many parents say bashfully when speaking of a child's failure in math. But they leave it at that, as if the child is crippled for life. Many teachers who see right-brain techniques as "giving in," fail to offer learning possibilities that would help a right-brained person.

Right-brained Eric, thirteen, was a paradox. He could recite biology facts to his mother the night before but the next day he would fail the multiple-choice test. Eric tended to become confused by the possibilities and he thought all three choices were correct. The wrong answers are called "distractors" by professional test makers, and they were powerfully distracting to Eric's right brain.

A right-brained child takes in all the answers at once, while a left-brained child takes a step-by-step approach and eliminates possible answers. Later, Eric learned to integrate left-brain logical skills with right-brain visualization and to evaluate each answer. After reading a test question, he made a "stop-action freeze frame" of the answer he had learned the night before.

Take advantage of the left-brain/right-brain *seasons*. During the summer, when children have fewer left-brain demands, introduce outlines or help the child organize his room. During the winter, emphasize right-brain skills; the child will be receptive to art, movement, and music.

A very right-brained child who seems to be uninterested in science and math but loves music and art, will need to be taught left-brain study skills such as organizing, note taking, outlining, and summarizing.

Annette, fourteen, loved horseback riding, dancing, and music, but she was failing school. She favored one side of her brain at the expense of the other. While we didn't want to discourage the things she enjoyed, she did need balance. Instead of saying, "Get busy and study; stop wasting your time in extracurricular activities," we told her how dancing and horseback riding were in fact using important parts of her brain. When she found out we considered horseback riding and dancing to be intelligences, she was quite willing to work on other intelligences.

The brain works best for homework when all the parts are working together as a team. The Six-Week Plan deals with the brain as a whole: Week 1 focuses on the organizational needs of the old brain; Week 2 focuses on the changing nature of all the child's brains; Week 3 focuses on the sensory access to the brain. The processes of motivation, concentration, and memory in Weeks 3 to 6 equally involve all three brains. Success, by our whole-brain definition, is more than getting the job done. Each of the three layers of the brain (and the two hemispheres of the Thinking Brain) must be satisfied and eager for the next learning encounter.

Three-Brain Homework

To help your child use all three brains for homework, say the following to him, "Imagine sitting down at the negotiation table and getting all parts of your brain and body to agree. Get each brain to sign on the dotted line." (Some people only get as far as a New Year's resolution, Step 1, and fail to get commitments from the other parts.)

Step 1. Make a left-brain choice to do the homework. Say, "I choose to do my math *easily.*"[10]

Step 2. Use the left brain's organizing ability to form the parts of the ritual (make a schedule, keep a neat notebook, etcetera). Ask, "How will I ritualize my math homework and how will I fit it into my other rituals?"

Step 3. Make a right-brain image of successful homework (see it, hear it, feel it).

Step 4. Have the Doing Brain agree to these rituals.

Step 5. Get the Feeling Brain's approval.

If you've gone through all the steps with your child, but she doesn't feel quite right about it, go back to Step 1. When it doesn't feel right, there is something wrong. Your child's system has an objection: She's not ready for it, the schedule needs to be adjusted, and so on. Return to the beginning and assess each step. Check that the child is able to do what you have asked. You may need to go through the whole cycle more than once with your child.

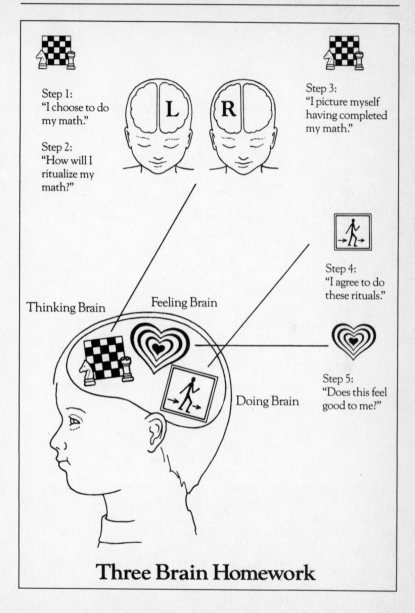

Step 1:
"I choose to do my math."

Step 2:
"How will I ritualize my math?"

Step 3:
"I picture myself having completed my math."

Step 4:
"I agree to do these rituals."

Step 5:
"Does this feel good to me?"

Thinking Brain

Feeling Brain

Doing Brain

Three Brain Homework

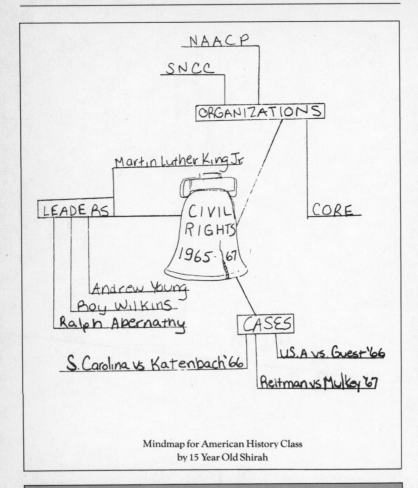

Mindmap for American History Class
by 15 Year Old Shirah

Mindmapping

Mindmaps are right-brained visual doodles useful for brainstorming, organizing ideas, daily planning, note taking, and showing "The Big Picture." Through color and the position of the lines, they also aid memory.

To some people, particularly right-brained visual people, mindmapping is superior to an outline. Mindmapping taps the images already in your brain. These images, however, since they are on the right side of the brain, need to be translated into words, largely a function of the left brain. With a mindmap, you can put the images down first and order them later. Also, mindmaps show relationships more clearly than do outlines, which only show hierarchies. To mindmap:

1. Collect your mindmapping supplies: a large sheet of white paper and a handful of colored felt-tipped markers. Relax; you don't need to be able to draw to do a mindmap.

2. Start with a central idea; draw a circle around it in the middle of the page. (Some children will need assistance initially.)

3. From the circle draw lines representing related ideas, using a different color for different ideas. (Some children, when first starting mindmapping, will use one color for everything. Let them do one that way, then show them how they can use different colors for different ideas.) Draw pictures or use key words.

4. From those lines draw "smaller" related ideas, and expand outwards. Some people like to use one word on a line; others prefer phrases or pictures and symbols.

Many children love mindmaps and seem to gravitate toward them, but others have to be convinced. Adults, especially auditory types, who may be unaware of their imaging process or who feel they are less artistic, may resist them.

We taught John to mindmap several years ago. He wasn't particularly artistic, but he loved to doodle. When the teacher introduced mindmapping to the eleventh-grade class, she wasn't particularly good at it, so John, a shy person, asked, "Do you want me to do it?" He mindmapped the entire chapter on the board.

There is no right way to do a mindmap, so judge not another's mindmap. Mindmaps are highly individual and

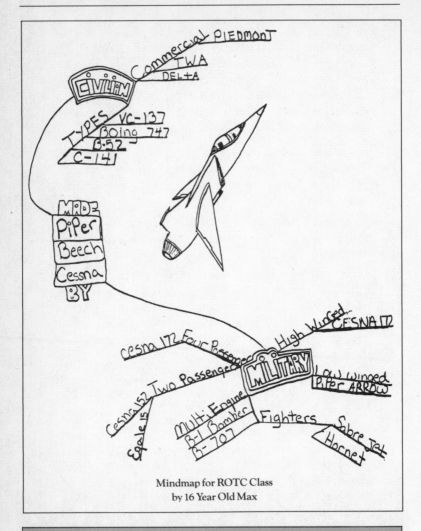

Mindmap for ROTC Class
by 16 Year Old Max

almost unreadable to another person. On the other hand, if the teacher is talking and the student sees the mindmap being made in the process of the lesson, it provides a point of reference—a "You are here" context. The teacher can refer to the mindmap to show what the class has already been over, and where the lesson is headed. Mindmap novels (character, plot, theme, setting) and use the mindmap as a memory device. Have fun with mindmaps.

Part Two

The
Six-Week
Plan

Keep in Mind

1. Start out with the structures and techniques we give you.

2. If something isn't working, find a system that will work for your child.

3. Be willing to present your child with structure after structure, until he finds his own way of learning and remembering.

The Six-Week Plan has helped hundreds of families make homework a daily habit. What was once the drudgery and emotional upheaval of studying becomes fun, productive learning.

The Six-Week Plan is a creative, rather than a reactive approach, keeping parents consistently involved in the child's main work. It provides help for the parent who knows every detail of every essay the child writes from September to November and assumes the coast is clear—until March when he discovers the child is failing. At the same time, the parent is not mired in the homework or doing it for the child.

The Six-Week Plan provides parents with a sense of perspective and control. Best of all, it takes much of the emotional intensity out of the homework situation. Containing as it does the game plan for homework, it eliminates the need for nagging, harassment, and fault finding. It serves as a buffer between the child's emotions and the parent's. Children love it because it gets parents off their backs; they get more done, but they also have more time to play.

The most basic reaction to the Six-Week Plan is relief: At last parents have permission to impose some structure.

Getting Started

Many parents feel ambivalent about setting up a system: They either have no structure at all or they have a different set of rules every week so that the child says, "Uh, oh, here comes another 'system'—what is it this week?" Other parents quit right when the change starts to take hold, playing the broken record entitled, "Nothing works on you" or "Everything I do is a failure. I might as well not have tried." All of these approaches discourage children, who desire a strong sense of continuity. It may seem paradoxical, but you need to provide both continuity and a system that works. If something isn't working, change it, but don't communicate that you're giving up.

For six weeks suspend your doubts, negative evaluations, and predictions. Think of the Six-Week Plan as an interesting experiment and allow the results to show themselves. How you view the schedule will determine how well it is received by your child.

This plan provides an intense look at your child's beliefs and activities surrounding homework. Best of all, it's only a six-week plan. That's about how long it takes to form a new habit, and it's a manageable piece of time: Anyone can do anything for six weeks. You may not need to use it at the same level of intensity all year. We don't intend that every parent do everything: Find the parts that fit your family's needs. You can adjust the plan and spend more time on each area, but we suggest a maximum of two weeks on each "Week." If you need to repeat, do so.

The Six-Week Plan will be useful no matter when you start. It is an excellent inauguration for the school year, but don't limit it to September. Reintroduce it in January if your child hits the traditional post-holiday slump. Anytime your child goes through a developmental stage, or a life transition (death, divorce, moving) where ritual grows thin, reintroduce the plan. Don't let your child go to seventh grade or to college without it.

Set aside time every day to work on the Six-Week Plan. Whatever amount of time you spend will help. Studies show that the parents of children who do well in school spend at least ten minutes a day talking with them about their homework. Just your child's awareness of your interest in his homework will help improve it.

In using a technique with your child, you may have to do it several times to perfect the timing. Rehearse it mentally beforehand and have the book in front of you when you do it. Timing, voice tone, and body language are everything.

Computer Helper

A computer will help greatly. If you have one at home, maximize its use during the Six-Week Plan. Use it to record the Homework Journal, the Daily Schedule, the Learning Log, et cetera. Select programs from the computer list for birthday presents and swap programs with other parents. If you are computer phobic, ask if you can attend your child's computer class.

The Parent-Child-Teacher Team

The Six-Week Plan is a team effort between you, your child, and your child's teacher. Let the teacher know that, although your child will be completing homework to the best of his ability, the focus will be on the *process* of establishing homework as a habit. Alert the teacher to the part of the process the child is working on so that credit is given for progress toward being able to do assignments. Talk to the teacher about adjusting homework assignments if they are too easy or too hard or inappropriate to your child's learning style. (If the assignments are too left-brained, read ahead to the chapter "Homework Helpers" in Part Four.) Send the teacher week-by-week results and assure him that nothing in this plan contradicts the school's organization and plan. In fact, this plan is to be enthusiastically shared. Whole schools have successfully adopted the

Six-Week Plan and teachers often say, "We've noticed an immediate change—the resistance toward school is gone."

Your child's role as the star attraction is to increase his knowledge about himself. He doesn't need to know the name of even one technique; the idea is that he is aware of a process that helps him learn. You can teach young children about the Thinking, Feeling, and Doing Brains, about visual, auditory, and kinesthetic learning styles, and about intelligences. A young child in our lab, for example, said, "It's easy for me to make friends because I'm good at social intelligences, and I can find my way around because I have good visual-spatial skills, but my math intelligence needs some help." It's helpful, for example, for a child to know that the teacher who makes charts and diagrams may be visual or that one who lectures or uses tapes may be auditory.

As your child uses new learning methods, other children may be quick to notice that he's different. (It shows when you're a Six-Week-Plan kid!) But children who laugh one minute, say, "Tell my mom to get me one of those notebooks," the next. "Everybody makes fun of me for mindmapping," said Martha, fourteen, "but they all borrow my mindmapping five minutes before the test."

Self-Assigned Homework

The Six-Week Plan involves self-assigned (in addition to teacher-assigned) homework, including previewing, mindmapping, memory techniques, the Homework Journal, and recorded tapes.

Children who are wary of anything that feels like more homework, or who fear that self-assigned homework cuts into their playtime, may be resistant, saying, "I already have enough homework; I don't want to do that, too." Help the child see that in the long run, self-assigned homework will save him time. It's the creative rather than reactive approach; it's working smarter rather than harder. (We say, "If you're going to do it, why not do it with a little style?") If possible, arrange for the child to receive extra credit in school. Teachers we've asked have given credit for completing computer programs, keeping the Learning Log, learning memory techniques, and doing a project on the brain or learning styles. Some have allowed the child to show others in the class how to do a memory technique or a mindmap.

The Learning Atmosphere

Sometimes the emotional atmosphere at home is so tense that doing homework is impossible. On the other hand, homework itself can become a stabilizing force. Many parents who are under emotional stress may find that the Six-Week Plan provides a set of rituals they can hold onto through divorce, change of job, or other upsets. One twelve-year-old had been very close to his grandmother, who served as his homework companion. After she died, he continued to use the plan. He found that being able to carry on with his homework rituals gave him stability in the midst of his grief.

Create an "energy field" for learning, a positive climate in which your child chooses to do homework. The fastest way to do this is to do your own homework at the same time. Set a task for yourself that is as difficult for you as your child's task is for him: Pay the bills while he does math, write letters while he writes a paper. If your child resists reading the books assigned in English, agree to read the same books. One father, in an effort to encourage his daughter to do better on the SAT, took the test with her. Another father, who had never read a fiction book, chose to read *The Lord of the Rings* while his son, who had severe reading problems, worked on his homework. Consciously *model* the behavior you want in your child: Do what you are asking him to do. Share your hobbies with him, talk about current events, let him see you reading and learning, with persistence and enthusiasm.

Homework Journal

At the end of each week, you will find a Homework Journal with questions that will guide you and your child in recording weekly progress. It will also help prepare you for parent/teacher conferences. To keep the Homework Journal, purchase two notebooks (one for you and one for your child) or use the computer. Or the child can keep his Homework Journal in a separate section of his school notebook. As you read, answer the questions and note any techniques you want to use with your child.

For the child's Homework Journal, use the questions at the end of each week as guidelines for discussing and recording the child's progress. He can write down his own answers or draw pictures in the Study Hints section of his notebook. He also needs to keep track of techniques that he finds particularly helpful, noting how he used them and modifications he made.

The first exercise each week is to list ten successes. Initially, your child may be resistant to listing his successes; he may think he's bragging. Teach him that it's okay to brag about himself. Also, listing the first three or four successes may be easy, but the last five may be difficult. Ten successes force you to stretch your idea of "success." This is part of the image-building process of the Six-Week Plan. Be extremely sensitive to any progress, no matter how small (he doesn't leave his coat at school anymore or he brings home his assignments four days a week instead of two), and give him acknowledgment and praise. Even if his grade is the same as the preceding quarter, point out how much he has improved. It may take time for this progress to show up in grades.

In reviewing your weekly "successes," don't forget to list something you or your child initially saw as a failure but were able to turn into a success. Maybe your child didn't complete his homework assignment because he played too long, but he started on schedule the next day. Maybe he failed a test but learned, after studying the test, how to pass the next one. Don't waste mistakes; use them to learn something for the next homework assignment.

The Six-Week Plan begins in the morning and ends at night. Regular meal and bed times help create the atmosphere of security in which learning can take place. If you follow everything in the plan—establishing ritual, honoring learning styles and motivations, and learning new learning technologies—all three parts of your child's brain will be satisfied and homework will be a very alive, stimulating, whole-brain experience.

An Overview of the Plan

Week 1: A Gentle Introduction to Time and Space In Week 1, establish home and school ritual to make homework automatic, not a choice. Get organized, buy lots of colorful supplies, and build excitement for the coming year. Help the child create a sense that "something's coming—I don't know what it is, but it is going to be great!" Introduce your child to time and space, gently. This week's theme: Identify your rituals.

Week 2: Developing Intelligently In Week 2, be aware of the developmental stages children go through and how you can adjust their homework to their developmental stage. Also, be aware of the wide range of intelligences, not just verbal and mathematical. Be on the lookout for your child's Teachable Moment. This week's theme: There are many kinds of intelligences.

Week 3: Learning with Style In Week 3, be aware of the different learning styles—visual, auditory, or kinesthetic—in your family. Discover your child's learning style by observing his eye movements, the way he expresses himself verbally, and his likes and dislikes. Adjust homework assignments to his learning style. Restore a range of sensory stimulation to homework. If an assignment is only visual, make it auditory or kinesthetic. This week's theme: What's your style of learning?

Week 4: Off and Running: Discovering the Motivated Child In Week 4, the goal is to discover your child's motivations at school and at home. Ask him: "What gets you motivated? What stops you from doing homework? What would get you to like doing your homework?" Listen carefully to the answers. Acknowledge his feelings. Find his Center of Learning Excitement, whether it's *Star Wars* or stamp collecting. Lead him through the Learning Comfort Zone. Use games and stories to engage him in the learning process. This week's theme: Uncover the motivation that's already there and transfer it to homework.

Week 5: Keeping the Eye on the Ball—Concentration In Week 5, help your child identify when he *is* and *is not* in concentration. Focus on doing away with external and internal distractions. Plan your child's entrances and exits from concentration. Have a goal to concentrate; take breaks. This week's theme: Prepare the brain to concentrate.

Week 6: Upgrading Your Child's Memory In Week 6, become aware of different kinds of memory. Learn the appropriate memory techniques for each subject. Be aware of how memory is different for older children and younger children. Stay away from memorizing. This week's theme: Memory depends on the senses.

How Much Homework to Expect Each Day

Second and third grades: ½–1 hour

Fourth to sixth grades: 1–2 hours

Seventh and eighth grades: 1½–2½ hours

Ninth to twelfth grades: 2–4 hours

The minimums are more important than the maximums. If your child has reached fifth grade and still doesn't have homework, or says "I did it in class," something is wrong; it's generally not possible to learn and practice new concepts and skills in class time by that level. (Some students and parents want the teachers who don't assign homework, but to the extent that homework represents learning and not busywork, this is self-defeating.)

The proportion of learning activities a child can manage by himself may increase from near zero in kindergarten to near 100 percent in high school.

Week 1:
A Gentle
Introduction to
Time and Space

Keep in Mind

1. Homework every night, whether the child has what he calls homework or not.

2. Establish when and where homework will be done.

3. Organize. Organize. Organize.

Dirty gym clothes, broken pencils, and old PTA notices to his mother fell out on our table when Nathan, ten, brought in his school things. He carried all this in a crumpled brown paper bag along with his treasure collection consisting of little bits of metal and dead insects from the school playground. When we asked about his homework assignment, he produced a piece of dirty paper so tightly curled that two heavy books were required to straighten it out.

(Nathan inspired us to adopt the Brown Paper Bag Technique to help children organize their schoolwork. The directive: Bring in everything that has to do with schoolwork in a brown paper bag and dump it on the table. Once they dump the contents of the bag on the table, they heave a great sigh of relief. We then help them sort through everything and begin the Perfect Notebook, described later in this chapter.)

Nathan is not the exception. We've seen homework assignments covered with tomato sauce from last night's pizza and books crammed with more school papers than they have pages. Some children are so disorganized that it's almost impossible to diagnose a particular problem. In fact, sometimes disorganization and poor study skills *are* the problem; parents and teachers are likely to call these children lazy and unmotivated.

Educators and politicians have called for a return to "basics"— reading, writing, arithmetic, and more recently, reasoning. But without the "basics" of organization, children are handicapped learners, and we see more and more such handicapped learners every day.

Matt, for example, is a gifted teenager with a minor motor disability. He knows he's smart but he has trouble putting things down on paper, and as the amount of paperwork increases, he gets further and further behind. The mound of assignments from his history teacher is particularly overwhelming, so he doesn't even look at it until 8:30 P.M.; he realizes then that he has to go to the library and it's too late. He decides he's lazy.

His mother asks, "Shall we just let him fail?" This strategy may at times be useful, but not in Matt's situation. Matt can understand history, but he lacks the ability to organize an activity. He often finds himself sitting at home looking at a question that requires a resource book he doesn't have, or can't find. Matt has to learn that as soon as he gets his history assignment, he needs to mark in red the items that involve going to the library and then mark on a calendar what has to be done and when. His mother needs to realize that this skill won't come naturally to him, as it has come to her. She must help him learn to organize his time. For Matt, basic organization is the difference between failing and doing well.

Often the disorganization of time and space represents an entire disorganization of the family. Leonard, nine, left his papers everywhere; his backpack contained his leftover lunch, uneaten, from several days before, and he spent a great deal of time making excuses for the homework assignments he never did.

When we began to explain Week 1 to the family with "Be sure your child has a clean desk," Leonard's father and mother looked at each other, and smiled, embarrassingly. "We haven't seen the top of a desk—Leonard's or ours—for a long time." They proceeded to explain their household, a model of disorganization in both time and space. Leonard's room was a hurricane; he couldn't make his way through the middle of it and his clothes hung out of his dresser drawer, which had no knobs.

His father was the "King of Mess"—his car was full of coffee cups and leftover food wrappers—while his mother was always late. She would just look at her watch and say, "Oh, it's eight o'clock. I'm supposed to be somewhere." Leonard's father was irritated by her lateness and she by his sloppiness. Their checking account was never balanced. Leonard, unfortunately, "inherited" the worst of both parents. He was messy like his father and late like his mother.

The Six-Week Plan became the impetus for the entire family to change, as the child became the model for the parent. When Leonard organized his notebook, his father organized his briefcase. When Leonard put a trash can in his room, his father put a trash can in his car. As Leonard learned to make a schedule, his mother bought stopwatches for herself and her child and set alarms during the day to remind her to get ready for appointments. As Leonard's parents observed their child's life being ordered, they ordered their own. New knobs appeared on Leonard's dresser drawer.

The organizational structure that homework imposes (or is intended to impose) is one of the most useful things a child will learn. It's how you get things done for yourself, how you manage your day, how you get from teacher-dependent to independent learning.

But too many children don't know how to do their "homework warm-up." While others are making home runs, they are still in the dugout because they can't find the paper they were supposed to hand in (it was in *some* book *somewhere*), and they forgot what pages they were supposed to read. With the "homework organizational warm-up," provided in Week 1, they get their first chance at a home run.

Organizing Space

A Place for Everything

Parents take two attitudes about a child's room: They nag her about cleaning up her room or they close the door and declare it "your territory." To reach a compromise, help your child clean up her room and teach her to organize in the process. Some children need to be told how to organize; you can't always expect them to know. For the young child's room, buy assorted colored baskets and colored stickers and sort everything in the room by color. You might want to put in an extra shelf or netting at the top of the ceiling for toys, or find a place to store them in the basement. Arrange things by categories so she can find them easily. Putting socks in the drawer with the blue dot and books on the shelf with the green dot lays the groundwork for good organizational skills. The structure of the room is a reflection of good mental structure. In a variation of this approach for the adolescent, use color-coordinated office supplies. (Buy them for birthday presents.) Give highly specific directions (more than just "Hang it up") for clothes, which tend to be the core of teenagers' organizational problems.

Set up a family "Don't Leave Home Without It" table by the front door for anything that has to go to school or work: books, schoolbags, keys, lunches, permissions slips, notes, notebooks.

If you aren't the most organized person in the world, ask an organized person to help (they usually love to put the rest of the world in order). If you're already a very organized person with a messy child, this week may be the most difficult; your strong beliefs about order may tend toward "holier than thou." Show your child how, instead of expecting her to "shape up." This week could give new meaning to the word "patience."

The Perfect Notebook

Help your child put together the Perfect Notebook. (This works best for fourth graders and older; simple variations may work for a younger child.) The Perfect Notebook contains everything your child needs for homework and is organized and hole-punched so it can pass this very tough test: When held by its spine and shaken (ouch!) nothing falls out. The Perfect Notebook contains sections for test papers and scores so that at least one thing in school— grades—will never be a surprise to you or your child.

Use a large, sturdy three-ring binder. Blue denim notebooks rarely last a year. Notebooks with Velcro-closing flaps are expensive but last a year and hold papers securely. If the teacher requires a separate spiral notebook for each subject, buy a larger notebook to hold these. When a notebook wears out, replace it.

Tape the daily school schedule on the inside front cover. From front to back, put the following things in the Perfect Notebook:

1. A zippered plastic envelope with erasable pens, pencils, erasers, colored pens, highlighters, and a small set of felt-tipped markers.

2. An assignment notebook (about 5 x 7 inches). Using one sheet per day, your child writes the subject name, date, and the assignment. Keep these pages from week to week so you can thumb back through them. For children who are used to writing assignments on little slips of paper, the assignment notebook may be a difficult habit to form. This is the child's Little Black Book; if it is lost—no matter how many times—replace it.

3. A three-hole-punched school calendar (September through June) where your child can write in long-term assignments. (This helps her get a picture of "three weeks from now.")

4. Set a separate section of the notebook aside for "The Homework Planner," divided with colored dividers into the following sections: Daily Schedule, Projects, Homework Choices, The Learning Log, Proofreading Checklist, Mindmapping, and Study Hints. In these sections your child will demonstrate that she is the ultimate authority on what works to help her learn. In addition, she will keep a Homework Journal of her progress, discussing the questions at the end of each chapter with a parent.

5. Set another section of the notebook aside for your child's different subject areas, each subject represented with a colored divider.

6. In the back, put a set of pocket folders labeled as follows: one for each subject, one "For Parents," and one for "General Junk" (for personal notes to friends or doodles and stickers). These folders will hold tests, graded papers, and anything else your child wants to save.

On the outside of the folder, she needs to write the subject, the date the quarter starts, and how the final grade is to be obtained (for example, 50 percent from tests; 20 percent from homework; and 30 percent from class participation, quizzes, the student's notebook, speeches, projects, papers, labs, and so on.) Have her list her grades as she earns them.

Your child will also need ruled three-hole paper with lines that are neither too faint nor too close together.

Home Supplies

Purple file folders with matching labels, notes that stick on the wall, and green and gold plastic magazine holders! There is an abundance of supplies to rescue the unorganized child or parent. Take advantage. Overdo it. Become an organization addict. Never must there be a child, like one we knew, whose parents were willing to buy three computers but refused to buy a pencil. Your child's study area can be as well-stocked as a business office. Indulge your child in supplies she really wants that will help her feel special and well-organized. Especially indulge small children in things like name and date stamps (to identify papers and drawings), that help them play with organization.

For the desk at home, provide a good dictionary and junior thesaurus in which she can underline words, a kitchen or digital timer or a stopwatch to mark study time and breaks, a large planning calendar, a file box in which to keep old test papers and book reports, a large set of markers, an art tablet for mindmapping, a hole punch and reinforcement tabs for three-hole paper, colored "tape flags" to mark text, colored index cards for vocabulary, a yellow or pink highlighter, a small tape recorder, an electric pencil sharpener, a stapler, Scotch tape, scissors, paper clips, Eraser-Mate pens, and "white-out." (Many teachers won't let a child mark through a word, but will let her "white-out.")

We also recommend purchasing copies of school books—either a complete or partial set—so your child can write in them and highlight key words and concepts. We have put children's schoolbags on a scale, and some have weighed almost fifty pounds! In such cases, having a second set of books at home may make homework seem "lighter." Before buying a book, ask the teacher if the book is going to be used on a daily basis.

Ritual

Homework Every Day

If your child has to make a Major Executive Decision every night, "Will I do my homework?" or "Do I feel like doing it?" the odds are she won't either feel like it or do it. In the Six-Week Plan, she will have all kinds of choices about *how* she does the homework, but *whether* to do it is not one of the choices. (In Week 4, you will experiment with a technique called "Helping Your Child Choose to Do Homework." From a motivational point of view, of course, it is better if the child does make her own choice, but for now, while she is establishing the habit, it's important that she not be burdened by too many choices. Establishing a habit means limiting choices initially.)

It's a mistake to ask, "Do you have any homework?" A child will say no every time. Even with ten vocabulary words due Wednesday, a book report and a science project due Thursday, and two tests on Friday, a child will still say, "I don't have any homework." (In all the years we have talked to children, we have never heard a child say that studying for a test was homework.) Children define homework in the most immediate, narrow sense—a written assignment that will be handed in and graded the next day.

Assume that every child has homework every day. The child needs to keep her appointment with homework at her desk, where, if she doesn't have any projects, books reports, and so forth, she can read, review, copy notes, make mindmaps and tapes, or anything else that will aid learning.

Homework, like teeth brushing, is a no-choice activity and the answer to "Do I have to?" is always yes. If this feels bad to your child's Feeling Brain, consider the favor to the Doing Brain, which craves pattern and sameness and could eat peanut butter and jelly for the rest of its life.

Same Time

Ritual is a commodity as rare as neat notebooks. With the lack of extended family, the abundance of divorced homes, and children shuttled back and forth, ritual has become less and less of a stabilizing force in children's lives. A home without ritual is a home with a high prospect of homework problems. At PTA meetings, when we are prepared to talk about intelligence, teachers say, "Tell the parents to give their children breakfast, tell them to have someone there when the children come home in the afternoon."

Divorced parents, particularly, may give up the rituals of marriage and the rituals of the child's life—conversation at the dinner table, a bedtime story, and holiday celebrations. When judges divide divorced families by the week, ritual is virtually destroyed. The small amount of ritual that remains centers around TV, with dinnertime starting "when the 'Cosby Show' is over."

In many families, dinnertime has become a kind of Meals on Wheels. We know a family where one child wants to go to Wendy's and the other to Roy Rogers; the whole family goes to both places and waits for each child to eat. This is the children's attempt to establish some kind of ritual no matter how bizarre. We recommend that the whole family have dinner at the same time each night with conversation and no radio or TV.

Bedtime ritual is also lacking. "What time do the children go to bed?" is too often a multiple choice question with the answer (nine, ten, eleven, twelve) depending on the child's mood and the nightly TV movie. In one family, Adam went to bed whenever he fell asleep, which varied by as much as three hours. In this kind of atmosphere, children become mentally disorganized and doing homework is almost impossible. When you ritualize bedtime, making it the same time every night, whether the child wants to go to sleep or not, within a week he will fall asleep and will be better prepared to learn.

Rituals make for consistency. Children who observe ritual through the day, will observe ritual at night. Children who observe ritual at home and with homework will observe ritual at school. If you've lost ritual along the way, call it back, welcome it home and be faithful to it every day. Structure and ritual, including regular meal and bed times, the evening cuddle, and the bedtime story, form the foundation for learning.

Some parents realize the importance of ritual but don't follow through with their plans. Mick's father and mother complained that despite their proclaimed allegiance to ritual and schedules, Mick, six, would not do his homework or go to sleep at night. Their schedule was very specific: 3:15 come home, 3:30 go out to play, 4:00 snack, 4:20 homework, 6:00 dinner, 6:45 more homework, 9:30 bedtime.

"How many days do you observe this schedule," we asked.

"Never," they said. "That's the problem."

Once you have a schedule, stick to it or revise it if it's impractical, but never throw everything out. Ideally, children need to do homework at the same time every day. However, given the demands of dance lessons, soccer team, and church meetings, this may not be practical. What is important is to establish a weekly homework pattern—on Tuesdays after dance, on Wednesdays before church, and so on.

Same Place

Your child needs to study in one place every night. We used to be staunch advocates of in-your-own-room studying, and we still believe that by fourth or fifth grade, it's best if a child is working at her own desk. But many parents at PTA meetings have convinced us that some children want to be with other people while studying, and we have allowed that some children can study in the dining room or den. Let the child study someplace, but only one place. (Many dining-room studiers may use a homework tray to transport supplies.) The child who studies in the dining room or den will require greater sacrifices by the rest of the family: that means no TV within ear or eye shot. Homework and beds do not go together. But coffee tables so the child can sit on the floor, and stand-up desks, especially for a kinesthetic child, may be very helpful.

Homework: It's About Time

Homework begins at the same time every day. Instead of nagging, use an alarm (watch or clock) in the afternoon to indicate that it's time to do homework. The alarm signals that "the special hour is here."

Children often exist in a sort of never-never land of time unconsciousness. A young child has a sense of spatial time in which an hour can seem like a minute and a minute like an hour, but she may lack a sense of serial (clock) time.

Children do not have built-in time predictors and live largely in the present moment. When told, "You have three weeks to finish this report," they may not automatically know how to spend one hour a day for three weeks as opposed to six hours the day before.

Start a "Gentle Introduction to Time" before the first week of school, when anxiety isn't a part of the equation. Plan time around things that have nothing to do with school—going shopping together, visiting a museum together, et cetera. Establish time rituals: Get your child dressed right after she gets up, before she eats breakfast, eat meals at the same time, and so on.

Once school has started, you can help her with a Preview of the Day and a Learning Log. Help your child orient herself in time by showing her where she's been, where she is, and where she's going, saying, "We're going to spend thirty minutes doing your spelling and then we are going to do your reading." Instead of saying, "You've been doing that for one hour and you still haven't gotten anything done," you might say, "You have one hour to work on this; let's see how far you can get." Honor your child's attention to a task; when she is in the middle of something, suggest, "In fifteen minutes, we'll need to leave. Can you finish what you're doing by then?"

Children who are too time conscious, who constantly say, "What are we doing next?" or "What time is it?" need to learn to "track" time without hurry. They need to learn to be in the present. When Debi asked, "What are we doing next?" about thirty times in an hour, we said, "Oh, the voice inside your head has a little clock with it." Then we helped her inside voice focus on saying, "What are we doing *now*?"

Help your child also plan an order of studying. If she needs to study French, Spanish, math, and science, alternate the languages with math and science. If math is the hardest subject, encourage her to do half of the math problems first, then twenty minutes of history or English, then the rest of the math problems. Save the most enjoyable homework for last.

The Homework Day

Preview the Day

If you've ever wanted to see a movie based on the preview, you know the power of advanced notification. The same is true for your child, who enjoys looking at the day's "coming attractions."

Ask your child in the morning: "What's going to happen today? What are you looking forward to? What are you going to learn today? What are you afraid of?" This helps her to look forward and express any fears or expectations.

Set the tone and pace of the day by creating another rare commodity in today's world: pleasant mornings, a relaxed time when "rush" and "hurry" are forbidden words. Play music and draw pictures or enjoy a game of pitch and catch. A child who leaves the house with a sense of emotional well-being will learn more than a child who arrives at school harried and anxious.

Preview Homework

The benefits of previewing also apply to homework. Introduce the ritual of previewing your child's assignments when she comes home from school. Ask "What do you have to do tonight?" Have her write all of her assignments in her assignment notebook. Open each textbook with her to see which pages are to be covered; look at each exercise, read the directions, and help her figure out what process the assignment will involve: studying, understanding, reading, skimming, researching, taking notes, working in a workbook, answering questions, outlining, or writing. You might say: "What kind of learning are you going to be doing? Are you teaching new material to yourself, reviewing, practicing, memorizing, or problem solving? How will you be tested on this material?"

Help your child estimate how long each assignment will take. If she has ten math problems, time her doing one, then multiply by ten. Likewise, with ten pages of English. For an essay, you might want to take time to do a mindmap or an outline, then estimate the time it will take to write the essay and proofread it. Have her write that estimate in the assignment notebook next to the assignment or on the daily schedule sheet. Play the Estimate Game! How close can she get to her estimate?

When we did this with Terence, a sixth grader, he was able to substantially reduce his estimated homework time. His father had said, "We can't stay long; Terence has six hours of homework." But when we helped Terence preview, it turned out that he had an hour and forty-five minutes of homework. He was delighted that we had "shortened" his homework.

Check out your child's long-, medium-, and short-term assignments. Help your child learn to pace herself, for example, to schedule the reading of a hundred-page book over an allotted time. Children really can't begin to do this on their own, especially before age ten. Children think school subjects go on forever and ever. Assure your child that she needn't learn the multiplication tables into the trillions. As you preview, help your child write down her goal, such as "I choose to understand these proofs." Help her keep this goal in mind, even if she thinks it's strange at first.

The first time you preview (and all good rituals take longer the first time), it is likely to take about thirty minutes and may not be the most enjoyable activity. But once you get into the habit, it will take about ten to fifteen minutes. After this mental preview, your child can put her books away, and take an afternoon break, preferably a fresh-air physical activity, or listening to music or drawing. Later, when she opens her books, she has confidence about her homework because previewing has eliminated her store of homework horror stories and that fuzzy feeling of the unknown when there is lots to do but she doesn't know how to do it.

The Learning Log

Children need to see a connection between the time they spend studying and their grades. But merely telling them that there is a connection is unlikely to make as great an impression, especially on the visual child, as charting a graph of how much time they spend on homework.

That's why we devised the Learning Log, a graphic representation of time, subject, and learning concepts. The purpose of the Learning Log is to record how your child spends her time. During this six-week period you may also want to record (a) the amount of time you spend reading aloud to your child, (b) the amount of time your child watches TV each day, and (c) how her breaks are spent.

Make sure the child understands the concept she's studying by listing it on the Learning Log. When James, ten, was asked what he was studying, he said, "You know, those little periods you put in math problems—math punctuation." He meant decimals, but clearly, he hadn't gotten the point.

Clarify the teacher's grading system. Students who know how they're going to be graded tend to do better. You don't want to make grades too important, but you do want to take them out of the magical realm and put them into the world of cause and effect.

One fifteen-year-old boy, who continually said, "I'm studying, don't bother me," was surprised when he got a D in math on his first interim report (especially since he liked the teacher). When we charted his study time on the Learning Log, he found that math time was less than ten minutes a week. His Learning Log profile was very similar to his grade profile.

Learning Log

How much time did you spend on your homework this week?

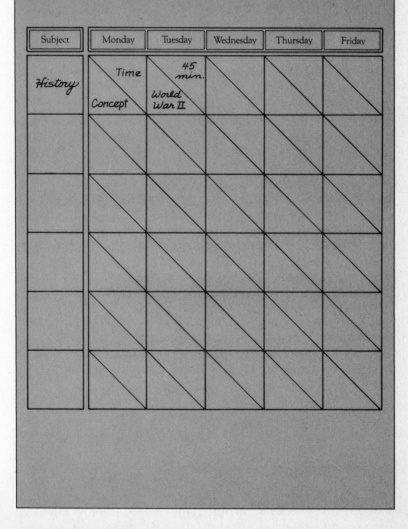

Subject	Monday	Tuesday	Wednesday	Thursday	Friday
History	Time / Concept	45 min. / World War II			

With another boy, we found that what he said was true, he actually *didn't* have time for homework. He had a paper route in the morning, a church event several nights of the week, and sports, Boy Scouts, and two types of music lessons in the afternoons. The Learning Log jarred the parents into seeing that they could plan homework first and schedule the child's other activities around it.

Break It Up

Young, physically active children may need a five-minute break every fifteen minutes; seven- to eleven-year-olds may need a break every thirty minutes; eleven and older, a break about every thirty to forty-five minutes.

A child can take breaks by either time or subject matter. Sometimes, if she is in the middle of a project, it is preferable to finish the task, then take a break. Sometimes one subject can be a break for another.

For a timed break, set a kitchen timer, but make sure your child really concentrates until then. Encourage break activities that allow your child to move her body and stimulate her senses, and that involve music, art, or movement (drawing a picture, playing puff basketball, juggling, or even raiding the refrigerator).

Review

Take a few minutes at the end of homework to review. Ask: "What did you study? What did you have problems with? What did you feel good about? Which skills and concepts do you *know* you know? Which do you need more work on?" If your child rushes and makes careless errors, train her to be an excellent proofreader. Make a game of this: Praise her for finding and correcting her own errors before the teacher does.

Review your child's day with her. When we ask a child, "What did you do in school today?" the answer is invariably, "Nothing." It is important for your child to be able to conceptualize what she *did* do in school. A review at the end of the day automatically reinforces the day's activities. Do verbal summaries, written summaries, weekly summaries, or summaries of subject units.

A daily review includes going over the day's class notes, and expressing the essence of the material in her own words, changing the notes into an artistic doodle, telling you about what she read or heard, making an outline, writing a story, or drawing a cartoon ("Once upon a time in France there was a short guy named Napoleon. . . .").

Spaced Review

Children will remember new material best if they do a "spaced review," reviewing material:

- ten minutes after it has been presented; then
- twenty-four hours later; then
- once a week for four weeks; then
- once a month for as long as you want the information to remain in current memory.

The Silent Partner: How Much Help Is Helpful?

Too many parents, in an attempt to foster independence in their child, give no help at all. Or, at the opposite extreme, they ask the teacher, "Do you want us to help with homework?" The teacher says no and the parents silently band together and help anyway, to the detriment of the child.

Jim, nine, made good grades on his fourth-grade homework but failed tests, a mystery to his mother and his teacher. Jim's mother sensed that something was not quite right, but when she complained to the principal and teacher, they said she was "overanxious" and that Jim was "a flower not yet in bloom."

We asked Jim's mother to stop doing his homework—he was totally dependent on her. We told the teacher that Jim wouldn't be getting assistance at home and the teacher agreed to help with skills correction.

Two weeks later, the teacher said in surprise, "He's not even doing fourth-grade work." As she adjusted his assignments to his skill level (not his mother's), Jim did his homework and began passing tests and increasing his skills.

When your child asks for help, we recommend a technique called "assist by questioning." Children get easily irritated and just want an answer, so when the child says, "Mom, do I put a comma after this clause?", it's easy for the parent to answer "Yes." But the child learns nothing. It's better for you to say, "Look at your proofreading checklist," or "Do you remember what a clause is?"

If you've helped your child quite a bit, write a note to the teacher, "I really had to work with Frank for him to understand this. You may need to go over this again." Have an understanding with the teacher about your role.

Homework deadlines soften even the most resilient parent, who may be tempted to do the child's homework for her. Don't. *Never, never, never* write a paper for your child that's turned in as her work. If the teacher then gives the "parent paper" a low grade, the child thinks the parent can't do any better than a C (your days as a homework helper then are numbered) and the child also thinks she can't write. We suggest that parents provide support and intelligence-balancing assignments as long as children need it. (See "Homework Hotspots," Writing in Part Four.)

Planning a Project

Gary, an extremely creative fifteen-year-old, had wonderful ideas for school projects; he would tell his ideas to his friends weeks ahead of time. But when it came to doing the project (for example, writing a speech), he became so lost in the planning stages that he ended up in despair, saying, "My hands are tied behind my back. I don't know what to do." He settled for a mediocre speech, or nothing at all, even though he hated "people who just get up and speak," without careful planning.

A child's lack of planning skills is especially obvious when it comes to projects. She may come home with little specific information about what the teacher wants, but just enough to rattle parents. One sixth grader said his assignment was "something to do with a movie, a newspaper, and a record album." He estimated that this assignment would take him three days. After much questioning, we discovered that he was studying punctuation in English and he needed to understand how to punctuate titles. He had to write one paragraph using titles from a movie, newspaper, and record album.

Choosing a subject for a project is also a problem for many children. Spending fifteen hours in the library deciding on a subject—something we've seen far too many children do—is entirely inefficient and helps little in learning.

PROJECT

| I Choose to: | write an essay on Feudalism |||
| for my social studies class ||||

Todays Date 11/22	Start 11/24		Finish 12/15
Description:	an essay describing how Roman		
and German life still influenced			
Feudal society	10 pages typed		

MINDMAP

read textbook mindmap write main idea type 1st draft

Write Essay

Brainstorm library read take notes

date	steps	helpers	supplies
11/24	mindmap from text	mom	color pens
11/25	Go to library	mom drive	note cards
11/27	Brainstorm all ideas		large paper
11/28	write main idea		
11/29	make outline		computer
12/1	rough draft	Dad reads	computer
12/2	teacher meeting	teacher	
12/4	second draft		
12/8	proofreading		check list
12/10	corrections		
12/11	Final draft		

Too often children fail to plan for the adult roles in their projects; they expect their teacher to know and to accept without question what they have in mind, and for their parents to be ready to talk to them about a project the night before it's due.

We helped Gary fill out a project sheet for a class project he was very excited about—a video presentation in which he interacted with puppets on the topic of recycling. For Gary, learning to set goals and break the project down into parts with a time schedule made the difference between passing and failing.

How to Plan a Project

1. Help the child decide on a subject that she is interested in, that meets the teacher's criteria, and that has enough, but not too much, information. Consider the competition: Is anyone else in class doing a similar topic? Would it be better to choose something else? Do a form of mindmapping called a "brain dump": Put the subject in the center, and put down everything you know, including resources, coming out from the center. Then, look at the brain dump and decide which things belong together and color code them with a colored pencil. Cross out the farfetched or the inappropriate. Go to the library and read on your topic. Talk to authorities.

2. Mindmap or "chunk down."

3. Outline the steps needed to do the project and highlight in red those steps that require other people's involvement. Get a commitment ahead of time from people that need to help you.

4. Estimate the time for individual parts of the projects. Then allow extra time if the project is highly creative or if you've never done anything in that format before (example: You've written a book report but not an analysis of a play).

5. Indicate materials needed—a compass, a metric ruler, a certain type of construction paper, Styrofoam, et cetera.

6. Make a timetable of when each step needs to be done.

7. Okay your project and the way it is to be done with the teacher; she may help you find additional resources and make suggestions about carrying out the project. Use a computer project-planner program.

How to Make a Schedule

1. Buy, or make on the computer, a planning notebook.

2. Fill in the parts of the schedule that are known—eating, sleeping, recreation, etcetera.

3. Fill in your chosen homework time, including time for preview and review for each day.

4. Allow break time.

5. Build in a "margin of error"—time that is not planned.

6. Update daily.

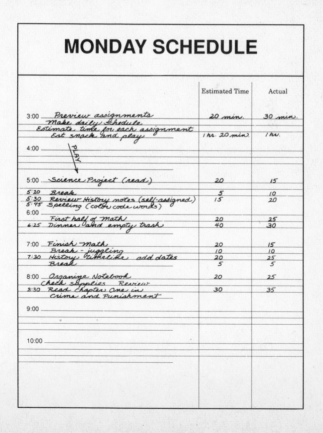

MONDAY SCHEDULE

		Estimated Time	Actual
3:00	Preview assignments	20 min.	30 min.
	Make daily schedule		
	Estimate time for each assignment		
	Eat snack and play	1 hr. 20 min.	1 hr.
4:00	PLAY		
5:00	Science Project (read)	20	15
5:20	Break	5	10
5:30	Review History notes (self-assigned)	15	20
5:45	Spelling (color code words)		
6:00			
	First half of Math	20	25
6:25	Dinner and empty trash	40	30
7:00	Finish Math	20	15
	Break - juggling	10	10
7:30	History titlelike add dates	20	25
	Break	5	5
8:00	Organize Notebook	20	25
	Check supplies Review		
8:30	Read Chapter One in	30	35
	Crime and Punishment		
9:00			
10:00			

Homework Journal

In Week 1, write the answers to the following questions:

1. List ten of your child's successes this week; list ten of your own.

2. What home rituals did you establish for your child—bedtime, mealtime, etcetera?

3. What homework rituals did you establish? What time will your child start homework, take a break, finish homework? Where will she do homework?

4. List the benefits of being organized.

5. How did you help your child get organized for homework?

6. How did you give your child a Gentle Introduction to Time?

7. What did you learn from previewing the day with your child?

8. What did your previewing homework tell you about your child?

9. What task will you be doing when your child is doing homework?

Week 2:
Developing
Intelligently

Keep in Mind

1. Honor the child's developmental stage.

2. Recognize that there are many kinds of intelligences, including musical, body, and interpersonal.

3. Evaluate your child's intelligences; use the strengths to pull up the weaknesses.

• Third-grader Glen was energetic, highly verbal, and very entertaining. For anyone who listened, he expounded on all creatures prehistoric—the Allosaurus, the Brontosaurus, the Stegosaurus, the ninety-two-foot Compsognathus, and the Iguanodon. From age four, he had been rattling off dozens of Latin names in front of guests at home.

His proud parents praised him and bragged about him—until he started failing school. By the time they brought Glen to us, his recitation of things prehistoric was wearing thin. Teachers and peers failed to be impressed with the "Dinosaur Kid." (We use this term to apply to any child whose verbal or logical skills are overemphasized at a young age.) Nonetheless, his test scores verified that he was very smart.

• First-grader Bobby was another Dinosaur Kid, only the fixation this time was the vocabulary of logic. Little Bobby proudly announced, "I know what a syllogism is. A syllogism is a form of deductive reasoning consisting of a major premise, a minor premise, and a conclusion. For example, 'All men are foolish. Smith is a man. Therefore, Smith is foolish.' " Bobby's parents were proud of his performance—all this from a six-year-old! But they were bewildered and very upset that he, like Glen, did poorly in school. When it came to reading, Bobby froze.

These "Dinosaur Kids" tell us a great deal about how a child's brain develops, how parents view intelligence, and what happens when a child's developmental stage is not honored. In the sensory-motor stage(up to age four), Glen most naturally would have been playing and moving instead of overusing verbal intelligence by rehearsing dinosaur names. Bobby's parents overemphasized logical intelligence during the fantasy stage(ages four to seven) when he could have been reading fairy tales.

Reciting the names of all the dinosaurs, or the names of five hundred fish, interferes with the four- to seven-year-old's process of development through "private speech." Without this self-talk, the child fails like Glen, in the third grade, because he can't get himself organized. The child becomes "stuck" at a developmental stage no longer appropriate for his age.

Bobby, now eleven, has problems with spelling, because he can't see images in his head. He knows the material perfectly, but he can't put it down on paper because his visual-spatial skills are poor. The left side of his brain is all tuned up—he can tell you the meaning of any word—but the right side has a bad transmission.

Fortunately, a Dinosaur Kid can be put back on the track when his parents understand the problem and engage the child in learning experiences emphasizing right-brain activities, including movement and visual-spatial relations. For example, we recommended that Glen do some block building and running in the park, almost anything nonverbal to balance out the high verbal input.

Week 2 of the plan focuses on identifying your child's developmental stage and how it relates to homework. We'll also look at the many kinds of intelligences and suggest ways you can help balance your child's intelligences through homework.

The Developmental Stages

The world children live in changes rapidly. Just as their bodies are constantly growing and changing, so, too, is their way of thinking and responding to what's around them. Their brains respond in a way that correlates to their developmental stage. A two-year-old, for example, will respond to food or a ride on the rocking horse, a five-year-old to fantasy stories, and a teenager to a mirror.

Within each stage, the child moves from helplessness to autonomy, from thinking concretely to thinking abstractly. At each developmental stage, the child emerges in a new body, as if he has moved to a new country. So radical are the differences from one stage to the next that you can't assume a thirteen-year-old will remember what you taught him at six: You may have to teach him to organize his time and space all over again. (Often when a child comes to us at age seven and comes back at age eleven, he doesn't remember ever having come to the clinic, so different are the personalities of each stage.)

The developmental stages proceed in a stair-step fashion. The child might be coasting along at the same level for quite awhile, then suddenly lunge forward into accumulating facts, or suddenly into abstract thinking. He can also regress to an earlier stage of behavior, such as thumb sucking or imitating a younger sibling. From birth to about age sixteen, a child passes through four development stages.

Sensory-Motor (Birth–Age 4)

The first crucial part of a child's development is bonding, a biological and emotional process that establishes what Joseph Chilton Pearce calls an "intuitive, extrasensory kind of relationship between mother and child."[1] Many of the homework problems we see stem from the child not having bonded at an early age. If he is not bonded with the mother at birth, he will later refuse to accept the teacher as mentor. (We don't mean to say that it's too late if a child hasn't bonded by a certain age. The mother of one hyperactive five-year-old "scared animal" child was sure she hadn't bonded at birth with her son. When we worked on bonding the relationship through holding and touching, the child calmed down significantly.) This initial bonding of the infant to the mother is the foundation for a series of bondings which occur throughout life; for example, bonding to family, earth, society, society's knowledge, a spouse, and to one's own offspring.

Very young babies learn through their bodies. When you look a three-year-old straight in the eye and say, "Don't put your hand on that," he immediately gestures with his hand in the direction of the object, not to disobey willfully but just to "hear" with his body. The main guideline in this stage is: Touch is more effective than words. Before age four, the left and right brain are not divided, and excessive verbal instruction (as with Glen and Bobby) will "skew" the division of the brain.

Very young children need to be using their bodies, exploring the world through play and spending much of their time outdoors. When they aren't, we see them later with learning problems. Five-year-old Vickie developed a motor learning disability—she couldn't jump rope, play ball, write, or draw—because she preferred playing indoors all the time with her Barbie Doll.

Magical Child (Ages 4–7)

Joseph Chilton Pearce has called this age "the grandest part of childhood . . . when a perfect balance is achieved between body, mind, and feelings."[2] The Magical Child is a step beyond the body-learning of the sensory-motor stage but he doesn't know where his brain is, where consciousness is located. When Faith told Stevie, four, that she was going to take a picture of him writing, he held up his hand so she could take a picture of his hand writing. When she asked Paul, age four, where his brain was located, he pointed to his stomach, illustrating the way he "thinks" with his body. "Use your head," doesn't say much to a Magical Child. You might as well say, "Use your foot."

At four to seven years, children are far more intuitive than in later stages; they believe in luck, remember their dreams (which are frequently bad) and have déjà vu experiences. They talk to animals (and the animals sometimes talk back), a fact you can use to enter their world. At our clinic, two stuffed bears, Oreo Bear and his brother Chocolate Chip, sit at the computer or beside the child to help with math problems. What a big help it is to have these two bears involved in homework! The idea is to preserve the magic and prevent school from taking it away.

Magic preservation means thinking of ways to communicate with a child on his level. When we caught Beth, six, peeling the wallpaper off the wall, we didn't say, "Stop, you're ruining the wall." Instead, we attributed human qualities to the wall and said, "Ouch. That hurts!" She laughed and tried gently to smooth the wallpaper back on.

Homework, up to the age of seven or eight, needs to incorporate as much fantasy as possible. Leslie, seven, refuses to work on the computer unless she has her brain hat on. If math and reading become something to cry over or dread, the purpose of the homework is lost and the child's positive attitude about a subject may be affected forever.

Acknowledge his fantasies, both good and bad. If he has a bad dream, instead of saying, "That's okay, it's not true," talk with him about it, and help separate fantasy from reality.

The Magical Child has little sense of time. He'll say, "It takes nineteen hours for us to get to the house from school," or "There are two hours in the day." Don't expect him to know how long a homework assignment will take or what "next week" means. It's a waste of time to say to a four- to seven-year-old, "Promise me you'll do your homework in the morning if I let you watch TV tonight." He'll promise anything because he's completely present-oriented. At this stage, it is not appropriate to teach him "responsibility" by pointing out the deal he made yesterday. He believes you are the crazy one.

The ego is developing at this stage and the child will brag and exaggerate. Some parents hearing, "I was the best," think they need to "break" the ego and deflate pride with "No, you weren't the best, you were second best." This kind of accuracy is unnecessary. Go along with his tendency to exaggerate. In fact, superlatives are a good motivating technique: "You are the best. You are the fastest. You have the most fun."

The Magical Child doesn't think logically. He'll say, "It must not be raining outside because I'm dry," or "Nickels are better than dimes because they're bigger." Or, as Jenny said, "A caterpillar is a girl because it has blond hair." Logical adult statements are lost on the Magical Child. When the parent says, "You're supposed to

Developmental Stages

1. Sensory Motor
2. Magical Child
3. Concrete Logical
4. Formal Logical

12-16 Years
Formal Logical
Judgemental and idealistic
Polarized thought
Abstract reasoning

7-11 Years
Concrete Logical
Compare and contrast
Sequence and classify
Collect facts

4-7 Years
Magical Child
Fantasy and Dreams
Intuition
Little sense of time

0-4 Years
Sensory Motor
Bonding
Motor actions
Physical communication

stay clean for church," the child doesn't understand the logical connection between staying clean and church. Given another chance to catch a grasshopper, he will get just as dirty the next time despite your logical explanations.

Appeal to these logical inconsistencies. When we gave Arnie, four, a piece of cake, he complained that his piece wasn't as large as the pieces his brothers received. But he was delighted when we pointed out that his piece of cake was longer.

In your attempt to preserve the magic, be careful about TV overexposure. Too much TV plays havoc with a Magical Child's fantasy world. It shuts down visual imagination and may inhibit the development of his imaginative muscles. When a Magical Child constantly "jumps" out of his own experiences and becomes a small intellectual, he short-circuits a developmental stage and may actually decrease his intellectual ability.

Concrete Logical (Ages 7–11)

In this stage the child becomes a small fact collector, rivaling the U.S. Census Bureau. He may astound you with the batting averages of six hundred baseball players, the names of all the presidents of the United States, or the dates of all the wars since the beginning of the world. He gains left-brain thinking skills, such as comparing and contrasting, classifying, defining, and sequencing. Fill his homework with facts, with sequencing activities, and with classification, such as, "Tell me all the kinds of animals in the reptile category."

Ten-year-old Kenneth illustrates the Concrete Logical Child's disdain for his past life as a Magical Child. When asked if he wanted to see a Halloween puppet show, he said, "Those things don't work on me anymore."

The Concrete Logical Child loves to keep records and charts. Becky, nine, kept detailed accounts of the stock market, comparing the ups and downs of her McDonald's shares to her friend's Jiffy Lube shares. She fussed when her parents didn't save the stock page of the newspaper, which she filed away daily. Lucy made detailed bar graphs of her wins and losses on the computer game, *What's My Logic?* These are prime opportunities to teach the data-gathering and chart-making skills needed for science.

The child will also welcome scheduling; at no other time is he so intrigued with tracking events in time. It's a big mistake, however, to assume that the child will be as meticulous about following the plan; his concept of time hasn't caught up with his ability to put things down in little notebooks. Becky, for example, charted her day—get up at 7:00, feed the dog at 7:20, eat breakfast at 7:30—but usually the schedule was unrealistic. Instead of saying to the child, "You made a schedule but you didn't follow it," help your child realize that a schedule is an estimation that needs to be continually revised as experience dictates. You might say, "You know, it takes awhile to put the dog's food out. Why don't you schedule more time for that?"

In grades three to six, concentrate on helping the child master both concepts and skills, such as the multiplication tables, reading, decoding skills, and handwriting. It's important to strike a balance between the two as well as between homework and play.

Continue concrete touchable experiences during this period. (Some parents mistakenly think that children have outgrown the need for seeing, feeling, touching.) If the subject is fractions, bake a cake using measuring spoons and measuring cups, or build a model using half and quarter inches. If a child is having trouble with math, use bean bags, glasses, baseball cards, anything he can see and touch.

Formal Logical (Ages 12–16)

The Formal Logical Child is oriented toward idealism and sees the world as good/bad and black/white. He enjoys cause-effect and "if-then" reasoning. During his apprenticeship to good judgment and abstract thinking, his reasoning is often poor and his data may be incomplete. It's a good time to teach thinking skills such as inductive/deductive thinking and divergent/convergent thinking.

In the process of forming his own personality, he rejects the ideas of his parents and teachers, sweeping them away with over-generalizations and stereotypes: "My father is very stupid," and "Everything is dumb," and "Teachers don't know how to teach."

He's busy creating a belief system and his theme song may be "Don't bother me while I'm building it." If he doesn't have his own set of beliefs about boys and girls, who's stupid, or what's in, he may embrace a ready-made set. For example, Julio, sixteen, adopted the sixties philosophy: he had long hair, listened to Beatles' music and begged to hear about the Vietnam War. Your job is not to challenge or confront your child, but to acknowledge. It's very important that the child have a nonthreatening adult with whom he can relate.

Expect the Formal Logical Child to love at least one subject each year, to be bringing books home every night and to be writing a great deal.

Homework and Development

Understanding the developmental stages is often the missing piece of the homework puzzle. For example, parents who have mastered communication with a Sensory-Motor Child may get into a power struggle or give up completely when, one morning, they wake up with a Magical Child who doesn't listen and won't do homework. Fathers, especially, because they usually spend less time with the child and may be unaware of subtle changes in development, tend to take this one-size-fits-all approach. A parent ignorant of the characteristics of the developmental stages is more likely to punish, to have "out-of-control" children, and to miss the golden opportunity to be in harmony with the child's natural phase.

Everything you do to match your child's developmental stage is a contributor to school success. Because school is often not in sync with a child's developmental stage, you may need to provide the right homework assignment at home to satisfy the demands of his developmental stage.

Samantha, six, failed first grade because the teacher said she was "immature." (Although "immature" is a popular note on report cards, we never use the term. It indicates a mismatch between school experiences and the child's developmental needs.) In school she acted silly, played imaginary games, and daydreamed constantly. But when she came to us, we found that all her test scores were very high. We discovered, after talking to her parents, that Samantha had no chance to be a Magical Child at home because they frowned on play and constantly talked to Samantha about "responsibility." Everything was so regimented at home that Samantha took the only course of action any red-blooded Magical Child could take—she played at school. Her parents' "homework" was to allow the Magical Child to revel in her magical kingdom.

The developmental stages are biologically rooted with their own timetable and a fixed sequence. You can't drastically change the rate of development.

It's very important that a child go through each developmental stage. Each level is a preparation for the next. If you force a child to think abstractly too early, you may get an abstract thinker who can't fantasize. If you push verbal too quickly and "cheat" sensory-motor, you get a very verbal child without good motor coordination who will have trouble with small motor development in school. If

Honor Developmental Stages

Sensory-Motor

1. Favor sensory-motor activities above others. If the child plays with small figures indoors or watches too much TV, compensate with outdoor, large motor activities, such as jumping rope, playing hopscotch, playing ball.

2. Limit the use of any device that inhibits total body movement, such as backpacks and strollers. Even walkers with wheels inhibit middle body movement—the child isn't sitting down, standing up, or learning to balance.

3. Use movement and music tapes for a natural introduction to colors, shapes, letters, and numbers. (See Educational Activities' Hap Palmer tapes in Part Five, "Recommended Materials," Videotapes.)

Magical Child

1. Welcome your child's fantasies; join him in them. Never dispute an exaggerated claim.

2. Use fairy tales, myths, and legends (and not biographies and facts) to make homework fun.

3. Use animal power ("Oreo Bear is going to do this with you") to persuade a child to do anything—eat, go to sleep, or do his homework.

you don't give enough concrete experiences, the child may be limited in his ability to do processes such as math because he can't see the image in his mind.

Sometimes he may appear to skip a stage; it usually means that he's just testing the waters of the next one and he may flip back and forth. If he does miss a stage, however, he can go back and "pick it up," although it's more difficult as he gets older. If the child has come too quickly out of the sensory-motor stage, for example,

Concrete Logical

1. Exploit your child's desire to learn facts, keep tables, and collect things. Buy notebooks, diaries, and photo albums to encourage collecting.

2. Help your child establish the habit of scheduling, but don't berate the child for not sticking to a plan as first constructed.

3. Encourage your child to pursue his nonschool interests, even those that may not seem immediately useful to you. If your child wants to collect stamps, don't say, "You won't have time to do your homework." Instead, help him develop his hobby.

Formal Logical

1. Since parents are temporarily out of style, encourage your child to have another adult as a confidant(e): an uncle, aunt, minister, or a best friend's mother or father.

2. This is a good time to teach formal thinking skills: logical (step by step to a single conclusion) and lateral (generation of many ideas). The Formal Logical Child will also enjoy learning about how his brain works.

3. Know that your child's social motivation—to look good, to fit in, to be accepted—may be more powerful than his motivation to do well in school. Encourage your child to associate with children who are successful in school.

we may spend a lot of time doing sensory-motor activities, especially "cross laterals" for integrating the right and left parts of the body.

We encourage talking to the child about what's happening to him as he moves to another stage. The minute he makes a change toward an older behavior, we'll say, "Do you remember when you used to cry about your homework?" Maybe it was only yesterday, but we reminisce as though it were ages ago. This puts time and space between the child and the younger behaviors he wants to grow out of. Children look forward to being older and this anticipation can be used to encourage them to acquire new skills. Instead of saying, "Maybe when you're nine, you'll finally learn how to spell," or "I wish you'd act like a nine-year-old," we'll say to an eight-year-old having trouble with spelling, "Let me tell you about nine-year-olds. They can spell very well. When you're nine, spelling will be no problem."

The Search for Multiple Intelligences

Every parent knows when a child says his first word, but how many observe the child's other intelligences—his first dance step, first block structure, first resolution of a problem with a friend? Verbal intelligences tend to catch our attention at the expense of other intelligences: musical, visual-spatial, bodily-kinesthetic, and personal intelligences, as well as wisdom, intuition, and street smarts.

To Bobby and Glen's parents, for example, intelligence meant fluency with words, good verbal memory, and the accumulation of thousands of facts. This is still the image that comes to mind for most people when they hear the word "intelligence." Add mathematical logic and you have what the schools and the vast majority of I.Q. tests call "intelligence."

Recently, however, experts have come to believe that there are many areas of intelligence. After studying kindergartners for a year, Howard Gardner, Co-Director of the Harvard Project Zero, now thinks there could be as many as two hundred intelligences. He has, however, identified seven primary intelligences.[3] Note that musical and linguistic intelligences appear at fairly precise ages, but other intelligences will be apparent at different ages in different children.

1. *Linguistic Intelligence* is a facility with words. It shows up in gifted children by age four (earlier in girls than in boys). It's used by writers, translators, actors, et cetera. Children with high linguistic intelligence will love to tell stories and play with the sounds of words.

2. *Logical-Mathematical Intelligence* is a facility with reasoning, visual thinking, and nonverbal problem solving; it is used by computer analysts, economists, and scientists. Children with high logical-mathematical intelligence will love puzzles, logical arguments, and computers.

3. *Spatial Intelligence* is the ability to image spatially rotated objects and to orient yourself in space (for example, find your way around a city); it is used by artists, architects, engineers, pilots, sailors, and some scientists. Children with high spatial intelligence will enjoy drawing or designing things; they may also like machines and may daydream often.

4. *Body Intelligence* is the sense of one's own body and how it moves in space; it is used by dancers, actors, athletes, and craftsman. Children with high body intelligence will enjoy almost any kind of movement.

5. *Musical Intelligence* is a facility with the sounds and rhythms of music; it is used by all kinds of musicians and dancers. The prime time for musical intelligences is between the ages of four and five, when auditory discrimination develops very rapidly. Children with high musical intelligence will be particular about the music they listen to and they will enjoy singing and playing instruments.

6. *Interpersonal/Social Intelligence* involves understanding people and how to deal with them; it is an intelligence used by politicians, salespeople, and psychologists. Tiny babies who are immediately attracted to other people are often demonstrating an early knack for social intelligence. Children with high social intelligence will enjoy being with other people and they will understand how to get things done that involve other people. They will often be the class leaders.

7. *Intrapersonal Intelligence* is knowing one's self and abilities and being able to control one's emotions; it is an intelligence used by writers, entrepreneurs, psychologists, and ministers. Children with

high intrapersonal intelligence can be opinionated and usually enjoy working on independent projects.

Two other intelligences are less well-defined: *Intuition* is having a "sixth sense" about an event or person without having any factual evidence. This intelligence is highly valued in business. *Common sense*, also known as "street smarts" or practical intelligence, is an ability to match the right action to the right situation.[4]

Each intelligence has a "prime time" to develop, but these times may vary among individuals. For example, Lindsey learned to swim by "just watching a fish," at age four when she was very kinesthetic and her body intelligence was high. She could have learned to swim at age eight or nine, but with a great deal more difficulty.

Catching this moment, however, depended on her parents providing her with the opportunity to be in water; otherwise she might not have learned at all. The flowering of the intelligences, unlike the developmental stages, depends on the support of the educational system and parents. If no songs are played around the house, a child may not develop his musical intelligence.

Many, if not most, of the children that we test, show an uneven intelligence profile; there are highs and lows. On the other hand, children without school problems who are good learners have fewer highs and lows among the intelligences. Six-year-old Betsy had a profile, for example, that was very high in intrapersonal and very low in visual-spatial. She could talk her way through many situations and was quite sociable, but she did poorly in school because she had not mastered visual-spatial skills.

It's a myth, however, that intelligence is fixed and that Betsy is "stuck." Our experience with thousands of children indicates that the right learning style matched to the right learning method will help bring the lows up to the level of the highs on the intelligence profile.

"It may be," says Gardner, "that intensive intervention at an early age can bring a larger number of children to an 'at promise' level."[5] We believe that homework can be this intensive intervention, particularly with the inclusion of art, music, spatial, and body intelligences to counterbalance a school's emphasis on verbal and mathematical intelligence. Recognizing also that social skills (how the child relates to the parent, teacher, and other children) make up a separate intelligence is a critical step toward bringing a child to an "at promise" level through homework. The parent must be attuned to both the developmental stage of the child and the promise of specific intelligences. If both parents are low in a particular intelligence (body, for example), it is unlikely that they will recognize a child's intelligence in that area (athletics). If both parents are very verbal, they may not notice or appreciate mathematical intelligence.

Parents can use the strong intelligences of a child to "pull up" the other intelligences. Patrick, sixteen, had a hard time with school even though he was obviously very bright and had the potential for a great artistic career. His gift for spatial intelligence was never acknowledged in school. Once his parents were aware of his other intelligences, their attitude changed. Instead of blaming him, they used his "nonschool" spatial intelligence to help him succeed. Their plan started with Patrick reading Shakespeare's *Macbeth*, a task he didn't enjoy. Patrick's mother asked his English teacher if he could do an art project to demonstrate his knowledge of the play. The teacher agreed and Patrick made a handsome set of drawings illustrating major turning points in the story. When his intelligence was acknowledged, Patrick even began to enjoy reading Shakespeare.

The Teachable Moment

Once you are familiar with the developmental stages and the intelligences, you can learn to recognize your child's Teachable Moment. Margaret, eight, begged for violin lessons, sang songs, and constantly pretended she was playing the violin. But because she had reading problems, her parents didn't want to "overburden" her. This was a Teachable Moment; her musical intelligence was at promise.

Look for your child's own natural development, rather than comparing him to the norm. Instead of saying, "He's four and he should be doing x," think about it this way: "He's four; what has he shown interest in? What is he already good at?" Let the child reveal his own Teachable Moment.

Sometimes parents miss a particularly poignant Teachable Moment because they think their child should be doing something else.

Roger's parents were concerned that, at age four, their son wasn't reading. After all, his older brothers had been reading since they were three. In addition, Roger's teacher reported that his attention span was short, he didn't listen, and he doodled constantly during class (an intelligence clue). What his parents didn't value as much as reading, however, was the fact that Roger loved to spend hours building intricate ships out of blue and red Legos. When one of his older brothers left a Rubik's Cube on the living room floor, Roger picked it up and quickly solved it, an ability he lost at age seven.

This was Roger's Teachable Moment when he could easily, almost magically, see complex spatial relationships. Later, when his parents learned about the Teachable Moment and realized that Roger's visual-spatial intelligence was now at risk, they reinforced his love for building by buying him games, construction sets, a back-yard building set, and an advanced Legos set with its own carrying case. He regained his Rubik's Cube ability by age eight.

If a child starts drawing cartoons, instead of saying to him, "Stop it. You should be doing your homework," incorporate the cartoons into his homework. Have him draw characters from his history lesson, or the letters of the alphabet.

Understanding the broad range of intelligences and the sequencing of the developmental stages are keys to understanding how the child can naturally love homework and learning.

Homework Journal

1. List ten of your child's successes this week; list ten of your own.

2. What is your child's developmental stage?

3. How can you adjust his homework to fit his developmental stage?

4. How can you help him ease into his next developmental stage?

5. Evaluate your child's intelligences. Which is he strong in and which does he need encouragement in?

6. What Teachable Moments have you noticed?

7. How can you use your child's strong intelligences to "pull up" his weaker intelligences?

Week 3:
Learning with Style

Keep in Mind

1. There is no preferred learning style.

2. All thinking is based on remembering and imagining.

3. Each child has her own sequence of learning strategies.

• Ryan came to us because he couldn't recognize the letters of the alphabet. "Each flower blossoms in its own time," Ryan's first-grade teacher said, but Ryan's father doubted the boy was just a late bloomer.

"You know, when I read to him he can't sit still," said Ryan's father, "and I tell him to sit still because it's important."

"If he wants to jump up and down, let him," we said. "Some kids learn better when they jump up and down."

Ryan's learning style—the way his brain takes in information —is *kinesthetic*. He learns through his body and his feelings; he learns better when his body is moving. When he has to sit still, his brain turns off. In school, it's frequently in the off position.

• Little Catherine, who has trouble with math, learns mainly through her ears. Her learning style is *auditory*. If she *hears* something, she remembers it. In math, she can *tell* you the answer, but she can't put it down on paper.

• Nine-year-old Gregory is a *visual* learner. He learns best when he sees a picture in his mind. He asked his mother to tape his spelling words on the ceiling above his bathtub so he can *see* them.

Ryan can't sit still, Catherine can't write math problems down, and Gregory can't spell the words unless he sees them. What's wrong with these children? Nothing. These children aren't uncooperative or obstinate. What they illustrate is that all children learn differently; they have different *styles* of taking in information.

In Week 3, we show you how to determine your child's primary learning style and how to adapt her homework to that style.[1]

When we ask children, "How do you remember your telephone number?", we find that kinesthetic children remember it by the feel of their fingers on the dial, visual children remember it by seeing the numbers in their mind, and auditory children remember it as the sounds that the numbers on a digital phone make. Some mothers calm their babies by rocking (kinesthetic), some by singing a song (auditory), and some by showing them their reflection in a mirror (visual).

Learning is intimately involved with the senses—a fact that, in our sensory-deficient schools, we tend to forget. Children are multi-prong learners, but schools are usually one-prong systems. It is estimated that "90 percent of all instruction occurs through the lecture and the question and answer methods." However, only about 30 percent of children learn best by listening.[2]

Most children (and most adults) are unaware of the brain's internal processes. Sometimes after only one hour of learning about their learning style, they begin to see how their brain works and how differently it may work compared to another person's.

All humans use all modes of learning. When we say Gregory is a visual learner, we mean he *primarily* (not always) uses *images* to interpret the events around him. When we talk about the learning style of a child, we mean how the child's brain processes information and in what order. For example, some people see pictures first, hear sounds or words second, and experience feelings third. Some people feel or hear something first and get pictures in their mind second. Because brains take in information so differently, no one learning method works best for everyone.

Four main ideas will help you understand the different types of learners:

1. *There are external and internal parts of learning.* Some children are extremely sensitive to what goes on around them; they don't miss a friend's new haircut, the funny sound at the back of the car, or any other external change. This iş an *external* learning style. Others are more attuned to what goes on inside their heads. Their internal movies, sounds, or feelings are stronger than outside distractions. This is an *internal* learning style. Obviously, all of us at times are more oriented to the outer world and at other times we are more inner directed.

2. *All information coming into and going out of the human body depends on five channels: sight, hearing, feeling, smelling, and tasting.*

3. *All thinking is based on remembering and imagining* as when a ten-year-old remembers her fifth birthday party or imagines her sixteenth.

4. *When a person is thinking (remembering or imagining), her eye movements, verbal expressions, and body movements indicate which part of the brain she is using.*

Types of Learners

We speak of six major learning styles: Visual External, Visual Internal, Auditory External, Auditory Internal, Kinesthetic External, and Kinesthetic Internal. To this, we add two minor learning styles: Gustatory and Olfactory. Remember that a child uses all these modes of learning, but one style often predominates. For convenience, we have used the terms, "the visual child, the auditory child, the kinesthetic child." A more accurate description is "a child accessing visual parts of her brain."

The *Visual External* child cares about how things look; she likes neatness and order and may constantly straighten things. She is good at proofreading. She may say, "I can't do my homework because I don't like the way the teacher looks." The Visual External child is careful about how she looks and may be critical of how other people dress or how they do things, such as load the dishwasher. She may keep her toys in order. She likes to draw pictures, do puzzles, and play games.

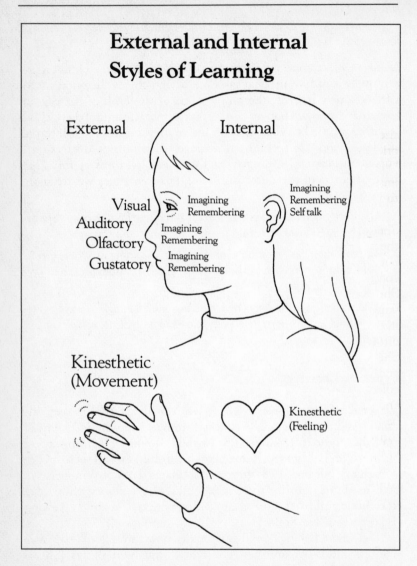

External and Internal Styles of Learning

External

Internal

Visual
Auditory
Olfactory
Gustatory

Imagining
Remembering

Imagining
Remembering

Imagining
Remembering

Imagining
Remembering
Self talk

Kinesthetic
(Movement)

Kinesthetic
(Feeling)

The *Visual Internal* child sees pictures in her mind, usually clear, color pictures with movement. Most children, consciously or unconsciously, have this ability, but children whose primary system is visual, know without question that they see pictures. (Children who have no trouble with "internal visualization" often don't realize that others, including their parents, may have little or no awareness of how to form pictures in their heads.) The Visual Internal child daydreams and may be an inventor. She sometimes complains of sounds interrupting her, and may watch TV with the sound off. She thinks faster than she can speak, plays with imaginary characters, and is usually a good speller.

She uses visual words to describe the shape, form, color, and size of something (square, blue, striped). She may be more internally oriented in general. In the Visual Internal child there are two modes: "visual remembering" or calling images up from the past; and "visual imagining," calling imaginary pictures up or cartoons, or being able to visualize the way things are going to look.

The *Auditory External* child is sensitive to pitch, tone, and rhythm. She hears when you call her. She may listen to TV but not watch the picture. She may like working with sound in the background, but she may be quite particular about what song, and how loud, continually flipping the radio dial until she hears the right song. She may say, "I love her voice," or "I hate her voice." Her own voice tends to be well modulated and interesting to listen to. She likes to talk and to listen, particularly to recorded tapes. The Auditory External child may prefer reading aloud to reading silently. She tends to tell stories with details about what happened to whom and who said what rather than stories with visual details about shape, color, and movement. She likes making car sounds (*Vroom, Vroom*) and siren sounds. She appreciates structure and rules. She likes to be read to. She makes imaginary animals talk to each other. She turns her head to the side when answering questions (prompting a visual parent to say, "Look at me when I'm talking to you").

The *Auditory Internal* child may go into "story mode," remembering precise story lines; she relishes telling about a movie or her day at school. She remembers songs and she may not be conscious of seeing pictures. She rehearses conversations in her mind and may "play" old tapes of things she's heard—for example, negative or positive statements from her parents: "You'll never be any good," "You'll never make it," or "You're wonderful," "You can do anything you want." The internal auditory voice usually appears at age five. Girls become auditory learners earlier than boys and tend to have better auditory skills. (Conversely, boys tend to be kinesthetic longer than girls.)[3]

In the Auditory Internal child there are two modes: "Auditory remembering" is remembering what you have heard before (words to songs, conversation, tonalities), and "auditory imagining" is imagining how things are going to sound that you haven't heard yet (the national anthem played in chimes, voice imitations).

The *Self-Talker or Strategizer* child talks to herself, sometimes out loud, while performing a task. Joseph Chilton Pearce calls this self-talk, the "yackety yack that goes on in your brain."[4] The Self-Talker actually shows the feeling part of Auditory Internal. When children get stuck on a math problem, we ask, "What did you say to yourself?" They begin to realize they are criticizing themselves, or calling themselves names, rather than using their self-talk to guide them through a problem. A child can't be self-critical and be a good Self-Talker at the same time. A Self-Talker is constantly evaluating. She may miss the teacher's instruction to "Circle all the incorrect words" because she's saying to herself, "I hate this teacher, I hate spelling, I can't pass this test."

A good Self-Talker will say to herself, while working on a math computer program, "Well, let's see, the numbers are getting smaller, so it must be subtraction or division. So let me try that."

The *Kinesthetic External* child rocks in her chair, plays outdoors until exhausted, and loves sports. She is sensitive to how her clothes feel, and may not care how she looks. She loves to touch the fur of animals. She enjoys movement in any form—dancing, climbing, aerobics, gymnastics—and has a good sense of balance. (Many children labeled "learning disabled" are kinesthetic learners.) Young Kinesthetic External learners love to use sandpaper, clay, felt, nylon, and burlap to help them learn. If you have a kinesthetic teenager, she may need more physical than verbal expressions (hugs instead of "That was good"). Let her study on the floor; don't force her to "sit up straight" in the chair.

The *Kinesthetic Internal* child is completely aware of her feelings. She may whine, be clingy, and sensitive, and cry or giggle a lot. She looks down and has an emotionally expressive face. When you scold her, she hangs her head down. She is quick to hug and to express feelings.

There are two other less prominent learning styles: *Gustatory* and *Olfactory*. You will notice these styles in children who have very discriminating food and smell tastes.

One sixth grader, when asked his earliest memory, said, "Dipping asparagus in lemon juice" at age three, and when we asked,

"What could help improve your schoolwork," he said, "If I had better food to eat." A nineteen-year-old boy who graduated from high school without having learned to read, showed no strong predilection toward any of the other learning styles. But we noticed that he had a keen sense of taste. When we suggested that he go to chef's school, he was sufficiently motivated to learn to read recipes, so he did learn to read and he became a chef.

The Olfactory learning style can be used to help children remember information. Evidence suggests that if people associate certain information with one smell, and can use that same smell at the time of a test, it brings back the state of mind in which they can more easily remember the information.

Eye Movements

We have videotaped hundreds of children to find out how they learn. Starting with questions such as "What is your telephone number?" or "Can you hear the sound of your mother's voice?" we observe their eye movements and verbal responses to these questions. We observe what they say, how they say it, and the *pattern* of eye movements. For example, in response to "What does your mother's voice sound like?", a child may *hear* her mother's voice internally (looking to the side), see a picture of her mother internally (looking up), or get a feeling about her mother (looking down). This sequence may happen within seconds.

(These eye movement patterns are cues to internal learning styles; there are no eye movements associated with external styles.)

You can observe the pattern of eye movements, words, and body movements by asking different children the same question: "Can you see the Washington Monument?" A visual child looks up and might say, "Yes, I can see the orange sunset in the background and the flags are waving." An auditory child looks to the side and might say, "It's *like* a pencil," but she may not see a mental image. A kinesthetic child may make a motion with her hands indicating the height and width. The idea is to determine which learning style the child is using most of the time.

If your child spends most of her time looking up, you can assume she is a visual learner. If her eyes look to the sides, she may learn auditorily. And if her eyes look down, she probably tends to learn

Learning Styles and Eye Movements

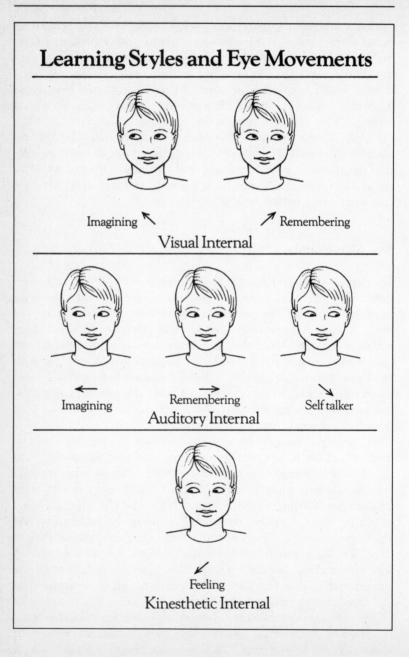

Imagining   Remembering
Visual Internal

Imagining   Remembering   Self talker
Auditory Internal

Feeling
Kinesthetic Internal

kinesthetically. The child who looks straight away with eyes unfocused is usually accessing either visual remembering or visual imagining, but ask questions to make sure. Closed eyes indicate remembering or imaging smell or taste or visual imagining. (Every child will fit into more than one category, but almost everyone has one main way of processing information.)

Ask your child, "Do you see pictures in your head?" The answer will either be, "Huh? What? I don't understand?" (auditory or kinesthetic), or "Yeah, sure," almost with disdain if she does (visual). One six-year-old said, "Sure, I see pictures. I can turn to channel twenty-two, twenty-seven, twenty-nine, and twenty-one. As a matter of fact, I see it all the time. Two dinosaurs are playing right now."

A right-handed child looks up and to the left for visual remembering, up and to the right for visual imagining, to the left side for auditory remembering, to the right side for auditory imagining, to the left and down for Self-Talk, down and to the right for Kinesthetic Internal. Sometimes these eye movements are reversed for left-handed children. (For example, a left-handed child may look up to the right for visual remembering and up to the left for visual imagining.) To be sure of how your child's eye movements relate to her learning style, you need to ask memory questions.

For reasons that are not quite understood, kinesthetic eye movements are not parallel to the visual and auditory eye movements. Usually, a child looks down when feeling, but when you ask about the content, you will find that feelings are based on combinations of pictures, sounds, and body feelings. She may be afraid of a horrible ghost (look down) but look up to see it.

Word Clues

What children say often gives away their learning system. Between the ages of two and five, children start expressing very strong preferences: "I like Sandra," and "I hate green peas." This isn't an attempt to be precocious; it's their way of partitioning the universe, of becoming who they are. Listen carefully to these likes and dislikes; they will often be a clue to their primary learning style. A visual child, for example, will say, "I don't like the way things *look*," or "*Show* me," "Look! Look!" or "I went blank on the test." An auditory child may like the way things *sound*—"Tell me, tell me," "That clicks," "You said . . ." or "You told me . . . Listen!" A kinesthetic child, will say, "Hold it, I'm stuck," or "I don't feel like it."

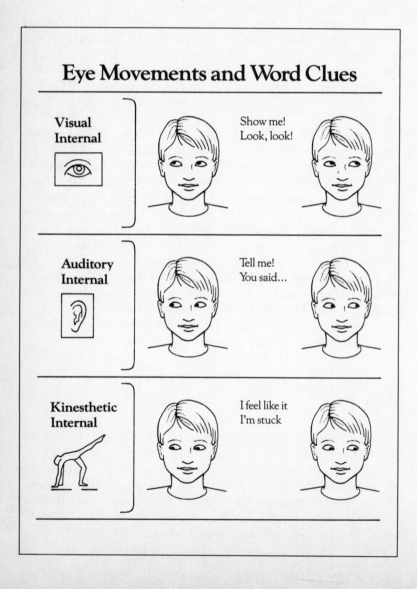

Eye Movements and Word Clues

Visual Internal
Show me! Look, look!

Auditory Internal
Tell me! You said...

Kinesthetic Internal
I feel like it I'm stuck

Auditory, visual, and kinesthetic learning styles are very *broad* categories. Within each style are many individual differences. In observing your child's learning style, no one activity is the final answer. But when you carefully observe and give the child the opportunity to show you her style, you will begin to see a pattern.

Family Learning Styles

"Oh, you're just like your dad," may be the sign of a learning style schism in a family. Mom, who is Visual External (keeps things neat), may consider Scott slovenly and disorganized, while Dad sees him as comfortable and well-adjusted. Scott gets caught in learning-style limbo between parents with vastly different brain processes.

Michael's father (auditory) was a lawyer who remembered facts easily.[5] He couldn't understand why his kinesthetic artistic son wouldn't sit still long enough to remember the multiplication tables, and why his visually internal wife didn't keep the house neat. On the other hand, he got along well with his daughter, who got straight A's and had no trouble in school. When he sat down with his son to work, Michael would constantly say things so he could get up— "I want a soda," "I need to sharpen my pencils"—anything so he could move around. His father finally blew up and said, "When you work, you work; when you play, you play."

The solution to this problem in family learning style was to play on the strengths of each family member. We used the mother's and son's artistic abilities to make a color-coded multiplication chart. Michael was allowed to move when he wanted to, and his father saw that what he considered "fooling around" helped Michael learn his math with ease.

Family differences in learning styles needn't be a source of conflict. On the contrary, they can be complementary and enriching for your child. Don't insist that your child conform to your learning style. Instead, acknowledge her style and accommodate her homework to it, but at the same time expand her repertoire of learning styles by showing her your own.

Neither Howard's mother nor his father valued his natural athletic abilities (Kinesthetic External). His mother was a Self-Talker, solved problems quickly, and was annoyed when father and son couldn't keep up with her. The Visual Internal father lived very much inside his own head. The mother thought Howard was simply "dumb" like his father. The parents were so tuned into their own internal processes, that Howard had no model for relating to the outside world.

When the family understood that it was okay for each member to have a different learning style, they stopped blaming and began building the bridges they needed to communicate. Howard's father used his internal visual ability to help Howard see himself as a star soccer player. He taught Howard to look at the pictures inside his head, which Howard had been unaware of before. Howard's mother, using her internal auditory strategies, helped him think through new soccer plays, saying, "Here's what I'm doing now, here's what I'm going to do next." In this way, Howard was able to expand his own thinking processes.

Victor, sixteen, was musically talented, had long hair and played in a rock band. (His learning style was an auditory/kinesthetic combination. He took in information through auditory means first then kinesthetic.) More than anything he wanted his father to appreciate his music. Unfortunately, his father, while kinesthetic, had poor auditory skills and refused to listen. Finally, the father blurted out, "You don't understand, I can't *hear* the music. I'm not deaf; I just have no way of hearing whether it's good or bad. It wouldn't matter if it was rock or country. I just can't hear it."

Victor couldn't believe it! How could his father not hear the difference? We explained that his father did not have the highly developed auditory style that Victor had. Eventually, Victor's father agreed to listen to the music and to acknowledge Victor's auditory abilities. At the same time, Victor no longer required his father to approve it, because he understood that his father couldn't.

There was another learning style difference in this family. Victor's mother was visual, dressed neatly, and objected to Victor's long hair and pot-smoking. Our conversation with her went like this:

"On a scale of one to ten, how much does it matter if Victor smokes pot?"

"Nine."

"On a scale of one to ten, how much does it matter that he has long hair?"

"That's a nine, too."

Her highly visual learning style had distorted her judgment. We finally got them both to agree that he would stop smoking pot in exchange for keeping his hair long, an exchange Victor was willing to make. Again, we were able to make learning-style adjustments that everyone could accept.

Applying Learning Style to Homework

Some learning styles are less well-suited to standard school curricula than others. The artistic, kinesthetic child whose thinking is also predominantly right brained (intuitive, imaginative, and more spatially oriented) will tend not to do as well in a traditional classroom as an auditory child whose thinking is chiefly left brained (linear, logical, and analytical).

Your job is to show the kinesthetic or visual child a different way to learn the same material and to allow her different ways to show what she knows. Each child is a little different; honor the differences; don't "correct" them. One child learning a computer program may need to get up and walk away from it for awhile; another may need to talk it through. A highly visual child may simply look at a math formula for the cube root of eight and understand it; another may need to have it explained.

You won't have to write spelling words on charts or record lectures on tape for the rest of your child's school life. Use the techniques initially, to help the child learn how to learn, or to overcome a particular learning problem. The final authority, your child, will accept or reject the parts that work, according to her own internal system.

If your child is the type who, as one mother said, "will spill a glass of milk, and then, not only will she not clean it up, she will walk right through it," she is probably also careless about proofreading her homework; she won't check the spelling, and she'll miss some of the punctuation. She's not Visual External. The idea is not to nag and tell her she's lazy, but to make her aware that it's not her natural style to be observant visually. Encourage her to compensate by slowing down and looking around. She may need a proofreading checklist for her homework.

When Ryan's father began to understand learning style, he stopped trying to harness Ryan's energy. Instead, he incorporated more kinesthetic activities, including hopscotch for math. He let him stand at his writing desk. Ryan, when he wasn't made to sit all the time, met him halfway. He calmed down and started to learn.

There is a "built-in" learning style for each subject area. (See Part Four, "Homework Hotspots.") Spelling is easier for visual children because it depends on seeing the word. Math, especially algebra, is visual, but also requires self-talk. The visual child who does well in math but has problems with algebra, needs to develop self-talk.

For years, knowing that each child needed something different, we searched for new teaching methods. But children almost always proved us wrong when what we recommended—even though it was education's most innovative method—failed to match their learning style. (The best of methods is only as good as its fit to the learner.) We finally opted for the obvious: We asked children to tell us "what helps you learn?" Some of the answers were surprising, and many times we didn't understand *why* they worked. Children will think of learning techniques that never occur to a learning specialist or to a psychologist.

Gregory, nine, told his mother to tape his spelling words on the ceiling above the bathtub. He couldn't explain why this might work, and she didn't take kindly to his suggestion, but was desperate for good spelling grades, so she complied. Later, we learned that rolling the eyes up and to the left helps access visual memory. Looking up helped Gregory see the word spelled correctly in his mind. When his mother honored his request, Gregory's spelling grades improved. Now we often recommend that parents of visual learners paste new spelling words on the ceiling over their children's beds so they see them as they go to sleep at night, or, less dramatically, to hold the spelling cards up and to the left for the children.

When a child fails to learn something, change the method of presenting the material. Change it into her learning style—sound it out, draw a picture, help her feel it.

Acknowledging learning styles allows us to talk about our differences less emotionally; we become less judgmental about others and less defensive about ourselves. We learn that Carla isn't being obnoxious when she taps on the desk and Joey isn't trying to be difficult when he wants to look at pictures instead of read. Children's differences are less attributable to absolute standards, good or evil, than they are to differences in ways we take in and make meaning of our experiences.

The Visual Learner

Tony, eleven, was very visual; he spent a lot of time watching TV and movies, and playing video games.

He would look at a math problem and say, "Yes, I can do it" or "No, I can't," but his lack of internal auditory skills kept him from having any "figuring out" strategies. His mother said he had not talked to himself when he was little and never played "let's pretend" games.

Instead of yelling, "Think! Think! Think!" (an all too common response by parents), we helped Tony create an internal auditory process.

There are many ways to help a visual child remember information. If she's learning the state capitals, put a huge map of the United States on her bedroom wall. For history, help her make a timeline going around her room, on which she can write in the dates of key events. Think how much easier it will be to conceptualize the timing of events if she can see the Revolutionary War to the left of the dresser, the Civil War to the right of it, the Great Depression beyond that, and the Civil Rights movement farther on. Put your family's birth and marriage dates on the timeline.

Make sure a visual learner has a large art tablet and a good set of felt-tipped markers. Nothing helps children learn a concept better than a larger-than-life illustration of the "Concept of the Week." When she is first learning division, put one division problem on a large sheet of paper on the wall; if she can see the model in her head while doing a problem, she will have more room in her "working memory" for the calculations. Little by little, she will incorporate the model into her memory and you can move the illustration from the wall to a file of helpful materials.

The Auditory Learner

If your auditory child is having trouble with spelling, write the spelling words very large and put them up and to the left over her desk, or over her bed so it is the last thing she sees at night. This helps imprint the words on visual memory. Practice spelling the words backward and forward. Spelling backward helps move the child's processing away from auditory and toward visual.

Even though school is best suited to auditory children, they can still have problems with certain subjects that require good internal visualization skills, such as spelling. Many auditory children who do not visualize internally tend not to be able to read and enjoy descriptive paragraphs as much as those whose minds are flashing with pictures from every phrase. Internal visual skills are the key to comprehension.

To auditory sixth-grader Christopher, the visual skill of spelling was difficult. Christopher spelled every word exactly as it *sounded*. He knew logically there was not a one-to-one correspondence, but he had little awareness of how things *looked*. Misspelled words looked okay to him.

Christopher learned to develop a better visual learning style, by first learning to recognize and mark words that looked wrong. (Initially he spelled words with no vowels at all and that didn't look wrong to him. A first step in spelling is to see if the word fits a correct pattern.) We also had Christopher practice imagining scenes with these instructions: "Picture the front of your house in your mind, now add the trees, the driveway, the mailbox." This process helped Christopher see things in his mind.

There are several ways to help an auditory child with reading. Look at factual information and make up a "Once upon a time." Turn facts into songs, write poems, varying voice quality and tone. Allow two auditory children to read a book together aloud, alternating chapters. Auditory children, especially, are never too old to be read to by the teacher or another child.

To help a child with low visual skills, we take a paragraph from a book and build the picture, make a movie in her head, line by line, saying, "Let's imagine this happening. Do you remember something like this?" Sometimes the first paragraph takes twenty minutes. The second may only take five minutes.

Danny, eight, had low visual skills. He could read, but he was very slow. After reading a paragraph about Indians running up the hill, he had no idea what he had read and could not respond to the question, "What does the Indian look like?"

So we read, "The Indian went up the mountain," then we said, "Now, let's make a movie of that. Describe your Indian and I'll describe mine. Does he have feathers? How old is he?"

Suddenly Danny was excited and said, "You mean I can do it any way I want to?" He had stopped himself from learning because he thought there was a correct way to imagine.

If your auditory child is visibly animated while talking about a subject but loses all interest while writing about it, let her talk her assignment into a tape-recorder and play it back, taking dictation from herself. Also, allow her to use appropriate background music for studying. (See Part Four, "Homework Helpers," Music.)

In some very auditory or self-talk children the auditory "channel" is full of negative self-talk that stops them from learning. Derrick, thirteen, was a high auditory/kinesthetic, low visual learner who had never been able to learn from a book. He could understand what he read for a moment, but it seemed quickly to evaporate. When he worked on a geometry program on the computer, he either jumped to push the keys to guess or he said, "I don't know what its talking about." And every time he tried to study, he heard his father's voice saying, "You don't make A's. I made all A's in school. Your mother had a perfect grade point average. What's wrong with you?"

We told Derrick, "Turn down the volume of the voices inside that compare you with other people. Take out the old, 'I can't' tapes and put in new 'I can, I know how' ones." We helped him simultaneously turn on his visual and turn down his auditory so that the pictures and sounds finally complemented his learning.

The Kinesthetic Learner

The kinesthetic learning style is the one least acknowledged in schools, and children who are kinesthetic learners are the ones most commonly referred for psychological help. For them, school feels like too much talk and not enough movement, touch, or personal involvement. These children tend to do things that may irritate parents and teachers, such as swiveling in their chairs, twirling their hair, or grabbing at nearby objects.

For the Kinesthetic External learner, make up a play, a dance, any kind of movement around what she's studying. Juanita, eight, a kinesthetic learner (she took three types of dance and gymnastics), reversed letters when she spelled, and read at primer level. All the learning specialists at her school, believing she was dyslexic, unsuccessfully tried to "sit her down" and make her do verbal phonics lessons. But after eight months of reading while standing up, walking, or jumping on the rebounder, she improved to third-grade level.

The Kinesthetic External learner may read better with her finger on the page or word. Never discourage this. Indeed, speed-reading courses often encourage this to focus the eye so it can see more material at once.

Ask the Kinesthetic Internal learner how she feels about something. Ask her to note her personal experiences in a journal. It's important to "pace" the Kinesthetic Internal child, to acknowledge her mood and to help her learn to change it, if necessary, for homework. The kinesthetic child likes to read about what she has experienced. For example, boys will read only about sports heroes, or the sport they play. Use these subjects to develop their interest in reading.

You can teach children about their own learning styles, as we do at the clinic. (Some of the children have won prizes for their science projects on eye movements.) Elementary schoolteacher Joan Armstrong-Brisson has successfully taught children about learning style in the classroom.[6] She tapes a magazine picture to the desk of each student, removes it ten days later, and asks each child to tell what her picture looked like, to illustrate that some children are more visual external. She points out to her class that "children with strong auditory skills are easily identifiable in the early weeks of school. They remember class discussions of three days earlier and have their hands up immediately to answer questions." To illustrate Kinesthetic Internal, she tells students that if someone looks down at his toes, it means he's having strong feelings.

By respecting learning styles, you can help your child adapt to school homework assignments that may be too narrow, teachers who teach with only one learning style, and parents who have different learning styles. Children must come to know that learning is inside them, to be elicited and released. It's not something to be given to them, but something they discover through their own internal processes.

Learning Styles

Visual External
Sensitive to visual environment
Learns by watching
Likes movies and museums
Is good at arranging objects, keeps the room straight

Visual Internal
Makes pictures in head
Recalls how things look
Likes descriptive novels

Auditory External
Learns by listening
Can listen to two conversations at once
Especially sensitive to sound
Sorts by how things sound

Auditory Internal
Hears words in head
Recalls melodies
Talks things over with self
Recalls sounds of different voices

Kinesthetic External
Likes dancing, sports
Likes to use hands
Learns by doing

Kinesthetic Internal
Sorts by feelings
Has strong body reactions to experience
Learns only when comfortable

Homework Journal

In Week 3, interview your child and observe and record her eye movements in response to the following questions. The child will access internal processes:

Visual Remembering
What color is your favorite toy?
What does your friend look like?
Picture your own room in your head.

Visual Imagining
Picture your mother standing on her head.
Imagine your best friend with purple hair.
Imagine a pink cow jumping over your house.

Auditory Remembering
Hum your favorite song and let me watch.
Hear the sound of a siren on a fire truck.

Auditory Imagining
Hear your father's voice speeded up like Donald Duck.
Imagine the sound of the largest bell in the world.

Auditory Self-Talk
What do you say to yourself when you're feeling bad?
Make up directions to tell yourself how to bake
a cake.

Kinesthetic
Imagine an ice cube melting down your back.
Feel a splinter in your foot.
Tell me about the last time you felt scared.
Imagine yourself in clothes that are too tight.
Imagine honey on both sides of your hands.

Also, note the following in your Homework Journal:

1. List ten of your child's successes this week. List ten of your own.

2. What visual, kinesthetic, and auditory teaching methods does the teacher use? What do you think her learning style is?

3. What learning styles do the members of your family have?

4. How can you adapt your child's homework to her learning style?

Week 4: Off and Running— Discovering the Motivated Child

Eleven-year-old Richard came to us because he was "unmotivated." He daydreamed constantly and had such poor motor skills that when he bounced a ball, it always hit his feet. He was in the lowest-level classes in his grade. It took Richard more than a minute to write his name. When he wrote, his shoulders drooped and his mind, as he put it, "just went off on other things." His mother, desperate to build some kind of fire under him, nagged and nagged without success.

Based on our belief that all children are motivated about something, we looked for an area where Richard was motivated—what we call his "Center of Learning Excitement." We tried the usual interests of eleven-year-old boys—computers, friends, camp—all of which drew no more than an "uh" from Richard, who kept his blond head down, and refused to make eye contact.

"How about movies?" we asked. Had he seen any movies he liked?

Suddenly, his eyes brightened, he sat forward in the chair and he looked up. He had barely gotten out "Yeah, *Star Wars*," before he proceeded into a rapid-fire, fifteen-minute description of the fantasy/adventure story of Luke Skywalker, Darth Vader, and the Jedi Knights. *Star Wars*, then, was our point of reference, his "Center of Learning Excitement."

"You really are turned on about this," we pointed out to him, "and you're really not very excited about writing, are you?" He agreed that *Star Wars* was in no danger of being preempted by writing (the most detestable thing in the world to him).

"We're going to help you learn to transfer the excitement you get from retelling the story of *Star Wars* to your writing. Do you believe you can do that?" we asked.

He smiled softly at the ridiculous suggestion of merging such sharply disparate worlds, and though he was very skeptical, he was somewhat intrigued with the idea, and agreed to experiment with it.

"Think about the excitement of telling the movie," we said, and his face brightened. "Now think about writing," and his face drooped. We encouraged him to notice this difference and to describe it. "I feel queasy when you say writing," he said. "When I tell about *Star Wars*, I feel good, like I've run a race and won, there's a tingling in my head. I see the pictures, hear the sounds, and feel the excitement."

When Richard thought about *Star Wars*, he had three senses going positively, but when he wrote, he had feelings (kinesthetic) only. And those feelings were negative. To get Richard motivated, we needed to turn on the other senses while he wrote.

"Think about writing," we said. "While you're thinking about writing, we want you to think of a moving, color picture. Get the picture of yourself having written something you really like and reading it in front of the class. Hear the sounds of the teacher saying, 'I really like this.' Get a tingling in your head and let the tightness go away." As we did this, he became visibly excited about writing and said, "This works like magic." As he practiced this motivation strategy several times in the next week, he began writing much faster and more imaginatively.

Motivation Strategy

Each child has a motivation strategy and Richard had learned his. He needs to hear sounds, see pictures, and have positive feelings. When he's only tuned into feelings, he's not motivated.

Sometimes a child hears sounds and then sees pictures, then has feelings. Sometimes he sees pictures first and hears sounds second. Motivation or lack of motivation is determined by the content and form of the sounds, pictures, and feelings inside the head and *not* by rewards and punishment on the outside.

Week Four will show you how to discover your child's motivation and how to help him apply it to homework.

We see dozens of report cards with children described as "lazy," "unmotivated," "not listening," and "not working up to potential." Yet we have never met a lazy or unmotivated child. We have met

What Goes on Inside Your Child's Head

We now have the "technology" to change feelings by changing the mind's pictures. This exercise will help you discover your child's motivation strategy.[1] Ask him the following questions about each situation and write down the responses. Watch his facial expressions, eye movements, and body posture. If he says no to the questions about pictures, ask about sounds or feelings. If he says yes to a question, then go to the follow-up questions for that category.

1. *Think of something you did that was easy for you.*

Do you see a picture? (If "Yes," go to A.)

Do you hear sounds? (If "Yes," go to B.)

Do you have feelings? (If "Yes," go to C.)

A. Is the picture: big or small; black and white or color; moving or still; vague or clear; near or far away? Does children whose natural inclination to learn was stifled by "dread pictures" of failing at homework, sick feelings in their stomachs at hearing the word "learn," and negative sounds in their heads telling them they will fail.

We believe in the theory of natural learning—given the right conditions children naturally like to learn. If you doubt this, watch a very young child, unhampered by fears, explore the world, ask questions, poke his fingers into things.

But as a child matures, Learning Obstacles, often beliefs and actions of parents and schools, get in the way. Your job as Chief Obstacle Remover is to pare away the hindrances (negative pictures, sounds, and feelings) and rediscover the motivation for learning and homework hiding just below the surface.

What Doesn't Work

First, here are several unsuccessful methods tried by parents (maybe you) across generations:

the picture have sound or is it silent? Are you in the picture? (Most positive pictures tend to be color, moving, and near to the person; negative pictures tend to be black and white, still, and far away.)

B. Is the sound soft or loud? Do you hear your own voice or someone else's voice? Is the voice fast or slow? What is the tone? (Positive sounds tend to be melodious, smooth, and unhurried; negative sounds tend to be grating, monotone, or too loud.)

C. Where do you feel it in your body—throat, chest, back? Is the feeling warm or cold? Is it tense or relaxed? (Positive feelings tend to be warm and relaxed; negative feelings tend to be sensed as pressure, pain, choking.)

You can repeat the above process with the following situation:

2. *Think about something you wanted to do but didn't.*

1. *Five-Miles-Through-the-Snow-to-School Lectures*. When the label "lazy" or "unmotivated" meets the parents' eyes, the response is predictable—Hardship Lectures 101 and variations thereon. Lisa said her mother delivered her "Do this for your own sake" speech. One father told his son, "When I was your age and I didn't want to write, the nun would beat my knuckles with a ruler." Another father who had reading problems in his youth, and struggled to overcome them without help, told his son, "You can get over it. I did." Another parent said, "I didn't need a computer and I went to Harvard." These parents refuse to give or receive help of any kind for their child.

2. *But-Your-Father-Made-All-A's*. When you hold up a parent as an ideal comparison to a child, the child always feels inferior. Parents are the best models (we'll talk about that in a moment), but their models shouldn't be so perfect that the goal is impossible for the child to attain.

3. *Cut-Out-the-Foolishness-Let's-Get-Down-to-Business*. This approach (also known as the no-pain-no-gain rule of learning) is advocated by too many left-brained achievement-oriented parents. These parents see children as small adults and expect them to be serious and disciplined. A game, a stuffed animal, or an allusion to a sports car that would motivate the child is too silly for these parents, who fail to believe in the power of play.

4. *Find-Out-What-They-Want-and-Take-It-Away-from-Them*. This is known in psychology as Behavior Modification. This frequently sung refrain, in which the parent assumes the side of management against labor, goes like this: "If you don't do your homework, I won't let you watch TV," or the converse, "If you read a book, I'll pay you twenty-five dollars." Tit-for-tat techniques are very tempting, especially when all your other "I'm being understanding" approaches have failed. But while "behavior mod" may be successful on your cat or dog, on children it is a dead-end street. It creates small, study-shy Frankensteins who do their homework carelessly and thoughtlessly so they can do something "more fun," like watching TV or playing outside. And the price tag is the conclusion that, "Homework is awful. It's just something you have to do so you can watch TV." This holds true, also, for the parent power move called "grounding," which has never produced anything

but passive behavior. "If I'm grounded," says the child, "then let's see how filthy this place can get."

Instead of "I'm really excited about my math project," a child thinks, "I should do my homework so I can get a better job" (the response of one "unmotivated" eleven-year-old who had no idea what her own motivation was). The Little Bargain Makers who are rewarded for homework with an ice cream cone always negotiate for a bigger and better ice cream cone.

Mark, sixteen, was a star athlete and a good-looking boy. Faithful to his one love, tennis, he played it in the morning and in the afternoon and his mind was preoccupied with tennis during classes. When he wasn't thinking about tennis, he was obsessed with the next punishment from his father for failing school. His prisoner mentality was such that he couldn't imagine not having "someone on my case" and said, "Well, I'd have to have some kind of punishment or I wouldn't do anything."

Believing that Mark had to be punished for his scholarly laziness, his father decreed, "You can't play tennis until you make A's." Mark, who had never made an A in his life, responded with total lethargy, moping around the house with even less enthusiasm for school than before.

We persuaded his father to allow him to return to his only true love, tennis, to recognize tennis as an achievement, and to help him "bridge" his success in tennis to school success. His father began praising his tennis achievements (which were indeed laudable) while Mark, with renewed energy, worked on getting organized for school. At the same time, we paralleled the athlete's pursuit of excellence to the champion student's pursuit of homework excellence by telling Mark: "An excellent tennis player doesn't mind doing five thousand hits to learn a stroke and that's what you have to do in history. Sometimes a good tennis player loses a game, but he always keeps winning in his mind at all times."

Know Yourself

As your child's Chief Obstacle Remover, you'll need to be a bit of an armchair psychologist. Examine your own beliefs, work habits, and expectations—all of which are passed on to your child, some-times unconsciously.

Remember Your Own Scraped Knees

When was the last time you were a learner? Was it yesterday or twenty years ago? While you have probably learned many new things about your job and about getting along with people over the years, most people think, "Me, a learner? No, learning is what kinder-gartners and teenagers do."

If you can't remember your own scraped knees the first time you rode a bike, how slowly the words came together the first time you read or how much water you swallowed when you first learned to swim, bring to mind a more recent learning frustration—learning how to operate a computer, or learning how to get along with a difficult boss. If you can't remember any "learning embarrassment," try learning how to juggle. When you say to your child, "I remember when I learned to ride a bike and I fell off," he knows that you acknowledge the frustrations of learning.

Examine Your Beliefs About Work

Your own motivation and happiness in your job are the core of your child's beliefs about work. If "Thank God, it's Friday" is your usual refrain, don't be surprised when your child hates work. If "I'll do it later" is your second most popular song, don't be surprised when your child takes a month to do a school project that could have taken a week.

Sixteen-year-old Laura's father and mother were upset that she put off doing her assignments until the last minute. She told her parents she was doing well in school, which they believed, until the interim report revealed the truth: F's in algebra and biology. When the family came to our clinic, we discovered that Laura's mother had spent hundreds of dollars on exercise videos which she hadn't used and classes she had never attended. Laura's father worked for a computer firm, and each night Laura heard him tell how other departments were backed up because he had not installed a new program.

Laura was tremendously relieved to be off the hook as "the prob-lem." Temporarily assuming the role of teacher, she helped both parents work out a schedule for their projects. When she said, "Just do it!" to her parents, the entire family broke through their pattern of procrastination. "Just do it!" became the family's battle cry.

Make a Portrait in Your Head

What expectations do you have for your child? What are the present and future pictures of your child in your mind? Look carefully; these pictures are self-fulfilling prophecies—children absorb them and conform to them.

Nine-year-old Jay was a problem child and his parents were at the end of their rope. Even when he made better grades for a year, his father said, "That's great but he'll probably lapse back into his old patterns." When we asked them, "How do you see Jay as an adult?", they looked down quietly and responded, "A total failure, a rule breaker headed for juvenile delinquency."

We suggested that the picture of him that they held in their minds was far more important than the one on the bedroom dresser and that they needed to send their current mental picture back to the development lab.

At first they resisted because the image of Jay the Juvenile Delinquent was so fixed in their minds. His mother said, "Yes, if he behaves better for ten years, okay, then we'll change our image." Poor Jay, locked into ten years of negative expectations!

The picture of eight-year-old Daniel in his parents' minds was equally undistinguished, particularly since, with increasing age he had been on a steady fall from grace. When he was born, he showed signs of superior intelligence that thrilled his parents. He talked, walked, and made Lego structures much sooner than his cousins. His parents dreamed that one day he would be the architect who designed their house.

But by the time he was eight, his parents had lost their dream. Daniel was loud, belligerent, refused to be read to, and was totally uninterested in making things. His mother described the picture in her mind: "Manipulative, not as bright as he was when he was younger, uncoordinated. I don't see how he can be successful in the future at all. I can see him living with us when he's twenty-seven years old."

We helped both sets of parents change their pictures by adding color, movement, and positive qualities to a future picture. For example, we said, "See Daniel having his own children, having a successful job, paying his taxes." Both Daniel and Jay began to alter their behavior in response to their parents' new expectations.

Be aware of yourself as a learner, as a worker, and as a portrait artist and then you can begin taking steps to motivate your child. The following section shows how.

Acknowledgment: Walk a Mile in Your Child's Reeboks

Imagine yourself in this situation: Every day you wake up and your body is just a little larger and different. You start work before some people are out of bed and every twenty to forty-five minutes you have to switch topics and bosses. You get tested on your performance at least once a week. Every year you have a different group of colleagues, some of whom you like or dislike so intensely you can hardly stand it. And through all of this you are trying to figure out where you belong in the universe and why your mother won't let you have the allowance you deserve.

This is the ever-changing world of youth, a microcosm far removed from the adult planet. Your passport to this world is acknowledgment. Acknowledgment is not just mouthing the phrase "I know how you feel." It's walking a mile or two in your child's Reeboks and feeling the sharp sting when you hear your name and "nerd" in the same sentence. Acknowledgment will keep you from immediately jumping into "Let's preview your homework" right after your child has had a big fight with the school bully. Acknowledgment dictates that you talk about the fight first, then ease into homework.

Acknowledgment of sixteen-year-old Jesse's other intelligences helped him see how he was spending his time making F's and D's. When we asked him to tell us exactly how much time he spent on what, it came to a very full day: six hours in school, two hours of football practice, two and one-half hours socializing. On the report card we gave him, we acknowledged his progress—an A in football, an A in hair combing, an A in socializing, an A in growing a large body. Once we recognized his success, he agreed to take small blocks of time from various activities for studying. He used some of his time talking on the telephone with his girl friend to do algebra, one day a week of football time to study, and he used study breaks in school to catch up on projects.

Many parents are speechless (and devoid of acknowledgment) when a child says, "I'm afraid my friends will think I'm a nerd if I bring books home from school." Express a *genuine* interest in the pluses, minuses, and interesting points of how your child thinks and feels.[2] For example, ask, "How many books could you bring home and not be a nerd?" Questions like this allow the parent to enter the child's world and help him sort out his beliefs.

Acknowledge your child's learning style, which means not insisting that he *see* the math problem when he might be able to *hear* it more easily. Acknowledge the talents of the right-brained artistic and musical children who have difficulty in school.

For some parents, the acknowledgment well runs dry during the teen years, when independence is the theme song. Acknowledging your child's culture doesn't mean saying yes to everything, but it does mean knowing his friends and acknowledging their importance to him.

It's important that you know with whom and where your child spends his time. No motivation technique will override the power of peer group pressure. If your child's friends make F's, it might be difficult for him to do otherwise. There are subtle ways to influence your children's friends: Invite them to go along on trips, invite them to dinner at your home. Parents who think they have lost their power are surprised when a child responds positively to suggestions to do something different. We suggested to one parent who despaired over her son's drug abuse to have his uncle in Iowa invite him out for the summer. The teenager drove a tractor and pitched hay all day and loved it. By the time he came back to school, he had grown far apart from the drug culture.

Motivation Techniques

Make a Choice

Help your child choose to do homework by creating a positive study picture in the child's mind. Help him imagine what it will look like or feel like when he's finished and is proud of what he's done. The idea is not just to finish homework, but to feel the pride of the accomplishment.

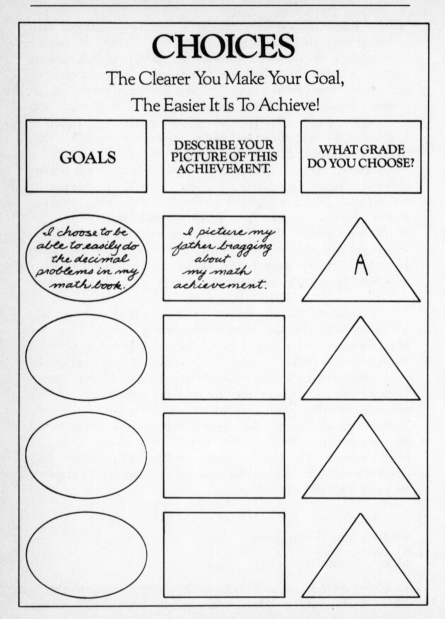

CHOICES

The Clearer You Make Your Goal,
The Easier It Is To Achieve!

GOALS	DESCRIBE YOUR PICTURE OF THIS ACHIEVEMENT.	WHAT GRADE DO YOU CHOOSE?
I choose to be able to easily do the decimal problems in my math book.	I picture my father bragging about my math achievement.	A

Say this to your child: "Imagine that your homework has been completed. It is accurate, looks neat, and is on time and you are very proud. Your teacher gives you a good grade and says, 'Very good.' To get this wish, you can make a choice—'I choose to do my math homework easily without upsetting myself or anyone else. I choose to make it fun.'"

Write down these choices and pictures and remind the child of his choices in the middle of a project when motivation may lag: "Remember what it's going to be like when you get there." This is not a one-shot process. Stay with this until your child is able to make the choice himself.

Often a child *wants* to do homework, but he doesn't want to do it just because "it's good for you," or any other adult reasons. Any reason a child comes up with is the right reason. So the trick is to help him come up with *some* reason, no matter how ridiculous. For more resistant children the conversation may go like this one which Cecil had with Jane:

"I want you to imagine making an A in math," Cecil said to Jane, a struggling student who squirmed in her seat.

"Why should I imagine that?" she replied. "I don't even want to do my math. I don't care what I make." (At this point, parents usually slam the book shut and stomp out of the room, exasperated.)

"Is there anything that would make you want to do your math?" (In our experience, most children request the unattainable—movie stars to assist them, a million dollars, instant fame.)

"Well, if I could have Tom Selleck help me do my math, I would want to do it." (Take the cue the child gives and use it to close the motivation gap.)

"So, under *some* circumstances, you could possibly make a choice to do your math?"

"Yes." (Once a child gives you any reason, fortify the reason, and make it concrete and present-oriented.)

Cecil continued, "Then, picture Tom Selleck looking over your shoulder each day as you do your math. See him smiling and hear him say 'Good work!' as you complete your math problems."

At this point, Jane's face lit up. Her attitude toward math homework was beginning to change. She began to look forward to doing her math—it became an easy choice for her.

This might seem like a leap of logic—the child goes from offering a reason for doing homework to thinking he has chosen on his own to do it—but it does work. Note the important difference between "want" and "choose." Wanting and wishing are passive, while choosing is active. The idea is to lead him to choose to do what he previously didn't want to do.

Examine the Stop Signs

When you ask a child, "What stops you from doing homework?", consider any reason a gem to be treasured. You can deal with these reasons and at the same time help children sort through their beliefs.

Children have as many irrational beliefs as adults do, and reasons appear funnier and more ridiculous when said out loud than when they stay in your head (where they sound perfectly rational). The trick is to let the child see that he, *in his own mind*, can overcome these beliefs.[3]

For example, to "I don't want to do my homework because my teacher has narrow shoulders," you say, "Let me get this straight. To be able to learn, your teacher has to have broader shoulders." (Instead of "You *should* do your homework; I don't care what the teacher looks like," you extend your child's own belief to a ludicrous point so that he rejects it completely.)

"Yes."

"Well, how, specifically, would your teacher have to look for you to be able to learn biology? What if the teacher were taller, then would you learn? Should the teacher wear shoulder pads?"

Lightly take it to an extreme. "In case we wanted to find a good teacher for you to learn from, what would we look for?"

At this point the child will laugh, as he sees what he thought was a firm belief about his own learning crumble. "Well, it's not that," he'll say, "I guess it really doesn't matter about my teacher's shoulders." This is the first step in helping the child realize that external criteria do not control his internal learning process.

The check on this technique is "Do you believe you can learn from anyone, no matter how they look?" The answer is usually "yes" with a big grin.

As you "peel away" the child's false beliefs, make the transition to what's really stopping him. "So it's not the teacher's looks that stops you from learning. Is it that you don't understand the history assignments?"

One of the more popular Stop Signs (among adults and children) is "I can't do my work because I don't feel like it." Children need to learn that they don't have to feel like doing something in order to start it. If children or adults required themselves to always feel like doing something, they probably wouldn't get much done. It's important to get this message across to children (especially kinesthetic children): You can want to do something but not feel like it. But not "feeling like it" need never stop you from actually doing it.

Find the Center of Learning Excitement

John's main passion in life was BMX dirt bike racing. Every weekend he was out on his bike with his friends, pulling "wheelies" and splattering mud over every inch of himself and the bike.

Enter vocabulary, a task he hated as much as Richard hated writing. So, starting with his passion—his Center of Learning Excitement—we encouraged him to use a computer program, Mindscape's *Crossword Magic* (See Part Five, "Recommended Materials," Computer Programs), to generate a crossword puzzle using BMX bicycle terms: banana seat, knobby tires, etcetera.

Astonished that there was a connection between his Saturday morning mud games and school, he said, "You mean something I'm interested in can actually help me learn?" This was the beginning of his interest in words.

A child's interests will be apparent in his conversation; listen carefully and notice what activities excite him. Go with his interest even if it's not particularly interesting to you.

Fifteen-year-old Rob was "unmotivated." His father and older brothers were all West Point graduates, and Rob was expected to follow suit. His dreams, however, focused more on how to get rich without working. He detested homework, and when we asked him to picture himself studying, Rob said, "I can't see my face; I can't see my whole body, just part of it. The picture is in black and white with no sound."

But Rob adored lacrosse. The lacrosse picture in his mind, in stark contrast to studying, was in red and green and purple with screaming crowds and Rob, the star, moving swiftly, boldly, across the field.

"It is possible," we told him, "to transfer your feelings of excitement from lacrosse to homework. Get both pictures in front of you—the small, plain picture of homework, on the left, and the large, bright picture of lacrosse on the right. Have you got both of those? Now we want you to let the homework picture on the left become as bright and as vivid as the lacrosse picture on the right. Put it in color, brighten it up. Let the positive feelings from the lacrosse picture go on to the homework picture."[4]

In this way, Rob was able to successfully transfer his feelings about lacrosse to the dreaded homework situation.

Be a Model

Ten-year-old Louie hated division. We tried contests on the computer, and even though this speeded up his calculations, he still complained, "I don't like this. Do I have to do it?"

"Here's the book," said Faith. "Do this at home." But before he left, she took the book, sat down at the table, pulled out a pencil, and started working on the problems herself.

"Stop," Louie said, grabbing the book away. "Those are *my* problems. You're using them up. Let *me* do them."

When Faith "modeled" enthusiasm for math, Louie liked the idea that somebody else could like what he thought was awful.

Doug had a similar distaste for history. According to him, no one could possibly like history. Not one single person in the universe! But by the next session, miracle of miracles, he had tracked down another student who enjoyed talking about the Battle of Bunker Hill and the signing of the Declaration of Independence. This was an incredible revelation to Doug and sparked his interest in things historic.

Sometimes a child doesn't know how to be enthusiastic or interested in something. He doesn't know how to act or what to say. He needs to be exposed to these behaviors and the parent is the closest model. You can model enthusiasm for homework and help your child create success pictures through voice tone, positive words, and body movements.

Make a Game

Kathy, eight, had one word to describe the vocabulary words she was required to do in a workbook—"boring." But as soon as we made it a game, calling out the words on the page and seeing how fast she could find them, she became intrigued. Games and play are keys to a child's motivation and learning.

We sometimes use UNO, a children's card game similar to Crazy Eights, to observe a child in the context of a game. You can learn a lot about your child during a game: Does he have enough motor dexterity? Does he cheat? Can he lose without crying? What are his strategies? Does he have any strategies that might be transferred to homework?

For a child who plays soccer, football, or basketball, we say: "How many times do you practice catching, making baskets, or throwing the ball? Well, we're going to do the same with punctuation. We're going to be your coach and we're going to go over punctuation the same way you learn to make a field goal." Some computer programs "induct" children into the Punctuation Hall of Fame. The most successful programs for children are in a game format. They have evolved a long way from simply having a workbook page transferred to the computer. In many games, a child competes with himself, an excellent motivator for children.

Make Sense

Motivation comes with feeling, hearing, smelling, tasting, and seeing, causing the brain to say, "I want more." Read it, draw it, hear it in a song, feel it and see it, act it out, dance it, make it concrete, build it, tear it apart, have the child tell and re-tell it to you. Taste it. Provide experiences in as many forms as it takes for the child to learn (he won't respond to all). To get his attention, engage him in his learning style. To make learning permanent, encourage him to learn through all the senses.

Often, before we start any kind of homework assignment, we have the child jump on the mini-trampoline, look at a visual stimulus, smell a flower, listen to music, or watch a nature video. Once the child is in a heightened state of sensory awareness, we sit down and breeze through homework. Often he has a breakthrough. Everything is dramatically easier with a brain that is stimulated through the senses.

The Learning Comfort Zone

One day, while playing a series of simple computer games with ten-year-old Ronald, we discovered that when we got to game seven, he didn't want to play anymore. "That's too easy," he said. At the same time he refused to go on to game eight because it was too hard

("And I know since the games have been getting harder and harder that I don't want to play anymore").

Clearly at this point no learning takes place because what the child has already done is too easy and what he will not attempt is too hard. When the child gets to a place like this in homework, the trick is to create an opening. Find some place, any place, where he will accept a small challenge. If it's math problem number seven that's easy, but math problem number eight that's hard, drive a wedge between seven and eight and create a space for him to learn. Search like Goldilocks for a place that is "just right"—a Learning Comfort Zone. On one side is "I can't," "It's too hard," or "I won't," and on the other side is "It's too easy" or "It's boring."

Not that the Learning Comfort Zone is always comfortable at first. In fact, a child may encounter fairly frequent turbulence (like an airplane going through clouds). We call this "learning embarrassment"—that scary feeling when you cross over to a higher level of thinking. The child expects something new and exciting, but what he gets instead is butterflies in the stomach. He needs to recognize this feeling as a sign that he is entering the Learning Comfort Zone.

Tell a Story

Alex, who was extremely frustrated with his failures in math, had a dream about a giant, shiny paper clip. He couldn't quite remember the dream, so we told him to close his eyes and we would finish the dream together. We said, "Imagine that giant paper clip, how big it is and how good it is. And *pow!* It killed the big bad math giant and you don't have to be afraid of math anymore." Alex adored this story, repeated it several times, and over the next few weeks began to enjoy math.

Stories motivate children (and adults) of all ages to learn in a way that a direct command—"Do your homework"—cannot. Children can be the proud owners of a treasure chest of success stories, such as the story of Colonel Sanders, who at age sixty-five, asked 1,009 restaurants to buy his chicken recipe before he succeeded. Children are inspired by Grolier's ValueTales series' *Dedication of Albert Schweitzer* or *The Curiosity of Christopher Columbus*. Children are ecstatic when honored as "Computer Queen," "SuperReader," or "He-Man of Math."

Use stories such as Baby-Wah-Wah to sneak around sensitive homework topics. We say: "We had this child come in here and his name was Baby-Wah-Wah. Now Baby-Wah-Wah, who some people called 'lazy,' didn't do his homework. Every night he stubbornly refused to do anything. And when his father asked him to study, he threw temper tantrums on the floor! Now what would you do with a child like this?"

"I'd tell him to get busy and do his homework," the child says. Week after week children inquire about Baby-Wah-Wah.

A variation on Baby-Wah-Wah for the older child is the "Success of Failure" story.[5] It goes like this: "We know some real nerds who make all A's and they need to loosen up a little bit to learn how to get D's. If I were to apprentice them to you for a day, could you teach them to know how to do that? How would you advise another child to get D's instead of A's?"

Initially hesitant, the child thinks and then says, rather emphatically at times: "I would tell him to take books home only sometimes. I would tell him not to turn in assignments on time. I would tell him not to listen in class."

Children (like adults) are better at dealing with the problems of others and have no shortage of advice. In the middle of "Success of Failure" it dawns on him that he has pinpointed the cause of his own successful failure. Anyone who did what he did, would have failed. Surprise! What he does affects what happens to him.

Families can also create their own family learning lore about the accomplishments of parents, other children, cousins, aunts, and uncles. This is *not* a variation on Five-Miles-Through-The-Snow-To-School Approach and timing is everything; when the child is misbehaving is not the time to give the opposite model. Instead of "You know, your father was in *Hamlet* when he was in college," and "Why can't you read Shakespeare?" tell the whole story, the good, the bad, the frustrations, so the child sees the accomplishment as a process he can imitate.

Melt Excuses

Denise, sixteen, was supposed to bring in an English paper to us so we could help her with it before she turned it in to the teacher the next day. The next morning, she walked in slowly, burdened with a multitude of excuses, starting with "I forgot my paper and I can't go get it because I have to pick up my mother soon," and ending with "I have to call my boyfriend, I don't have a pencil, and I don't know where my book is."

We proceeded to slowly thaw the excuses, one by one, until she eventually had no iceberg to stand on: "See if your mother can get a ride with a friend. Call your boyfriend for five minutes. Here's a pencil, and we'll go to the library and get the book you need." By unemotionally answering all her objections we helped her finish her work.

A variation on this is to reverse roles so that you become the person giving excuses. People have less tolerance for hearing excuses than for delivering them. When Kathy, eight, resisted reading, Faith became the resistant student. Kathy said, "I'm the teacher. Now read." Faith said, "I don't wanna and I'm not gonna," at which point Kathy said, "Just shut up and do it." When we returned immediately to her reading assignment, she laughed with embarrassment at her own resistance. "I don't want to read," she almost said, but laughed instead, and put her hand over her mouth, with an "oops."

How to Talk to Your Child

Kimberly, age seven, had trouble reading and remembering number facts in second grade. But she had a wonderfully curious mind. She asked questions constantly, to which her mother offered very factual answers. When Kimberly heard a siren in the distance, and asked, "What is that?", her mother replied, "A fire alarm." We suggested that her mother respond, instead, with something that might acknowledge Kimberly's wonderful curiosity and also stimulate Kimberly's thinking, such as, "What do you think it might be?" or "Why do you ask?"

Children ask questions because they have a hypothesis. To give them a short, factual answer stops their curiosity short. Kimberly, when given the opportunity, offered a stream of very clever answers. She hypothesized that a fireman was letting his little girl sit in the driver's seat of the fire engine, and she had accidentally hit the siren button. Although Kimberly was behind in the basics, she was well ahead in creative thinking. You can use children's curiosity to find out more about the world that motivates them.

If the child says, "I can't do this," or "This homework is too hard," or "It's not important," and you respond, "Oh yes, you can," what you are, in fact, saying to your child is, "You are lying." It's better to say, "I know how you feel," and do your best to understand, then proceed.

When you give feedback and words of praise to your child, be specific. "Isn't he wonderful" may be rewarding for the parent, but it is of little help to the child. Instead, say, "You organized your paper well," or "You really stuck with the math problem." Effective feedback does not blame. Rather than saying, "You *didn't* stick with the math," get information so you can help the child. You might say, "Does that math problem seem too long or too hard? Do you know how to do it?"

Plan for the Plateaus

When your child is learning he will probably hit plateaus when, like Dorothy on her way to Oz, he wants to "turn back." Let him walk gently along the flat parts of the yellow brick road and even walk backward. This does not signal a total retreat!

The data collected at our clinic over the past ten years shows that we've been able to increase intelligence remarkably in children in a short period of time. But intelligence increase is not a steady progression. It's more like this: The child goes along for weeks and months with no changes, then there's a dramatic breakthrough. Then more weeks and months follow and nothing happens until the next breakthrough. If you plan for the flat periods, the plateaus between the breakthroughs when progress seems to have halted, you won't be frustrated by them.

And sometimes your child may have to imitate a car without four-wheel drive stuck in the snow, rocking backward and forward to get out. He'll go back to problem six, even if he's up to problem nine, or he'll jump forward to problem twelve.

Children who see the big picture before they understand the component parts may have to go forward to learn something more complex, then return to the simpler. We've seen children read even though they haven't been taught reading skills. Instead of going over the beginning consonant blends, "st," "ch," "th," and so on, a child may easily read, in context, words with those same blends. Zigzag between the parts and the whole.

Sometimes parents and children start the Six-Week Plan on

Sunday. On Monday, after setting a personal record for "Time Spent Studying," the child receives a sixty-nine on a test and everyone throws up their hands and says "Nothing works." This is not to be seen (felt or heard) as anything but one little zag backward. It is certainly not failure, but rather a perfectly natural part of improvement.

Homework Journal

1. List ten of your child's successes this week. List ten of your own.

2. Identify your child's feelings, pictures, and sounds about homework.

3. What does your child see, feel, and hear when he is motivated? When he is *not* motivated?

4. Identify ways you've tried to motivate that haven't worked.

5. What is the portrait of your child in your head? How can you change it?

6. Identify your child's cultural pressures.

7. Has your child made a choice to do homework?

8. What stops your child from doing homework?

9. What Center of Learning Excitement could you use to motivate?

10. How did you "model" enthusiasm for homework to your child?

11. How did you plan for the flatlands and zigzags?

12. List games you've used this week.

13. Where is your child's Learning Comfort Zone?

14. What stories did you tell your child to motivate him?

15. How did you melt your child's excuses?

Week 5: Keeping the Eye on the Ball— Concentration

• Eight-year-old Stephanie was failing school because she couldn't concentrate. She did her homework at the dining-room table, but what her brain had to battle at the dining-room table made it impossible for even the most dedicated student to concentrate: "The dog barks, Mommy is talking to Daddy, the TV is on, and I listen to rock music."

• Bruce, a highly distracted seven-year-old, was remarkably preoccupied with his own appearance and dress. One day, after we had worked with him for over a year, his mother asked, "Do you think it makes a difference if his desk is in front of a large mirror?"

While the outside barriers to a child's concentration are significant, the ones on the inside may be just as distracting. If you monitor the thoughts traipsing through your child's head during any two minutes of a given day, you'll probably find a rowdy bunch of drunken monkeys—"What grade am I going to get in this class? Suzie doesn't like me. I wonder if I should tell Mom?"—a mishmash of ideas, notions, desires, and thoughts ranging from the mundane to the imaginary.

For normal everyday awareness, the abilities of the brain to drift on to different thoughts can be pleasant; it allows your child to enter imaginary places, picture friends who have moved out of town, and think of the person she wants to become.

But when it comes to asking the brain to stay tuned to one channel for homework, concentration is often not automatic. Most children we see do homework in the most scattered way possible. To concentrate, children say, "I try real hard," or "I just force myself to think about it." Because they haven't learned concentration techniques, they believe concentration is painful. It may be harder than ever to concentrate in the distracted modern world, but fortunately, we know how to train the brain to do this.

Note: As much as 10 percent of boys, and a lesser proportion of girls, have what is called an Attention Deficit Disorder (ADD) because of delayed development of part of the Doing Brain. They are easily distracted and may or may not be hyperactive or have other learning disorders. It requires a skilled clinician working with dedicated parents to properly diagnose and treat ADD. Treatment includes lifestyle changes, such as creating a calm emotional atmosphere, giving more leeway for physical activity, cutting down on homework problems, and sometimes taking medication (Ritalin is one) to help normalize the old brain function. Neurological conditions such as tics or undetected seizure disorders can also interfere with concentration.

The Brains to Concentrate

To concentrate, a child needs routine and organization for the Doing Brain and emotional security for the Feeling Brain. The Thinking Brain needs to be the executive in control, to *choose* the focus of concentration, rather than to have it decided on by precedent or emotion. A child worrying about a parent's drinking problem or embarrassed about her own reading deficiency cannot easily concentrate.

Obstacles to Concentration

The War Between the Brains

For a right-brained child, lack of concentration may be the result of a war between the brains. While the left brain asserts, "I want to concentrate on homework," or "I will study American history," the right brain disagrees, supplying more vibrant pictures of playing outside. A right-brained child (particularly when working on a left-brain task) may have a hard time ignoring the pictures. When asked to do a writing assignment, for example, the right-brained child may be concerned about whether it is fun and what the visual form is (ink or typed), while the left-brained child thinks about structure—"How many pages?" Often the right brain wants the whole result of concentration, but the left brain is needed to employ *steps* to get through the task. To concentrate on the assignment, both brains need to work together. Help the child to use organizing strategies of the left brain (through outlines, project sheets, and timelines). Use the right brain to envision the goal and to energize the task.

Overstimulation by Today's World

One part of the Feeling Brain, the amygdala, plays a central role in helping children concentrate. The amygdala regulates sensation in the brain. It has its own "set point," the level at which it recognizes novel stimulation. In far too many children, however, the set point has been raised too high by the overstimulation of mini motorcycles, MTV, hard rock music, and certain "twitch" (all you have to do is quickly "twitch" to hit a button) computer games. When the amygdala expects the high-level sensory stimulation of a motorcycle, but instead gets homework or school, the brain rejects the lower-level stimulation and the child, unaware of the cause, concludes that "school is boring, parents are boring, everything is boring." Once the amygdala is set too high, the brain rules out everything that doesn't match the driving need for greater sensation.

"Twitch" computer games are highly appealing to some children, especially those with Attention Deficit Disorder. Supplying stimuli at the rate of several impulses per second, they lock in the wavering attention and the child enters a rare state of absorption. We recommend no more than twenty minutes of these highly addictive games at one time. (See Part Five, "Recommended Materials," for a list of quality computer programs.) The high intensity of today's society can make schoolwork seem flat by comparison, in the same way mind-altering drugs do.

Of course, you can't say to your child, "Your amygdala is out of whack." Neither can you expect her to switch overnight from Michael Jackson's *Bad* to Mostly Mozart. Parents need to be ingenious in finding ways to skillfully (and gradually) redirect the child's attention without making her feel deprived. At the same time, parents can raise homework stimulation by making assignments more interesting and involving more senses.

Dwight, ten, came to us because he couldn't read. What he could do well was to sing constantly, in his head, the words and music to innumerable rock songs, heavily laden with sexual themes and powerful beats, such as "Like a Virgin."

"Do those songs go through your head all the time?" we asked.

"It never stops," he said.

Dwight's auditory brain was totally preoccupied. He had such a good auditory memory that if he had been reading, his auditory channels would have been engaged in self-talk with strategies such as, "Let's see, what does this mean?" Instead, they were absorbed with pounding and highly sensating beats.

Dwight's parents were successful in substituting a highly kinesthetic alternative—soccer—so that Dwight was so tired when he came home that he didn't notice that he had forgotten all about TV and rock music. His parents also suggested that he listen to music without words while he studied. Dwight gradually learned to turn down the competing sounds in his head.

Substitution is the most successful way to cut back on rock music and TV. Each family can determine their own schedule for withdrawal.

Television: The Number One Distraction

Another challenge to the brain's attempt to concentrate is television. Too many parents can't see this connection. We've seen children fail school while the parents buy them a new TV for their room for Christmas. Almost all children we see with learning problems have a TV set in their bedroom.

One of the first things we recommend when children have homework problems is to limit TV. We tell parents that if the child is coming to our clinic to increase visual-spatial skills, for example, we can't compete with forty (or even ten) hours a week of TV. We recommend no TV during the week and only a limited amount on the weekend. Two hours a week of well-chosen TV is plenty. Some parents find this recommendation quite startling. But the question we pose is "What would your child be doing otherwise?"

Television is particularly harmful to the preschool child whose ego is just forming, as noted by Joseph Chilton Pearce:

"When blank staring takes place before a TV screen . . . the child bonds to the chaos of that screen. He is not being egocentric as designed by nature, but exocentric—he is being constantly pulled outside his center. The *screen* is the center of his world and impinges upon him. Whether this impingement is cartoon mayhem, commands to buy corn flakes, instructions on how to spell Sesame Street or read the encyclopedia, *is absolutely of no consequence*. . . . No content . . . can overcome the dramatic split of Self that the mechanism itself induces."[1]

And yet, according to Marie Winn, author of *The Plug-In Drug*, "Even the most conservative estimates indicate that preschool children are spending more than a third of their waking hours watching television."[2]

If a preschool child watches TV thirty-seven hours a week, his attempts at sustained concentration are constantly disrupted and his attention span is shortened just at the critical moment when it would naturally be growing longer. Watching TV cartoons trains the child's attention span back to a second-by-second stage, and it may interfere with the developmental stages. Some children will survive and do well despite this, but later in school they may have learning and concentration problems.[3]

Many parents agree that TV is too powerful but feel powerless to control it; the "electronic baby-sitter" is a central organizing device for the family. For some families, TV time may be the only time they spend together. "Let's all watch less TV now and instead do some learning activities," is sure to go over as successfully as "Do your homework now."

Some families can go cold turkey. In others, the TV mysteriously "breaks" (this works with small children) and still others use TV locks and limits. They only allow the child to watch the Disney Channel or less than two hours a week. Watching nature videos during studying may be a good way to "wean" some children from TV.

One father, who taped over three hours a day of soap operas for his daughter, wondered why she was depressed and uninvolved in school programs. The family broke away from "soaps" first by not taping on Thanksgiving. Then, they stopped taping during family vacations, holidays, summertime, and when the daughter was in school.

TV Weaning

1. Don't make TV watching an issue; don't nag about how awful it is.

2. Substitute other stimulating experiences for the child: games, playing outdoors, art, involvement in organizations.

3. Try this: No TV during the week and selected programs on the weekend.

4. "Sesame Street" counts as time watching TV.

5. Modeling is important. Parents need to watch less TV if they expect their children to do the same.

6. Substitute good videotapes.

Concentration: Definition Please

Concentration is the ability and desire to maintain interest over time; it requires dealing with inside and outside distractions. Concentration for children never is the picture that many adults have in their minds—sitting still in a chair and doing a workbook page, night after night.

The elements of concentration have been most aptly defined by University of Chicago Professor Mihaly Csikszentmihalyi, who has studied the experience in mountain climbers, surgeons, dancers, and chess players.[4] He has identified a certain state of deep and very pleasant concentration which he calls "flow." He has defined its components this way (we provide homework example in parentheses):

1. Your personal capacities match the challenges of the activity (a child is asked to do a math problem she knows how to do).

2. Feedback is immediate (she sees that the answer is correct by checking her math).

3. You forget about the distinction between what you are doing and why you are doing it (she forgets that this is a homework assignment she's *supposed* to do and perhaps *supposed* to dislike).

4. Consequently, you don't have the opportunity to worry about the things you worry about in normal life (she stops worrying about the fight with her friend).

5. There is a feeling of potential control (she *likes* figuring out this graph!).

6. Self-consciousness disappears and you don't think about whether you are failing or succeeding (no comment).

7. There is a lack of time consciousness (she forgets that she missed "Alf" at seven-thirty).

8. When all the above seven are present, the activity becomes an intrinsically rewarding experience (math is really fun!).

Unfortunately, the kind of pleasant concentration Csikszentmihalyi describes is rare in most children's lives, especially at school. He notes, "If you begin to look at how often these conditions are present in a classroom situation, you can see that it's not very often . . . the clock time is so important in schools, there are 50 minute periods . . . everything has to be ruled by those periods. You don't have time to get lost in what you're doing . . . most kids are extremely self-conscious in the class room because they know that their performance is being judged. . . ."[5] But at home you can help your child achieve the kind of concentration Csikszentmihalyi has described.

Development and Concentration

Concentration means different things at different ages. For a five-year-old child, it involves staying with a task and doing it to completion, not sitting at a desk and contemplating abstract thought.

For an eight-year-old, it might mean staying with a game of Trivial Pursuit.

Different techniques are required in different developmental stages for teaching a child to concentrate. There are several ways to teach a very young child to concentrate. Narrow your child's choices and simultaneously teach her to focus on one thing. One couple taught their five-year-old that he had a special playroom in which he played by himself while they did their work. If you buy several computer programs, make a commitment to one program (and hide the rest if you have to) before going on to the others. When we tell children that we have twenty new computer programs, they get all excited and want to rush through each one of them, not giving more than three minutes of attention to each one; they're always convinced the next one will be better.

There is also the Alternating Toys Technique (for up to seven years old), in which toys are divided into "toys for the car" and "toys for bedtime," etcetera. Similarly, instead of putting out massive amounts of toys, give the child one toy and get her interested in it. If she throws it across the room, pick up the toy yourself and "model" concentration by showing your own interest in it. Suddenly, you'll see her trying to get it back.

The Magical Child (ages four to seven) drifts between the conscious and unconscious worlds, and you're most likely to help her concentrate by entering her fantasy world. Instead of saying, "Put your bears away and concentrate on these math facts," you might say, "Oreo Bear and his brother, Chocolate Chip, are going to do their math." This pulls all the energy of fantasy into concentration.

The Magical Child will also do something that looks like just the opposite of concentration—she daydreams or seems to "space out." Burton White at Harvard's Child Development Center found that very happy children had only one detectable factor in common, and that was that they spend much of their time in blank staring.[6]

You can use this daydreaming to teach the child that she can control her own mind, that she can choose to daydream or choose to concentrate. You might say, "Think of Uncle Bob. That's a daydream. Now let go of that image and let's read this paragraph. That's concentration." Children need to daydream; it is the brain's natural break. But they can be aware that they are doing it and learn to "tag" it as one state of consciousness.

By about age seven, when the child moves to the Concrete

Logical stage, she may concentrate on small facts in an attempt to connect them into an overview of the world. She wonders, for example, if the ocean at Virginia Beach is the same ocean as the one at Hilton Head. She is absorbed by competition, games (Pictionary, Wheel of Fortune), boys playing with boys, girls playing with girls. Some of these children will be able to study with other things going on around them, while others may be completely distracted by the smallest interference. Because they're growing rapidly, physical needs must be considered. *Immediate* feedback is more necessary here than ever before; they want to know right away if they are right or wrong. Computer instruction does this perfectly. If you can overcome a preteen's objections from the beginning—"I don't feel like it," "I don't want to do it," she will become absorbed and enjoy the absorption.

Teenagers may have a particularly hard time concentrating since their Feeling Brain tends to rule, and being with friends is the number one priority. Teenagers dislike being alone. Csikszentmihalyi, in *Being Adolescent,* notes: ". . . of all the contexts in which they [teenagers] found themselves, this is the one in which they felt worse."[7] But Csikszentmihalyi notes that the teenage years are also a wonderful opportunity to learn concentration skills. "One of the major opportunities for growth in adolescence is to learn how to use solitude as a way to reach one's goals, rather than as something to escape at all costs."[8]

What children really want is to know you are with them. You don't have to be with them physically to convey this; you can create it with words: "I'm looking forward to hearing in thirty-five or forty-five minutes how you did this assignment." Reinforce the importance of your child's working in her own room by coming in and putting your hand on her shoulder, or ruffing her hair, as she sits at her desk, rather than waiting for her to come to you for a rewarding experience.

Learning Style and Concentration

A child's learning style is also a factor in developing her ability to concentrate. A child who is too kinesthetic may not be able to study if her clothes don't feel right, a very auditory child will be disturbed by sounds, and a visual external child will be distracted by a messy room. If a child's self-talk is very loud, she will have trouble concentrating; auditory memory will be difficult, especially if every time she sits down to study her internal voice pipes up with, "You are terrible at math."

Acknowledge your child's learning style: A visual child might need to remove excess papers from her desk; an auditory child might need to put in a different music tape; a kinesthetic child might have to squirm in the chair.

Ray, for example, was a "wiggle worm," so kinesthetic that his limbs twisted and jerked with every thought. To help him concentrate in front of the computer, we put him in an office chair with wheels; his body was able to move around, but his brain could concentrate.

Meredith is also very kinesthetic and warms up to concentrate by juggling before she does her homework (an activity that a visual or auditory parent may fail to recognize as a form of concentration.)

Notice what your child naturally concentrates on and what learning style is exhibited by that activity. Distractions to one child are fuel for concentration to another child. Nature videos during homework are very calming to children who are less visual; a very visual child may be pulled out of her auditory and kinesthetic modes by *any* visual stimulation. Play nature videos with the music off.

Help Your Child Concentrate

Prepare to Concentrate

Molly, seven, came in one day all excited about a friend's birthday party, describing the red dress she wore, her friends who were there, the chocolate cake they ate, and the funny hats they wore. Molly needed to work on her homework. How did we prepare Molly to concentrate? First, we did what psychologists call "pacing." This meant seeing, feeling, hearing, where Molly was, acknowledging that, and then leading her from there to homework. We said, "Tell us about the party for five minutes first, and then we'll do homework." Pacing is one form of preparation to concentrate.

Another is to perform rituals, such as straightening your desk. To concentrate, prepare the way a batter prepares to go to bat: He swings bats in the on-deck circle, knocks imaginary mud out of his spikes, scratches, and chews gum. The child might form the habit of putting on his favorite hat, arranging pencil, paper, and other learning tools and setting aside a snack. All these rituals march the Doing Brain into action and put the Feeling and Thinking Brains on hold until needed.

Previewing (see Week 1) is a prelude to effective concentration. Previewing a task allows a child to see the whole and to note the parts: What am I going to end up with and what are the steps involved? With a preview checklist in hand, when a child begins to concentrate on each part, she will still be able to track the overall project.

Set a Goal

A child can't really concentrate unless she knows what she's concentrating on; she needs a goal. Ask your child, "What do you want from algebra?" After the initial shock and the proverbial answer—"nothing," begin to suggest possible goals: to do the hard problems in a current chapter or to read algebraic sentences. Let her have a clear goal about this homework session.

Use the energy of the ego to concentrate on a goal. Seven-year-old Arnold, who loved superheroes, bragged endlessly that he could beat anyone at karate. But he wouldn't concentrate on reading; he always flipped back to superheroes. So we asked Arnold, "Do you want to be the best reader in your class? Do you want to beat everyone in your class?" From that moment, his goal was to become a superreader. He had no trouble concentrating after that.

Children sometimes believe that homework assignments are endless. They can't concentrate because they see no end. Monica, for example, was overwhelmed by the multiplication tables. We helped her concentrate by delineating the task clearly, which changed her belief that it was endless and too hard. We showed her all of the multiplication tables on one chart. Colored in blue were all the facts she already knew. She knew "two times three," and when she saw the chart she realized that she also knew "three times two." In fifteen minutes, Monica was able to memorize fifteen multiplication facts.

Give Me a Break

Children need to be aware of their concentration rhythms, including when to take a break. Breaks are not frivolous, unnecessary play, as many parents believe, but an important part of the learning process. They are not rewards; they are renewals.

Peter Russell, author of *The Brain Book*, says that even when you feel like continuing, "in fact, it is still better to take a break." Russell notes that interrupting yourself "can lead to higher recall of the material. . . ."[9]

Plan the amount of study time and the amount of break time and the activities to be done in each. To help your child concentrate, set a timer for twenty minutes to keep track of her study time. (In the child lingo of breaks, we say, "Twenty on and five off.") Before your child's break, plan an activity for her reentry into concentration. For example, you can refocus your child's attention with a concentration exercise (see Sidebar).

Your child can use the break time to get fresh air, food, listen to a different kind of music, walk around the house, throw darts or a nerf ball.

Plan Your Exit

If a child is very absorbed in learning, coming out of this state of mind can be disorienting. Children need to learn how to exit gently from the fragile state of concentration. Before starting homework, you might say, "When it's time for us to stop, how do you want to do that? Do you want me to tell you? Do you want a timer to go off? Do you want to have dinner?"

At the end of a homework session, write down what you've done and where you plan to start again. One writer we know never gets up from writing before he has designed a very easy reentry step (like the astronauts reentering the atmosphere): He spends the last ten minutes of every day planning what he will do the next day.

Concentration Exercises

These things may take time at first, but the results are well worth the effort. Say the following to your child:

1. Become aware of the movies in your mind. Slow down the movies and hold on to one frame. Practice holding an image in your mind for longer and longer times.

2. Take a deep breath while concentrating on the number one. Breathe out on one. Take a deep breath concentrating on the number two. Breathe out on two . . . and so on until you reach the number ten. But every time you break concentration, start over on the number one. This is a quieting exercise that will clear your mind for the task at hand, and help get you into a relaxed state of concentration.

3. Begin watching your thoughts as they go through your mind. Every time you spot one that's a memory, say "memory, memory," to yourself, and just gently return to watching. Do the same for fantasies and talk. If you find yourself having a fantasy or listening to talk, just say, "fantasy, fantasy," or "talking, talking" and go back to watching. Label each thought in this way. If something else happens—such as hearing music—label that, too. If you're not sure what it is, just say "Thinking, thinking." Continue for three to four minutes at first, working up to about ten minutes.[10]

This is an introduction to helping a child move from external to internal processes. In order to orchestrate the states of consciousness, a child needs to know what she's thinking when she's thinking it. A child is concentrating when she's focusing on a thought.

Homework Journal

1. List ten of your child's successes this week. List ten of your own.

2. Identify your child's outside distractions—TV, radio, family arguments. How have you been able to reduce them?

3. How are you eliminating or reducing high sensating stimulus such as MTV, TV, and rock music?

4. Identify inside distractors—internal auditory criticism such as, "I'm not any good at this." How are you eliminating or lessening these distractors?

5. How does your child's developmental level dictate her way of concentrating?

6. How does your child know when she's concentrating and when she's daydreaming?

7. How does your child's developmental stage and learning style influence her way of concentrating?

8. What ritual does your child use to prepare to concentrate? (Experiment with several.)

9. Identify your child's goals in at least two subjects.

10. Do background music or nature videos interfere with or help your child's concentration?

11. Does your child concentrate better with people or by herself?

12. What is your child's concentration/break schedule? ("Twenty on, five off," for example).

Week 6:
Upgrading Your
Child's Memory

Keep in Mind

1. Reduce the use of rote memorization.

2. Increase the use of senses to remember.

3. Use memory helpers.

When we ask children how they remember, the most frequent answer is, "I go over and over it," or "My mother drills me on it." Some children even think reading means memorizing words. "You mean I don't have to memorize every word in the English language to be able to read?" they ask. Others are so hooked on memorizing that they fail final exams because memorization doesn't store information in long-term memory.

Memorization—going over and over the amendments to the Constitution or twenty Spanish words or the fact that Beethoven was born in 1770—is the least effective way to *remember*. Repeating words without connecting them to meaning is like trying to hang your clothes in the closet without hangers.

"Try to remember" is also not a good way to activate your child's memory. Certainly the human brain remembers things it doesn't intend to remember. But children do not naturally develop *strategies* for remembering; they need to be taught how to remember. They need to know that they don't just look at something and automatically remember it. When one group of fifth graders was asked to read and recall a four hundred–word story, they did no better with five minutes extra to study because they didn't know how to use the extra time to review.[1]

Don't leave it up to the child to form his own memory techniques. If his system fails, he feels stupid and thinks he can't remember. If it does work, he tends to stick with that system, however faulty.

Wendy, an eighteen-year-old extremely visual student came to the clinic with memory problems. She was studying biology and statistics, and she was very slow at math. After testing her, we talked about how people remember things and we suggested that she use a memory association technique.

She looked up, as if to say, "You have no right to invade my brain," and we said, "Well, how do you remember what nine times seven is?"

She paused, curious that she had never thought about it, and suddenly said, "Let's see, that's sixty-three, which is blue and yellow." She realized for the first time that whenever she tried to multiply, colors popped into her head. She had no idea where the colors originated.

"You're a good image maker," we said. "Look in your brain and tell us why six is blue and three is yellow. At some point you attached a number to a color. Where did you get them?"

Suddenly, she exclaimed, "Oh, the numbers are on my elementary-school classroom doors." She quickly drew a picture of the doors and the colored numbers at the top of each door.

As a visual child, it made sense for her to associate colors with something she wanted to remember. But when she remembered numbers along with a corresponding color, it created "excess baggage" in her mind and brought her math ability to a halt. When Wendy realized that the memory system was faulty—the colors had no meaningful connection to the numbers—she practiced visualizing the numbers without colors and her math speed increased dramatically. Over the next two to three months, we helped Wendy use her visual learning style to mindmap, and she began to use memory helpers.

Wendy was on the right track, however, with her color-coding system. Relating pieces of information in a systematic and meaningful way is a big assist to memory. Children can learn to create these networks of meaning.

How Memory Works

The Memory Filing System

The brain is a complex filing system. If you "write" information on a computer disk and take it out a year later, nothing on the disk has changed—what you wrote is perfectly preserved. But human memory changes and reorganizes. Every experience that enters influences the whole of memory. "The brain is a library of loose-leaf books, constantly adding new volumes," noted Carl Sagan.[2]

A memory is stored in cross-referenced files throughout the brain. There is not one "math homework file" in the manner that "Math.5" on a computer disk contains all your math problems. In the human brain, the memory of math homework may be stored as an algebra formula one place, the strategy for figuring out which formula to use in another, the fear you have of math in another, the memory of the teacher in another, the feel of your desk in another, the memory of your father helping you in another. This multistorage is obvious when you remember only the formula but not the strategy or when you remember who helped you but not when.

A nicely organized memory file cabinet has many categories. The more categories you create, the more associations you can make and the more things you can remember. Deliberately filing in more than one place within categories is the key to retrieving memories.

Chunking

A nicely organized memory notebook has *chunks* of information. A chunk is a pattern of ideas and concepts. The idea is to recognize a pattern in information (the brain's favorite pastime) and either break it down into smaller chunks or glue it together to make larger chunks. Placing information into the brain in neat chunks makes it easily retrievable.

Nine-year-old Jimmy was required to write a report on "trans-

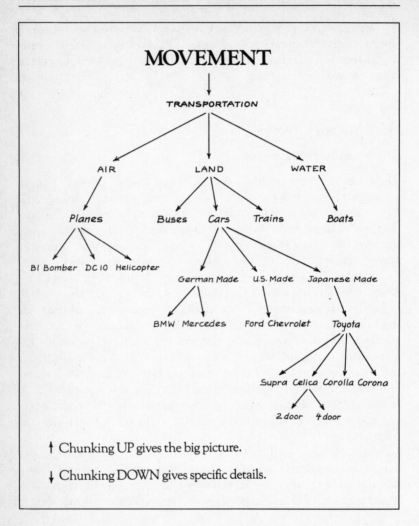

↑ Chunking UP gives the big picture.

↓ Chunking DOWN gives specific details.

portation." He couldn't think of anything to write and when he looked in the encyclopedia he was overwhelmed. "Chunking down" —taking the subject and breaking it down into parts—helped him learn and remember a topic that otherwise meant nothing to him.

We wrote the word, "Transportation" in the middle of the paper and from there we "chunked down." We started with types of air, water, and land transportation. Then, in each of these categories, we "chunked down" again: for example, types of planes—helicopters, DC-10s, B-1 bombers.

You can help children learn to break down and glue together chunks of things by drawing a map around the assignment and asking questions to stimulate thinking. In the above example, we asked: "What is transportation a part of?" (movement). "What's parallel to German cars?" (American and Japanese cars). "What is the broader category—cars or Mercedes?" (cars). This builds the child's ability to form hierarchic thinking, which in turn strengthens memory.

Sometimes children have trouble remembering because they zero in on the small chunks but never get "the big picture." Sixteen-year-old Bob, while focusing on the age requirements for U.S. president, senators, and representatives, was surprised to find that there were senators at both state and federal levels. He was sure the book had made a mistake. In a month of painful study about the details of running for public office, he had failed to see the Big Chunk—that there was a judicial, executive, and legislative structure for the state as well as federal governments. Once we drew a picture of the three branches, he had the scaffolding to hang the facts on.

Use a Big Chunk question to create this scaffolding in all subject areas. Memorizing a chronology of battles from Antietam to Gettysburg will help few children understand the Civil War. But to answer the question, "Why was the Civil War not just about slavery?", a child needs to understand the economic dependence of the South on Blacks and the industrial nature of the Northeast. The Big Chunk question provides a structure for remembering details, which are difficult to remember in isolation.

Developmental Memory

So you know that memory is stored and retrieved in chunks, that memory reorganizes when it's stored, and that you need to learn how to remember. But you also need to know that not all children remember in quite the same way. A four-year-old does not remember the same way an eight-year-old does, and a kinesthetic learner will remember differently than an auditory or visual learner.

A four- to seven-year-old may remember a fantasy about the great green giant who planted purple plants, but he forgets his telephone number. An eight-year-old may remember six hundred baseball cards but not what day to take out the trash.

By one estimate one out of ten young children has a photographic memory, but nine out of ten of those particular children eventually lose that memory; only 1 percent of adults have it.[3] Children seem to "dull out" by using inefficient memory techniques. Being forced to remember things they don't understand and not having a way to remember seems to "stunt" the magical brain. Help the Magical Child hold on to his cartoon-type memory with dancing images and colorful fantasies. Especially with younger children, use body involvement in all memory activities—clapping, stomping, hopping, and acting out. Movement creates a patterning (for example, when you "draw" a circle in the air), which is the basis for visual-spatial memory.

Young children do not rehearse spontaneously (go over something in their minds without being taught), perhaps because their internal auditory voice doesn't come in until age five. They can, however, easily be taught to rehearse.

To remember the alphabet, for example, the teacher, when presenting the letter A, can give the direction, "Now say it to yourself." Without this instruction, a child may repeat the letter aloud, but may not repeat it inside his head.

Five-year-old Brenda did not easily remember the letters of the alphabet, but when learning therapist Gerry told her, "Remember this letter," she stopped, closed her eyes, and said the letter over to herself while Gerry said it to himself. This extra step of saying the letter to herself helped her build "auditory rehearsal memory."

The prime time for factual memory (Concrete Logical) is about age eight, when children start collecting things and will ask repeatedly, "What kind of rock is this?" Encourage your child to remember license-plate numbers, telephone numbers, baseball cards, or the names of leaves. Although ten- and eleven-year-olds begin to categorize spontaneously, there is a limit to the memory effectiveness of categorization. In fact, we get many referrals of children in this age group who have gotten by without techniques, but who start to suffer when the school demands for memory are increased. (TV may have also usurped their visual memory.) This is the time to teach outlining and notetaking to help them organize their thoughts on paper.

A Concrete Logical Child will be unable to remember (even though he may assure you that he has) an abstract concept ("heaven")

Notetaking for the Visual and Kinesthetic

For many students, notetaking is not an automatic process; it's very easy for the auditory child but not so easy for the visual or kinesthetic child. Here's how it works: First, the child has to be attuned to what is being said and not be distracted by the visual (how cute the girl next to him is) or the kinesthetic (his own headache).

He then needs to be able to hold on to the internal auditory information long enough to reword it into a shorthand. Remember, all thinking is based on remembering and imagining. If he's doing this successfully, he compares what the teacher says (auditory external), "The freeing of the prisoners on Bastille Day was July 14," to what he already knows (auditory remembering), "I think I read about the French Revolution in the *Tale of Two Cities*," and anticipates what the teacher will say next (auditory imagining), "Was it a good idea to free those prisoners?"

To help a child learn these auditory skills:

1. Teach him to tune out distractions by focusing on a single sound.

2. Have him listen to two minutes of speech while writing down only five key words to focus on the main idea.

3. Teach him to recognize voice emphasis in sentences; emphasized phrases provide keys for understanding content.

4. Teach him to be aware of pitch, tempo, and rhythm; say the same sentence while varying each of these qualities so he will be better able to hear and interpret them.

5. To increase auditory skills, say longer and longer sentences and have him repeat the sentences exactly.

6. Have him repeat strings of digits forward and backward.

without a concrete image ("angel"). For over a year Kerry, nine, tried to remember the Tae Kwon Do creed without success. When we helped him think up concrete symbols for each line (a muscled arm for "Might for Right"), he had no trouble. When you talk about concepts such as democracy, peace, love, independence, and so on, always supply a visual symbol.

An adolescent can use the association technique called "method of loci" on a Shakespeare sonnet, keywording on a chemistry chapter, and mindmapping on a history text. He will usually reject, however, a memory device introduced the night before a test. Encourage him to practice these techniques first on material that he is not in the process of learning—a grocery list, the names of music tapes, et cetera. Once he's practiced the techniques, he can learn to apply them to the early stages of studying, such as notetaking in class.

Emotions and Memory

The best-organized memory files in the world won't work under adverse conditions. An emotionally upset child will seem to have "lost" his memory. Every time Carl had a fight with his younger sister, he seemed to have no memory at all when he sat down to do his homework. An adolescent, particularly, may have difficulty remembering homework information when his feelings overrule.

Mitzy, age nine, was a perfectly good student and had no memory problems before her parents got a divorce. But with the new living arrangements, she spent half the week with her father and half the week with her mother. "I have on my mother's dress and this is my father's stuffed bear," she said. She always wondered who would pick her up from school on a given day.

Even though Mitzy had actually learned her number facts previously, she forgot them when divorce was imminent. "She's slacking off. She just got lazy," said her teacher, who was aware of the situation but didn't believe that Mitzy's memory could be affected by the upsets at home. We convinced Mitzy's parents that her ability to remember in school was affected by her not knowing where she was going to spend the night, and they agreed for one parent to have her during the school week and another to have her on the weekend. Her memory improved rapidly. (In fact, we've gone to court numerous times to testify that the child's mental abilities are affected by the shuffling back and forth between parents during the school week.)

Children can learn how to use memory of positive experiences to their benefit. Using a technique called "circle of excellence," they learn to control feelings, to access good feelings, and to frame and remember them when they want to. Help your child remember, "I've been in this kind of anxious situation before and I got out of it." Have your child remember when he really felt good about something. For Jill, it was diving off a diving board. Any time she was going to study for a test, or wanted to achieve, she stepped into her imaginary circle of excellence. It works like this:

Think of an event where you were excellent. When you have the event clearly in your mind, imagine a circle on the floor and step into that circle. Now connect the event and the circle: Imagine being in that event as you're in the circle. The successful feelings you have can then be transferred to the anxious situation.

When Mitzy started saying, "I can't remember my math facts," she stepped into her circle of excellence and remembered how proud she was of learning to skate and ride a bicycle, and then she could more easily remember her math.

Memory by Learning Style

The child's learning style determines whether you need to color code the multiplication tables, sing them, or make a path on the floor and hop by twos and threes. No child needs to learn the multiplication tables without smelling, feeling, seeing, hearing, or tasting them (Remember Gummi Bear Annie).

Barry, a large, sports-minded (kinesthetic) seventh grader, was required to remember the types of clouds and atmospheres for his science class. Sitting down and trying hard to remember was very difficult for this kinesthetic learner, so learning therapist Terri suggested that he assemble a "memory shoebox" containing a collection of things of different shapes and textures from his room—his toy car, a favorite rock, a piece of cotton, and a candle. For each layer of the atmosphere, Barry pulled an object out of the box and made a mental association between the two. The rock, for example, was tied to the stratosphere; the cotton stood for the cumulus clouds. After reading a paragraph, he moved the cotton around like a cloud to remember cumulus. He and Terri reviewed the layers of the atmosphere and types of clouds in the same session, then put the memory tool away. If Barry got stuck, he went back to the box.

Because Barry was kinesthetic, moving while he learned was the magic he needed to trigger his memory. He was still able to identify the layers of the atmosphere months later with no problem.

Some children remember visual images better. A World War II battle might lend itself to a picture, or a wall map. Some artistic children like to draw cartoons to remind them of concepts in a book or class. George's mother used to take his history chapter and draw pictures of the ideas to help George remember them. Eventually, George was weaned from the pictures and now he makes internal visual images. These internal images tend to be remembered better when there is color and interaction—a boy riding a bicycle rather than just a boy and a bicycle.

For the kinesthetic or visual learner, play a game of "Gossip." Let one child tell a short story and whisper it to the next family member or class member until the story has been retold several times. The last child tells it aloud. The final version is unrecognizable compared to the opening version. This illustrates how a child imagines what he doesn't remember, hence the importance of notetaking.

Auditory memory may be more appropriate for some children; Read a poem in a "Mickey Mouse" or "Donald Duck" voice; this auditory imagining exercise may provide enough variation to store the poem in memory. (Try reading this week's Keep in Mind suggestions, at the beginning of the chapter, in a funny voice.)

Set what you want the child to remember to music. When Faith was in the fourth grade, the class sang the multiplication tables each day. Sing "Old MacDonald Had a Farm" with the vowels, "A, E, I, O, U" in place of "E I E I O."

Some children can remember the rhythm of a song and not the words. To teach syllables of words, tap out the rhythm on a drum as you say each syllable, or use a metronome.

Kinesthetic memory is the memory of athletes and dancers, of musicians and actors. If you ask a musician how to play, "The Star-Spangled Banner," he might say, "I can't tell you how; I just have to be at the keyboard." (He's really saying, "My body has to feel it.")

The body sometimes remembers more accurately than the conscious mind, especially in learning-disabled children. When Jenny, a nine-year-old dyslexic speller, was asked to orally spell ten words, she reversed the "a" and "i" in "straight" and put a "u" before the "er" in "answer." She only spelled three of the ten words correctly.

"Pretend," we said, "that you are writing a word with the eraser on the pencil and make the motions on the table top. When she did this kinesthetic movement, she spelled five more words correctly. Now, before Jenny spells, she "writes" the word kinesthetically.

Relaxation and oxygenation of the brain are important to memory. Physical movement is a good way to increase oxygenation: Walk, jump, or stand up rather than sit to memorize. We find it helpful (in some cases imperative!) for children to jump on a rebounder when reviewing the multiplication tables, or to walk while reading. Others need to move their shoulders, wiggle their toes and fingers, relax their jaws and shoulders. Some people find that reciting while walking backward improves memory.

To stimulate the sense of smell to improve the memory, we use "Scratch and Sniff" stickers or scented felt-tipped markers. Look at a fact, or draw a diagram using the stickers or markers, then smell the fragrance associated with the fact in your mind. Some students have taken the "Scratch and Sniff" stickers to school to stimulate memory on a test.

To learn the water cycle, you can "smell code" the stages with markers: (1). evaporation from oceans—blueberry; (2). clouds—melon; (3). rain on continents—lemon; (4). groundwater to streams—cinnamon; (5). groundwater to plants—apple; (6). evaporation from lakes and streams—grape; (7). transpiration from plants—mint. (Use a smell code with this week's Keep in Mind suggestions.)

Memory Helpers

Mnemonic devices, we used to think, were a form of medieval torture devised by people with exceptional memories for people with unexceptional memories. We thought that the cure—"one-bun, two-shoe, three-tree," or associating Martha Washington with the stereo (method of loci)—was worse than the disease. The name alone—mnemonic devices—conjured up images of Frankenstein.

But our experience has shown that these memory helpers provide powerful connectors in the brain, increasing a child's ability to associate and to imagine. We have seen them bring about improvements among the poorest students. Any entry into memory is a help and these techniques seem to form a powerful web of associative ability in the mind, causing an increase in overall memory. Nonetheless, many parents and children resist (with a capital R) using memory helpers.

Ross, sixteen, was very nervous every time he had a test, complaining, "I have a bad memory." He "memorized" Spanish words by going over and over them, writing them on his hand, and repeating them the morning of the test. He studied "*Bolsa* means purse," but when the teacher tested him on "purse" he could not come up with *bolsa*.

When we suggested mnemonic devices, such as associating *bolsa* with balsa wood and seeing a wooden purse, he said, "That's a lot of effort. I have to think of all that? Isn't that going to use up a lot of space in my brain?" Even though his own system was poor and made him incredibly nervous, he clung to the familiar.

We explained to Ross that memory is the reorganization of what you already know. On a computer, it's true that an image "uses up" a large amount of "memory." But with human memory, creating images is the most efficient way to remember. Memory helpers tap into this preexisting land of images, and when you're through with them, notes John Hayes, "the key word which is useful for initial learning disappears without harmful effects like a builder's scaffolding when it is no longer needed."[4] Ross decided to give the system a try.

"Ross is not studying," said Ross's mother, who called the night before the test. "He's not memorizing; he's just sitting around drawing pictures." We assured her that this was part of his studying.

The next day, still afraid that he didn't know it, and somewhat accustomed to the feeling of panic, he started "memorizing" in the morning. But to his surprise, he made an A minus on the test, retained the information, and continued to use pictures to help him remember.

Many students don't readily come up with good mental images. (Perhaps the result of too many prepackaged television images.) They may have developed an unnatural resistance to imaging, like Donald, twelve. When we asked him to imagine the Eskimos fishing after he had read a paragraph about Alaska, he blurted out: "You're not supposed to put a picture in your mind unless you know the picture the author had in his mind. When you look in your mind, you won't see the same thing that the author is writing about. That's cheating."

When using mnemonic techniques, some individuals, particularly teenagers, try to get by with mediocre pictures and ordinary associations. When trying to remember an association between jack-o'-lantern and refrigerator, Sharon said, "Oh, I can remember that because I kept my Halloween pumpkin until it was old and shriveled." But the next week when learning therapist Winnie said, "refrigerator," Sharon said "old, shriveled pumpkin" instead of "jack-o'-lantern." To help Sharon create a more effective association, Winnie said, "Make a visual image of yourself at the refrigerator door. See the shriveled pumpkin and take the paring knife and carve a face on it." Adding the movement part (kinesthetic) helped her make the connection.

Be aware that children do not always easily transfer the following memory techniques to a new situation. When they study the amendments to the Constitution one week and the presidents of the United States the next, it may not occur to them to use the same memory techniques. By the same token, they may try to apply a technique to a situation that is not suitable. Children need to have a repertoire of memory techniques and a knowledge of what types of situations each one works best in. You may need to repeatedly suggest different memory techniques and encourage the child to practice using them. Have the child practice the techniques in isolation first; he shouldn't be learning the technique at the same time he's learning new material.

Method of Loci

In the "method of loci" memory technique, the child visualizes a place and attaches what he has to remember to things in the location. Researchers have shown that students using the method of loci do from two to seven times better than those who do not.[5]

Mary Ellen, who was in her senior year of high school, only read what she had to read and resisted digging deeper. For her, schoolwork literally went in one ear and out the other. Nervously, she tried to memorize Macbeth's speech in Scene V, which was no small undertaking.

As she read a passage, she thought of walking in the door of her bedroom, looking from right to left around the room, identifying objects that she loved—her stereo, her boyfriend's picture, her stuffed penguin—and attaching a line to each object.

As she read, "Tomorrow, and tomorrow, and tomorrow, / Creeps in this petty pace from day to day," she imagined standing in front of the stereo and made an association between the line and the object. She thought of the "pace" of the music attached to the stereo. Then, to the next line, "To the last syllable of recorded time," she imagined standing in front of her bed and thinking it was time to get up. "And all our yesterdays have lighted fools / The way to dusty death. Out, out, brief candle!" she attached to her stuffed penguin and his white fur, which got dusty sometimes. She continued with the associations through "Life's but a walking shadow, a poor player; That struts and frets his hour upon the stage." And she easily remembered the speech.

When Ross, another student, first came in he was rehearsing to the hilt before he learned to use method of loci to remember the amendments to the Constitution. He used a route in his house from the minute he awoke identifying twenty-two places, and he tied the amendments to the places. For the right to bear arms, he saw a pile of bear arms in the corner of his room. Freedom of religion became a group of priests and nuns sitting by a lamp in the living room where he usually sits. One time through and he had it down.

Be careful what you choose as a location; for some children the house is too emotionally laden. Susan, a nineteen-year-old, stopped cold when we suggested that she use the closet in the front hallway of her house for place number one. "When I open the front closet," she said, "all this trash falls out. If you think my mind is disorganized, you ought to see the house." It was disturbing for her to think about her home, so she chose her history classroom instead. (At the same time, we worked on helping her organize her house.)

Elaborate and Exaggerate

To remember, use humor, exaggeration, and just plain silliness. Elaborate on the information and allow it to go into many different circuits. Many parents mistakenly think that "exaggeration is lying and humor takes away the seriousness of the subject matter." Yet even adults want to know more about geography and history when they read Donald Duck's travels around the world (for example, riding a horse through the Grand Canyon) in the *Disney World Encyclopedias*.[6] This kind of humor and elaboration are an effective form of overlearning that imprints things in memory.

Justin, ten, had two months to remember the states, their abbreviations and the capitals. Because he was very auditory, his mother came up with sentences such as "We're going to Augusta, Maine, in the month of August; We had tapioca pudding in Topeka, Kansas; We went to Juneau, Alaska, in the month of June; I met a lassie from Tallahassee, Florida."

Five nights before the test, she also helped him color code the U.S. map—five yellow states, five purple states, and so on. When she said "yellow," he named the states. Justin also had to learn the names and locations of counties in Maryland. He remembered the names by making connections to his relatives—a cousin named Anne for the county Princess Anne, two uncles named Frederick and Howard for those counties.

Jeff, eleven, had to learn the zoological phylum of worms. To remember the round earthworms, called "Annelida," he rolled on the floor and pictured his Aunt Anita. For flat worms—Platyhelminthes worms—he made himself *flat* on the floor and thought of "fatty helmet."

Randi, fourteen, had to learn one hundred dates in Roman history. Taking half sheets of typing paper, she drew pictures of each date and a symbol, such as a dagger for the assassination of Julius Caesar. She put the paper in chronological order around the top of the wall in her bedroom so that she would have to look up to put them into visual memory. She had learned almost all of them by the time she had finished drawing them.

Overstudying and overlearning are very good experiences for the child to have early on. To do this, encourage the child to use several elaborative techniques on one assignment. The child who goes into the test knowing that he knows, replaces the anxiety in his head with positive questions, such as "Let's see, what could they possibly ask me?"

How Not to Forget

If you want your child to remember to do anything in the future, especially something he's likely to forget, "future memory" is an

Ridiculous Image Guidelines

1. Imagine an object doing something it doesn't ordinarily do (make a tree fly).

2. Make the figures out of proportion (a tree as tall as the Empire State Building).

3. Multiply the image (a million flying trees).

4. Put the whole thing into action (a million flying giant redwood trees speeding across the United States that skid to a halt in a New York airport).

effective technique. To help him remember to bring home his chemistry book, for example, say to him:

"Find the place where you need to remember something. If it's at your locker, make a picture of yourself in front of your locker. When you open the locker, volatile chemicals, streams of red, blue, and orange, pour out on your feet, spelling the word chemistry on the floor. Other chemicals make popping sounds as they come out of your chemistry book."

Be sure the child sees himself in the picture, that the picture is coded in as many senses as possible, and that it is exaggerated. Use bright colors, loud sounds, strong odors, sticky or rough textures, and overstated movements.

For Those Who Don't See Pictures

The ability to form mental images is vital to good memory. Though we all make images, some of us are much more aware of them. When you ask a child to make a mental image of something, it's okay if he says, "I don't have a picture of it." These children can learn to become more aware of their internal pictures. The exercise goes like this: Say to your child, "Look at a candle. Now close your eyes and see the after-image of the candle. Look at the candle again and close your eyes and image the candle. Hold on to it longer." Start with simple designs and go to more complex things.

When Bridgette tried memory helpers, she complained that she didn't see images. Learning therapist Terri said to her, "Walk around the room, stop in front of that vase, and focus on it. Tell me as many details about it as you can." Bridgette enjoyed this little "achievement test" and rattled on about the shape and style of the vase and the pink flowers painted on it.

"When you are ready, close your eyes," said Terri, "and tell me about the image inside your head." This helped Bridgette create vivid images in her mind.

Point out ways that the child already images and bring the images from the unconscious to the conscious mind. Start out with, "Do you remember your first bicycle?"

"Yes."

"Well, I see you already do image. Let's imagine something else: Picture yourself having a space suit with a jet on the back that flies you through the air."

With effective memory strategies and good internal imagining, your child need no longer resort to ineffective memorization. With a well-organized memory file cabinet (in which he has filed material by senses), he can remember almost anything.

Homework Journal

1. List ten of your child's successes this week. List ten of your own.

2. Which *ineffective* memory systems is your child now using?

3. How can your child use "chunking" to store and retrieve information?

4. How does your child's developmental stage affect what he remembers?

5. How do your child's emotions affect his memory?

6. How does your child's learning style affect how he will remember things?

7. What kind of elaboration techniques can your child use?

8. What kind of memory helpers does he like?

9. What subjects can he use method of loci on?

Part Three

Grades
and
Testing

The grades and testing system has changed little in the past fifty years. Parents' beliefs about grades are based on how they were evaluated as students and, whether those methods were fair or not, they are as entrenched as the SAT now is. Few parents are willing to rock the grades and testing boat.

And yet, the trend is toward a radical departure. Gradeless schools with a larger number of alternative ways of evaluating will be the hallmark of the future. According to Howard Gardner, of Harvard, these schools will evaluate the intelligence of students through a process portfolio, "a collection of projects the child has done through the school years which demonstrate the intelligences, such as musical, visual spatial, interpersonal, etc."[1] But until these changes become widespread, we suggest that parents make every attempt to stretch the current concepts of evaluation at school.

Here are questions parents and children frequently ask about grades and testing.

Questions Parents Ask

Q. *What do grades tell me about my child?*

A. Grades are a measure of conformity to school standards. They primarily reward the left-brained, auditory child and are of primary interest to the left-brained parent. The kinesthetic emotional learner is least successful with grades because so little is taught in her learning style. Grades are indicative of a narrow range of intelligences, and may or may not reflect learning.

Remember that a test is only one measure; there are many ways to evaluate a child's progress, including daily class work, homework, and projects. With optimum learning, a test is a mere formality to show off what a child already knows.

Q. *Then how can I know my child's real achievement?*

A. There are many ways to evaluate what a child does other than with grades. Keep home records about what your child knows. Have a family yardstick of knowledge: Does she have a good sense of history and geography or does she think Egypt is a state? Collect a sample of writing at the same time every year and note her progress. Collect her art, make a portfolio of reports and creative writing. Have a special shelf for anything your child collects, such as rocks, leaves, bugs. Videotape acting, dance lessons, karate, and voice lessons. Keep a running list of what your child reads.

Q. *My child made an A the first quarter and a B the next in the same subject. Did he learn more in the first quarter?*

A. Not necessarily. It's a waste of time to compare grades from quarter to quarter. Curriculum content is often uneven, with more review in the first half of the year and more new material in the second half. As the curriculum changes from grammar to composition to Shakespeare, or from lab experiments to textbook information, the child may or may not be equally prepared in each area. Also, children have "learning cycles." Roy, for example, always does better the first quarter. When a pattern like this emerges, he's telling you when he has problems. Use this information to do the Six-Week Plan in the second quarter. Be aware that the teacher may have "cycles" too. Some teachers don't give A's the first quarter, because "the kids won't have anything to work for." Discuss and clarify the teacher's grading policy.

Q. *I give my daughter one dollar for every A she makes on her report card. Is this a good idea?*

A. No. Don't reward or punish a child for grades. We realize this is radical advice; one fifth grader told us she was the only child in her class who didn't get money for good grades or punishment for poor grades. Rewarding for grades makes children dependent on outside rewards and lessens their internal ambition.

Q. *The teacher wrote "immature" on my son's report card. How do I interpret this?*

A. "Lazy" or "immature" are never appropriate words on a report card. These words portray a negative mindset and, with this prediction of failure, it is almost impossible for the child to succeed. Find a real explanation for these terms. Ask the teacher, "What is my child doing when you call him lazy?" If she says, "He's sleeping during my first period," then the solution may be more sleep for the child. If the teacher continues to view the child negatively, discuss with the principal the possibility of moving your child to a different classroom.

Q. *What if the teacher grades unfairly?*

A. This is probably the most common complaint we hear. When a child begins school, she may think teachers are "unfair" because they don't pay as much attention to her as Mom and Dad do. Reassure the child that this isn't unfair. It is unfair, however, to grade children on behavior alone (as opposed to their academic performance.) It is unfair for a teacher not to return papers. If you think the teacher has made a grading error, go to the teacher and ask how the grade was determined, and what your child could do differently next time. For example, on a math test, Peter worked out a problem correctly, but copied the answer incorrectly to the other side of the paper. His grandmother complained that the teacher was unfair. But the teacher may have been willing to change things had the grandmother pointed out Peter's error. It's also important for children to know that they can learn from a teacher they perceive as unfair.

Q. *My son is fifteen and making A's but has no homework. Should I be concerned?*

A. Yes. At that age, he can expect to have two to four hours of homework every night. He might be placed in courses that are below his achievement level, and could do better in a more accelerated course or with outside stimulation, such as a photography course.

Check on the homework policy of the school. We have often suggested that high school students who need a challenge sign up for a college course.

Q. *Last year my daughter made A's, but this year my son is struggling to make C's with the same teacher. Should I make the same requirements of each?*

A. Neither you nor the teacher need compare one child to another. Never let grades be a barometer for how you treat your child. Know your child's learning style so well that you understand why Roger, the creative, right-brained child, will probably get lower grades than Sue, the avid reader.

Usually, poor grades are the result of mismatched learning styles (between student and teacher) or mismatched assignments (over or under the child's skill level.) Suggest that the teacher individualize the homework assignment by allowing your child to do more or less, give a different kind of assignment, and you can supplement classroom material with at-home work, geared to your child's learning style.

Q. *My child freezes up before tests. How can I help?*

A. Find out what your child is seeing, hearing, and feeling and help her change the pictures, the sounds, the feelings. One child said, "When I sit down to study, in my mind's eye I see the teacher handing my paper back with red marks." We had him remember vividly a time when he received high grades. He then practiced remembering that. Every time Audrey, thirteen, took tests at school, she burst into tears and was practically unable to mark her answer. We encouraged her to take as many kinds of test as she could find, just for fun: word quizzes in *Reader's Digest* and women's magazines. Over time she became convinced that tests were fun.

Encourage the teacher to allow a child many ways to answer, including video evaluation, stories, and multiple choice. Take-home tests are some of the best because they allow the child to work out answers over time, with assistance.

Q. *What can I do when my child gets an F on a paper?*

A. Train your child and yourself to think of an F paper as Feedback (Our rule is Never Failure, Only Feedback.) Quickly save it from the trash can and use it to help your child see why she missed. The following questions will help your child know what to do differently next time: What kind of question did I miss—was it an information question, a problem-solving question, or an opinion question? Did I miss the question because of something I didn't read or remember from my notes or the book? Was I the only one to miss the question, or did others miss it?

Q. Until my child's grades come up, is it a good idea to sign a daily report card?

A. We must have seen a hundred or more teachers use this, but we have never seen it work. The parent often forgets to sign it and the child is held accountable at school. She is embarrassed to be treated like a small child in front of the other students. The teacher could provide a weekly or monthly report or just let the parent know that the child is having trouble.

Q. What does it mean when my child makes A's but scores low on standardized tests?

A. Your child may have learned to play the school game, but not how to learn. She may be storing information in short-term memory (long enough for one test) but not in long-term memory (more than six months later). She may be insisting that she can concentrate while listening to music that is actually interfering with brain function.

Q. The whole school teaches to standardized tests. How can I change this?

A. Unfortunately, this is a prevalent problem. Notes Arthur Costa, President, Association for School Curriculum Development, "What was educationally significant and difficult to measure was replaced by what was insignificant and easy to remember."[2] Standardized tests encourage teachers to teach to the test and students to memorize test answers instead of think. In addition, art, music, and creative projects are the first to get the ax when standardized testing reigns. We suggest that a coalition of parents, perhaps through the PTA, take on this issue. Suggest video evaluations, portfolios of children's creative writing and art passed from grade to grade, so that at the beginning of each year a teacher can meet a student and smile because she has seen what good work the student does.

Q. *How much preparation can I expect the teacher to give my child before a test?*

A. This varies. Some teachers will do nothing more than announce the test, while others will provide a test review sheet the night before. As the student begins taking the test, a teacher can give a "guided walk-through" to involve the whole brain in test taking. This helps students recall the pictures, feelings, and sounds that were present when they learned the information. It's helpful if the teacher says, "Look at exercise number one. Jot down some rules that remind you what to do. Look at section two. Remember that funny picture of Mozart I showed you in class? Remember how snowy it was the day we learned it? You know everything on this test. Even if you think you didn't learn it, search your brain and see where you might have stored it."

Teachers might also give time estimates for difficult questions, such as "This question will take approximately fifteen minutes."

Q. *What do I tell my child's teacher about our divorce?*

A. In school the teacher may observe the child's emotional ups and downs during this time and lower the level of accountability. Encourage the teacher to give second chances to help your child succeed, and to talk with you frequently. In some situations, we've encouraged the teacher to give passing grades to preserve the mental health of the child.

Q. *What about timed tests?*

A. Timed tests are very unfair to some children who are simply neurologically slower. It is impossible for them to speed up. Even administrators of the SAT now allow learning-disabled students to take untimed testing.

Questions Children Ask

Q. *I'm failing French. It's only January, but the teacher won't let me out of the class. What are my options?*

A. This happened to Elizabeth in ninth grade French. She was required to stay in the class and was told, "There is nothing you can do to pass." When she protested, the teacher said, "You must stay in and you must fail." With a great deal of effort, we were able to get her out of the class. We firmly believe that a child needs to be given the opportunity to pass a particular class up to the last day, even if it means they will have to do twice the amount of work. We have made arrangements for children who were hopelessly behind to go back and complete all the assignments in a subject so that they could pass.

Q. *How can I know what grade I'm going to make before report cards come?*

A. When we ask children, "What are you making in science?" they don't know. Younger children especially (and a surprising number of older children) see grades as a random, uncontrollable experience, like winning or losing the lottery. To remedy this, make a folder for each subject and list the subject, the date the class begins, the concepts to be studied, and how the final grade will be determined. Keep marked tests and papers in the folders.

Grades and papers are important feedback. If teachers don't return papers, ask for them back. Your father or mother may need to ask the teacher exactly how you're being graded. On the folders, list your grades as you earn them. At the end of each quarter, put the old pocket pouch in your home filing system, and put a new pocket in.

Q. *How are grades averaged?*

A. Jesse, nine, couldn't understand why he was failing when he made eighty-nines on tests. He didn't think it made much difference that he was making zeroes on his homework; he discounted this by saying that the teacher would drop the lowest grade. When we averaged two eighty-nines and a zero, he couldn't believe it. He was awed that a zero would bring his grade down to failing. Make sure you understand what effect a zero has on your otherwise good grades. Play around with averaging the scores of your tests and papers to see what an A, B, C, does to your present scores.

Q. *How can I best study for a test?*

A. Ask the teacher what kind of test it is (multiple choice, true or false, essay), what it covers (class notes, textbook, homework assignments), and if it's possible to get a test review sheet, which many teachers give out. Then make out a list of what you need to do to prepare for this particular test. Examine your anxiety level about the test and think about what you can do to reduce it. It may help to go to the classroom early and study for five minutes. Think about the teacher's normal test pattern: Does she usually start with matching, then have true or false, then essay? Sit down and make up a test that is as good as the teacher's test. Study for the test so that "you know that you know that you know." This means going beyond just being able to recognize the right answer if supplied.

It's important to know if it's a book-made test or a teacher-made test. We had one young man who was usually a very good student but who failed every chemistry test while the rest of the class made A's. It turned out that all the tests were in the back of the book, but he hadn't discovered them. Book-made tests usually don't reflect what is taught in class. The disadvantage is that you know that it's possible to miss all the classes and still pass.

When you arrive at the test, look it over and figure out the type of questions. Bragstad and Stumpf list seven kinds of questions: 1) *memory* (recall): "What is the definition of solid, liquid, gas?"; 2) *translation* (restate the same idea): "Tell me in your own words what you read about gases."; 3) *interpretation* (use known information to solve new problems): "While reading this story, look for ways that African families are like ours."; 4) *application* (transfer learning to new situations): "Find the page in our social studies book that tells about Booker T. Washington." (draws on previous knowledge of how to use an index); 5) *analysis* (take apart): "What problems do you see in grouping mankind under the headings of white race, black race, and yellow race?"; 6) *synthesis* (put together): "Write a different ending to the story of Indian Bill."; and 7) *evaluation* (judge): "Did the colonists do right in throwing the tea overboard at the Boston Tea Party?"[3] Teacher-made tests tend to have more memory-type questions.

Be aware that you will need to think differently to answer these different kinds of questions. Your brain will need to change gears, pulling out information in different forms. For essay questions, which could be translation, interpretation, analysis, synthesis, or evaluation, mindmap your answer quickly.

Q. I studied for a test three and a half hours and still failed. What can I do to help me pass?

A. Take that F paper, get comfortable, put on your favorite music, and embark on a high-level learning journey. Imagine yourself as a brain explorer about to shed some light on a dark cavern of your brain. Examine your gut feelings as you read the questions you missed. Write down all the excuses you can think of for having missed each one. Get the original material and research your mistakes. Keep seeing and hearing the right answers.

F papers represent more potential learning than do A papers. At least you know what you don't know. Your perceptions of what was important to study and how to study it were not on target. This is a golden opportunity to improve your aim.

Examine the paper closely for patterns of errors. Recall your own judgments about what was important, and compare this to what the teacher thought it was important to study. Did you miss questions you really knew? Was the format of the test helpful or did you have difficulty adjusting to it? What does the test tell you about the teacher? Go back through the test and cover up the answers and answer them correctly, with the book open. This procedure remarkably improves test-taking ability. Once you are past the initial anguish, this practice reshapes future studying and test taking.

The Parent/Teacher Connection

- "I have several like him every year," said Michael's teacher. "We'll just sit on him till he does it."

- "I can't do my homework because I don't like my teacher," said fourteen-year-old Jessie.

- "Oh, Marian always acts up when she's bored," said Marian's mother to the sixth-grade teacher. "I guess you're just not a good enough teacher."

All of these situations could have benefited from a parent more attuned to the importance of working out a good relationship with the teacher. As managers of the child's education, too many parents are flunking Diplomacy 101. Unskilled in the high-level negotiation skills necessary for good parent/teacher relations, they are either the Overly Cautious Parent at one end of the continuum or the No-Teacher-Is-Good-Enough-for-My-Child Parent at the other end.

Whichever type of parent you tend to be, there is a better way. By creating a three-way learning team, including you, the child, and the teacher, you can deal effectively with your child's teachers and help your child love to learn from all teachers.

The Overly Cautious Parent sees the teacher and school as the ultimate authority and fears rocking the boat. This may be the parent who only has an eighth-grade education and feels inadequate because he can't do his child's homework. He is paralyzed by the thought that "If I make a disturbance, my child won't be treated fairly." This is a very legitimate concern, especially when it's the only school in town or the school is hard to get into.

BETTER: Caution is in order, but not so much caution that you fail to speak up. You can use a mild-mannered approach to register a complaint generally rather than specifically. Instead of saying "That math homework was too hard for my child," suggest, "My child feels that there is too much homework. I wonder if you could compare it to what others in the class feel." Ask, "What can we do as a team to help him learn? What is our structured plan for helping my child? If he isn't motivated, how can we motivate him? When he's behind because he writes slowly, is it possible for him to have shorter assignments that he can experience doing better?"

Empathize with the teacher's position in school structure. Teachers have had more than enough "top down" direction and often feel that no decision is theirs. Noted one high school teacher, "No teacher wants to hear from the principal." Go to the teacher first and do your best to resolve the problem before you go higher up.

The No-Teacher-Is-Good-Enough-for-My-Child Parent feels that his child must be the exception in every case. "Don't let my child go on a field trip in the rain," he will say, not allowing the child to have the experiences other children do. This parent (singularly disliked by teachers) asks questions that immediately bring a defensive response from the teacher, such as, "Have you ever taught before?" and "Do you get along with the principal?"

BETTER: One mother assumed the role of "Gentle Persuader." When her daughter was asked to draw a genealogy chart, she looked at last year's perfect charts and asked the teacher, "Oh, I'm supposed to do this chart?" "No," said the teacher, "the child is supposed to do it." "But these charts are not done by children," said the mother, pointing out the obvious overinvolvement by parents. The mother suggested, "Let's write down exactly how much the parent is supposed to do and how much the child is supposed to do." The teacher then became aware that the parents usually ended up doing too much of the project and allowed the project to be done in class rather than at home.

Check the Teacher Pictures

Before you meet with or comment on your child's teacher, check the file cabinet in your brain labeled, "Teachers I Hated" or "School and Other Disasters." These little file folders with negative pictures of teachers are sometimes tucked inconspicuously into your subconscious until they get their cue: the first time your child comes home with a bad grade.

Paint a picture of a successful relationship between your child and the teacher. Many parents clear their throats and raise their eyebrows to the ceiling when we suggest this image, as if we had said, "Imagine winning the lottery." Still, make the picture as vividly positive as possible and, meanwhile, look for another file (sometimes lurking far back in the recesses of your mind) called "Favorite Teacher," one person who inspired you at an important time in your life. Share this picture with your child and project only positive images.

Know the Teacher

At the beginning of the year, establish a relationship with the teacher and let him know that you want to follow your child's progress, that you're interested in innovative learning techniques and that you will assist wherever you can. Let the teacher know that you are open to two-way communication. (In high school the teacher's attitude is usually "Call me; I won't call you.")

Find out the learning style of your child's teacher: Does he talk a lot (auditory), draw diagrams and charts (visual), move around the classroom (kinesthetic external). Is he very open to children's feelings (kinesthetic internal)? Remember that it's the child's learning style that needs to be matched, not yours; a visual parent may not like the messy classroom that a kinesthetic child finds very comfortable.

The right teacher is the most important factor in the child's placement. If your child is labeled "learning disabled" or "gifted," don't automatically sign up for the classes designed for children in those categories. The regular class may be better if the learning style of the teacher is more compatible with your child's own style.

We've found it helpful to appeal to a teacher's original dreams and feelings about teaching, saying, "Remember what it was like when you first started teaching. I want my child to feel your enthusiasm for teaching." Most teachers still have some idealism about the excitement of inspiring young minds.

Let the Teacher Know You

The Good

Getting to know the teacher is no time to be shy about your child's achievements. Don't wait for your child to be discovered. Point out his star qualities (creative, active, and so on), his interests (rock collecting, soccer, ballet, reading), and your ambitions for him (to have a good year in school, to be able to make friends).

Kate's teacher thought that she was "spaced out" and distracted until her mother explained to the teacher that Kate had a very vivid imagination, thought up her own stories, and often made up songs and dances. Armed with this insight, when the teacher saw her staring into space, instead of chiding her for not paying attention, he inquired, "What interesting fantasy are you having?" Often the teacher, too, found Kate's fantasy more interesting than the subject he was teaching. But he brought her back to the subject, while acknowledging her fantasy at the same time.

Share learning-style information with the teacher so that he can be aware of your child's learning style. No one can expect to gather all of this information in one day, one week, or one month. But over time, the teacher can learn to see patterns in eye movements and verbal behavior. (When he does, teaching becomes exciting again and students will pick up on this.) Always keep in mind that the final objective is to help and inspire your child to learn.

The Not-So-Good

As you're getting to know the teacher, let the teacher know about you and your family—both the good and the not-so-good. Be your child's champion and share some family learning lore with the teacher, but also let the teacher know when the champ is down or the family is sailing through rough waters. Some parents say, "I wonder if it's important to tell the teacher we're getting a divorce." Yes, let the teacher know that your child may be going through some hard times. At the very least say, "We are in a family crisis, please know that my child may have more trouble than usual."

Barbara's first-grade teacher was convinced that Barbara was lazy until she found out that Barbara's parents were going through a divorce and that she was being shuttled back and forth between them. Once she was aware of this, she allowed Barbara to do a little less work for awhile. Teachers may revise their expectations when they know the reality of the home situation.

With inadequate home information, teachers may not realize how severe the repercussions of school failure are. Phil's math teacher called home and reported that he wasn't doing his homework. Phil's father, having threatened earlier to throw him out if he goofed off in school anymore, made good on his promise and put the boy out of the house. When Phil told the teacher the situation, she made adjustments, allowing Phil to hand his homework in a day late, just as long as he did it.

Speak No Evil

Whatever your assessment of your child's teacher is, the best approach in front of children is: "Speak no evil of teachers." We've heard parents say in front of the child, "His teacher is totally incompetent." This gives the child little chance to form his own opinion. He loves his parents and, knowing his parents don't like the teacher, he sides with them (and does no schoolwork). Thinking that it pleases his parents, he becomes Agent 007, whose top mission is to spy on his teacher, saying, "Mr. Sanders is always wasting our time talking about Vietnam," or "Mr. Sanders misspelled 'appreciation.' " He also learns to give credit to someone else for his failures and successes. Janice, for example, says she got into sixth- instead of fifth-grade spelling because, "My mother gave the teacher a lot of trouble." Support the teacher and work out any differences with him away from the child.

How Your Child Sees the Teacher

Children will do anything for a teacher they like, and sometimes, nothing for one they don't like. They want someone they can love to learn from. Developmentally, the child first bonds with the parents, then expects the same attention and care from other adults, particularly teachers. Teachers, understandably, are in an impossible situation; they can't give the same focused attention parents give in the early years. But they can do small things that make a difference.

At one junior high school, the children told us, "We've never spoken to the teacher personally." The school had made it a policy for teachers not to speak individually to a child. At our suggestion, the school reconsidered this practice and the teachers began making a point of saying something to each child, even if it was as simple as "I like your sweater." The children, motivated by good relationships, immediately started doing better in school.

Helen, a six-year-old adopted child, had not bonded with her adoptive parents. Everything, including eating and sleeping, was a struggle. Her first-grade teacher, who emphasized skills development, said she wasn't trying and gave her D's and F's. The parents and teacher agreed that Helen needed to be moved to a class with a more motherly teacher, who would treat her like one of her own children. After she was moved, Helen quickly began learning to read and eventually bonded with her own parents.

When a child is not bonded to the teacher, be prepared for what seem to be irrational aversions by your child to anybody standing at the head of the classroom: "Men teachers with small shoulders are wimpy," or "I can't learn from a fat teacher." The fact that they can learn from a wimpy, fat, limp-shouldered teacher with a shrill voice is "awesome" to most children, whose models are good-looking, trim, TV entertainers. Help them separate learning from the teacher's personality or appearance.

Understanding learning style (and a little about human behavior) will help a child understand his teacher's habits. Instead of your child saying, "I hate that teacher," he may find the teacher's habits interesting. For instance, "My teacher is too picky about the way my paper looks" becomes "I need to pay attention to how neat my paper is because my teacher is visual."

Write a Consumer Report

The principal of your daughter's school calls at the beginning of the school year with this news: "I'm sorry, Mrs. Jones. Jacquelyn's math teacher is one of our worst teachers. You're just going to have to make up for the teacher's lack of skills and teach her math this year."

As unlikely as this scenario is, too many parents falsely assume that they will be alerted to inconsistencies in their child's education. Remember that for better or worse many school systems are in the business of saving face and will not send out a consumer alert. Your job is to act as "informed consumer," to work in conjunction with the teacher and school to help your child learn the best way he can. Ideally, your "reading" of the school and the teacher is objective and unemotional.

Many elementary-school teachers will be quite frank about their subject preferences. They may say, "I hope he gets a good math teacher next year; he's getting a good dose of reading with me." Some principals, knowing the strengths and weaknesses of each teacher, may use this criteria to place children. It's foolish for parents to close their eyes to the inequalities in teaching skills, particularly in elementary school.

When evaluating the school, be aware of the Unacceptables. This is a Parents' Bill of Rights regarding practices that do not further the development, intelligence, or education of your child. To the credit of many school systems, these practices are generally not acceptable to teachers and principals either. Unfortunately, however, they do still exist.

Ask, "What can the school provide this year? What was my child weak in last year? Is the school strong in art or music? Is it stronger in math, but weaker in reading? Is there a subject that is routinely preempted for fire drills, assemblies, and special elections?" Then plan to compensate in the areas the school ignores or devalues.

Ask, "How well are the Seven Intelligences represented?"

1. *Linguistic Intelligence*

The school emphasizes all forms of language work.

2. *Logical-Mathematical Intelligence*

The school is strong in math and teaches thinking skills.

3. *Spatial Intelligence*

There are 3-D objects to work with and visual spatial activities.

4. *Body Intelligence*

Movement is encouraged, not punished.

5. *Musical Intelligence*

Music is present in the whole curriculum, not just music class.

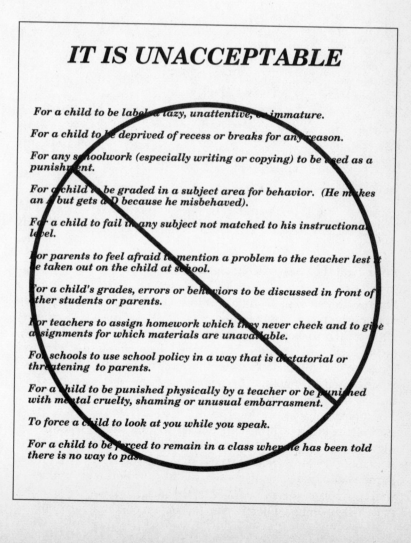

IT IS UNACCEPTABLE

For a child to be labeled lazy, unattentive, or immature.

For a child to be deprived of recess or breaks for any reason.

For any schoolwork (especially writing or copying) to be used as a punishment.

For a child to be graded in a subject area for behavior. (He makes an A but gets a D because he misbehaved).

For a child to fail in any subject not matched to his instructional level.

For parents to feel afraid to mention a problem to the teacher lest it be taken out on the child at school.

For a child's grades, errors or behaviors to be discussed in front of other students or parents.

For teachers to assign homework which they never check and to give assignments for which materials are unavailable.

For schools to use school policy in a way that is dictatorial or threatening to parents.

For a child to be punished physically by a teacher or be punished with mental cruelty, shaming or unusual embarrasment.

To force a child to look at you while you speak.

For a child to be forced to remain in a class where he has been told there is no way to pass.

6. *Interpersonal/Social Intelligence*

There are many flexible group processes, so the child is with a variety of children.

7. *Intrapersonal Intelligence*

The school helps students learn about personal relationship skills.

Evaluate the School's Homework Practices:

1. What is the school's homework policy?

2. How often is homework assigned?

3. What is the make-up policy?

4. What kind of motivation strategies does the school use?

5. To what extent will the teacher see that the child has the correct assignment?

6. How would you rate the teacher's enthusiasm?

7. What is the learning style of the teacher?

Four-Star Homework Assignments

Procrustean, an obscure innkeeper in ancient Greek mythology, ran perhaps the first Holiday Inn—with a twist. Taking a one-size-fits-all approach to hospitality, he insisted that every guest fit every bed; if they were too short, he stretched them, and if they were too long, he cut off their feet. In the modern world of homework, Procrustean has sometimes been up to his ways—making every child fit into the same homework guest bed, regardless of learning style, developmental stage, or interest.

Parents and teachers need not let this be. Individualizing assignments is one way that teachers can help create Four-Star Assignments in the new homework. The creativity for these individualized assignments must come from parents and children as well as from teachers. Parents can encourage teachers to give the same assignment on different days to different children, for example, so that the children who did the assignment on Wednesday can help those who will do it on Friday. One teacher has a fish bowl for young children to draw special assignments.

Other teachers allow the child to come up with his own assignment idea, saying, "Do whatever you have to do to learn the material and come back and tell us about it." These kinds of Four-Star Assignment choices give power and motivation to the students of new homework.

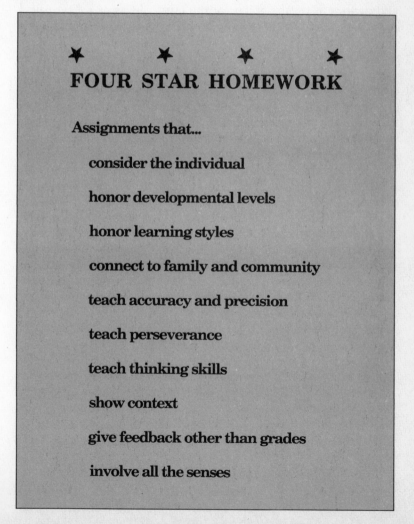

FOUR STAR HOMEWORK

Assignments that...

    consider the individual

    honor developmental levels

    honor learning styles

    connect to family and community

    teach accuracy and precision

    teach perseverance

    teach thinking skills

    show context

    give feedback other than grades

    involve all the senses

Kyle, a tenth grader, was failing Spanish and was uninterested in the topics the teacher supplied for an oral report about Nicaragua. We encouraged him to ask the teacher if he could substitute an assignment of his own design, then asked Kyle what he could do that would spark his interest in Spanish. Well, there was this one girl, Juanita, who he thought was very pretty and she was from Nicaragua. He had been looking for a way to approach her.

His teacher agreed to his idea—to compose a song in Spanish and perform it on the guitar for the class. He wrote a love ballad secretly dedicated to Juanita, performed it for the class, and made an A.

As teachers begin to honor learning style in assigning homework, they will find that they are emphasizing verbal skills less, and movement and art more.

Some teachers consider these homework options too time-consuming, thinking the more diversity, the more work for them. But more and more teachers are realizing that with a few creative changes, such as having children teach each other, the teacher can actually save time. When a teacher lets children who understand a concept help other children who do not, he speeds learning and connects the child to other children. Rather than saying, "We know you know how to do it, let the others do it," the teacher might let the child show others, saying "You be responsible for helping everyone learn how to use a computer disk." To the child who says, "I've got my drawing in first," say "Good, you can show someone else how to draw a horse." For the child who has perfect notes, say, "Maybe you could take notes for the class on the overhead projector so they can see how you take notes." This creates children who learn to solve problems as a team. Or teachers can identify "learning-style consultants"—a visual student, a kinesthetic student, and an auditory student—who can help other classmates with those particular learning styles. The idea is not to change one homework assignment, but to change the philosophy of homework in general.

Many teachers, schools, and communities are making imaginative, stimulating homework assignments a reality and doing it in a spirit that connects the child to the family and to the community. Homework committees, composed of parents, students, teachers, and business leaders help formulate good homework assignments. In an effort to respect family life as an integral part of learning, some teachers hand out assignment sheets previewing the entire week on Monday, so parents and children can plan around home activities. Other teachers provide an answer or guide sheet for the parent.

Homework hotlines staffed by retired people, teachers, and other volunteers relieve parents of uncertainty about what is due, when and how it should be presented.

In Jacksonville, Florida, a hotline is installed in the county professional library and teachers are trained to assist students in finding the solution on their own.[1] The operators answer an average of 130 calls a night and are able to assist 90 percent of all callers, the great majority of whom need help with math. Jacksonville has also designated fifty-eight schools as "Homework Assistance Centers" with a team of teachers ready to help.

High school students are learning perseverance, through a year-long English assignment that allows them to rework one paper continually. Using checklists to find their own errors, these students learn accuracy and precision.

Through homework assignments that show process, students are learning that thinking is their goal in education.

In thinking classes, students talk among themselves about how they are perceiving a problem, about the strategies they are going to be using, and how they will know when they have the right answer. While the teaching of thinking has up to now been reserved for the gifted, Dee Dickinson, Director of New Horizons for Learning, said in a December 1985 speech at Washington, D.C.'s Cosmos Club: "There is a fine wind blowing . . . it's a change across the whole system. Teachers are beginning to take the initiative on teaching thinking."

Many people believe that thinking should be taught only through the subject areas. However, our experience has shown a remarkable increase in school-type intelligences when children are taught thinking as a separate subject. But given that many students may not have time in their full schedules for a separate course, homework assignments are excellent ways to teach your child how to think. Teachers and parents can make thinking assignments from Mind-benders, de Bono Lateral Thinking Skills, Feuerstein Instrumental Enrichment, Harvard's Project Odyssey, as well as dozens of Sunburst Communications computer programs (see Part Five, "Recommended Materials," Computer Programs).

Dr. Luis Machado, former Minister for the Development of

Human Intelligence in Venezuela, told our clinic in a speech here in March 1976, "I can't think of anything better than that every family would have homework assignments that teach thinking skills." Four-Star Assignments in thinking involve creative thinking rather than just logical thinking, "problem finding" rather than "problem solving," and intelligent guessing rather than step-by-step procedures.

Through assignments that ask students to measure their own houses, children are learning to apply the math they learn in school. Through assignments in which children learn how their city is laid out and the history of major streets, children learn geography.

Through assignments that are graded by other students, children are learning that they can learn from each other. One teacher puts a student's papers on the overhead projector as the whole class works on it. Children are learning through games and through assignments done on computers that homework is fun. This is the new homework.

Part Four

Homework Hotspots and Homework Helpers

OUR BRAINS ARE not divided into subject areas. As you've seen in the Six-Week Plan, one part of the brain does not take care of math, another of science, and another of literature. Imagine a crystal-clear skull in which different colored lights correspond to the many intelligences. Red is visual-spatial, blue is linguistic-logical, green is interpersonal, and so on. Then, if we could watch a child's brain light up as she worked on math, we might see red and green come on. For history, we might see blue and green. For each subject area, different intelligences will light up but there will also be some overlap. If a child then has mastered certain intelligences (and processes within these intelligences), she can apply them to any subject.

And yet the body of knowledge we learn in school is divided into subjects. A child is more likely to say, "I'm having trouble in math," than (more accurately), "My visual-spatial skills are a little rusty." Because the child's, the school's, and your reference point is "subject" rather than the brain process, we've included the following Hotspots and Helpers (organized by subject area). First, a few cautions and considerations.

Avoid Homework Band-Aids

Under the stresses of parenting, you may reach for the usual home-work Band-Aids: Rules and Practice. Three out of four homework doctors, in fact, recommend Rules and Practice. We don't.

Rules in grammar, rules in reading, and rules in languages are largely ineffective. Most adults don't need to know what a "short A" is in order to pronounce a word. Memorizing a list of rules unrelated to concepts may help a child pass a test, but it won't help her think. "Even if brains worked faster," notes writer William Allman, "that might not be of much help, because humans are just simply awful at using rules. Given a problem, they seem to use almost everything but rules to try to solve it."[1]

Practice also has its limits. David Perkins, Co-Director of Harvard Project Zero and an Associate of the Educational Technology Center at the Harvard Graduate School of Education, says: "One of the most important results emerging from this science of learnable intelligence is that practice is nowhere near enough. . . . If you want to learn to skate, all right, straight practice will get you there. . . . If you want to learn to *think* better, straight practice typically accomplishes nothing."[2]

Children must learn *how* to do something. If the teacher says, "Do these problems exactly as I do them," the child doesn't learn the *how* unless the teacher says, "Now I'm moving the decimal so I can divide the large number."

Be alert to two things about the subject areas: 1) the learning style of the subject, and 2) whether what is being taught is conceptual or neuromuscular.

Subjects Have Learning Styles

Every Homework Hotspot uses particular parts of the brain and is matched to a certain learning style. In general, visual children will do better at math, auditory children will do better in languages, and kinesthetic children will do better in sports, art, and music. Children who have an auditory-kinesthetic connection will do well in music and dance. In general, visual children will have trouble with languages, auditory children will have trouble in math, and kinesthetic children will have trouble in spelling. An auditory child, for example, may try to memorize the steps to do a math problem, and be temporarily successful. But she may have problems later when she fails to see the application.

Skills: Conceptual or Neuromuscular

Each school subject depends to a greater or lesser degree on two types of performance: conceptual and neuromuscular. Reading this book and thinking about how to make use of it requires the manipulation of ideas, concepts, or images. This is conceptualization, largely a left-brain, logical, and linguistic intelligence. On the other hand, neuromuscular skills, such as handwriting, spelling, and learning math facts are more dependent on habit, automatic reactions, and movement. (More learning disabilities fall under this category than under dyslexia and attention-deficit disorder combined.) Some children will just naturally be better and quicker at spelling, handwriting, and adding numbers; others will need more help.

Jason, for example, was a gifted fifth grader with a learning disability; he could talk about ideas at the eleventh- or twelfth-grade level, but he had trouble with spelling, handwriting, and math facts. On an individually administered exam, he scored in the sixteenth percentile in math computation, but in math concepts he scored in the ninetieth percentile.

Ignoring his thirst for new concepts, the school system unfortunately focused on Jason's lowest point of aptitude. His teachers tried to help him subtract nine from sixteen, which he had to count on his fingers. So even though he understood square roots, he was stuck in remediation and spent the whole of fourth grade working on math facts. He was so curious, he took the book home and taught himself powers and bases.

Fortunately, this year Jason has a teacher who encourages his conceptual skills, while allowing him to work on his neuromuscular skills. Now Jason uses computer spelling checkers to correct his papers. He's studying new concepts in math but at the same time he's attending a remediation class to catch up on his math facts. He uses whatever device will help him while he's learning concepts, but puts the calculator or spell checker away when he's catching up on neuromuscular skills.

(Certainly there is a sequential nature to skills. But many children will defy that list by skipping up and down. Some children mix up letters of the alphabet but can read on a sixth-grade level. While most children do need to learn a lower level first, many can skip around.)

We recommend writing and producing stories while the child is learning to write, typing while learning handwriting, using calculators while learning math facts and spelling checkers while learning to spell, being read to while learning to read. We recommend thinking like a scientist while learning the facts of science, dancing while learning dance steps, singing while learning the notes, language play while learning grammar, drawing while learning the techniques of art. When the child can experience the process and the product while learning the skills, she experiences the excitement of learning.

Change the Beliefs

Whatever the Hotspot, if the child begins with, "I'm a bad speller," "I can't do algebra," or "I'm no good at that," work on changing those beliefs first, using the motivation techniques we've already discussed in week 4. Note the nuances of language when talking about skills. There is a large difference between, "I am a poor speller" in which the child seems to "own" the inability, and "I don't spell well." Instead of "I'm a poor speller," encourage the child to say, "I'm a good speller, potentially." Encourage the child not to align her whole self-concept with her performance in a given subject.

Be careful of what you say in your child's presence. She may pick up a lifelong prejudice by overhearing parents or relatives say, "I was never any good in algebra," or "What's the sense of learning grammar?"

Homework Helpers to the Rescue

Whichever Homework Hotspot your child is stuck on, there are a number of general Homework Helpers that will help her, no matter what the problem. Three of the Homework Helpers—art, music, and movement—are the so-called frills of the American educational system. They are the first to get cut by the Tax Hatchet and are most often known as "no-work" classes.

But art, music, and movement are essential to homework. They are the fortifiers parents can use to make homework fun, to recharge the brain and to stimulate creativity. Aside from their own inherent pleasure, they assist the child in learning any subject area, as does the fourth Homework Helper: computers.

We live in an age where unprecedented technological and educational products are readily available. No longer does a child with a learning problem have to struggle to get by. The child who is unable to visualize geometrical figures can get help from a computer program that rotates the figures in space. Computers are excellent for drill and practice, and are by far the best teachers of logical and creative thinking skills. In the future, workbooks will be replaced by computers, the ultimate Homework Helper.

Writing

Up to second or third grade, a child's writing experience may consist of X's on workbook sheets. Suddenly, with very little warning, he is told, "Put it in your own words," and writing becomes a problem. For some, writing a sentence is a painful punishment; the only way out is to copy from the encyclopedia. Many of these children have no trouble at all telling stories, but when they try to write, the words get stuck somewhere between the brain and the hand.

Teaching Your Child to Write

1. Encourage your child to "hear the voice inside you." Hearing the internal auditory voice is crucial to generating ideas in writing.

2. Ask, "What does the voice in your head sound like?" If it sounds grumpy, tearful, or bored, experiment with helping him change it until he has the tone he would like to express in his writing.

3. If a child can't write, have him talk into a tape recorder, transcribe, then revise. This allows the auditory external to begin creating the internal auditory voice.

4. Help the visual child who has difficulty translating mental pictures into words by modeling internal auditory dialogue. Ask him questions you want him to learn to ask himself; for example, on a

test, "Which answers can I eliminate based on my knowledge of geography?"

5. Sit at the word processor with your child and take dictation from him. Visually external children are delighted to realize that a writing assignment they thought would take hours can look good in such a short time. This helps them value their ideas.

6. Increase the opportunities for written communication. Have a spiral notebook in a special place to pass notes back and forth. One child wrote, "I hate my chores." The mother responded, "I'm sorry you have to do something you hate."

7. Separate creativity from revision and proofreading. Creativity is brainstorming without censorship. Allow your child's right brain to create ideas free from left-brain rules about spelling and punctuation. Make up an individualized proofreading checklist of the child's most persistent errors; put it in his notebook so he doesn't have to memorize rules. Help him proofread after he's finished writing.

8. Have your child discover his own errors by prompting him: "There is one capitalization error, and two misspelled words. Can you find them?"

9. Keep a portfolio of your child's writing experiences. Over time, he can develop criteria for measuring his improvement.

Reading

In our clinic we have seen hundreds of children with reading problems, but, with the exception of severely retarded children, we have never seen a child we couldn't teach to read. If you want your child to learn to read, just read to him and have him read to you at least forty-five minutes a day. (A child is never too old to be read to.) It's important that reading be a permanent daily homework assignment.

On the other hand, take a child's reading problem seriously. The consequences of not being able to read in this society are quite devastating.

Ask the teacher what reading approach is being used with your child. If that approach is not working, ask the school's reading teacher to assess for alternative approaches. No one method of learning to read works for everyone. Half the children learn to read with any type of systematic instruction; the other half need more specialized methods, depending on the individual child's balance of left- and right-brain skills, learning style, neurological integration, and psychological well-being.

The Development of Reading Skills

1. You can start a child reading early, but research shows that by fourth grade children who started early and those who started later even out.[1] In fact, reading before age five may overemphasize verbal intelligence and the child may be bored with first-grade reading instruction.

2. Good future readers have usually learned the alphabet by the end of kindergarten. If your child is six and still has not learned the alphabet, we recommend testing by a clinical psychologist. The testing could show the special methods by which a child could learn to read.

3. Reading is primarily an auditory internal process. Both the eyes and the hands (braille) can be used to take in the symbols, but reading takes place when sounds and symbols meet in the auditory internal system.

4. It's important that children be taught phonetics, not phonics. Phonetics uses word patterns to teach reading (for example, the "ight" and the "ide" patterns); while phonics uses rules (for example, the vowel is long when there is an "e" on the end of the word) that do not hold true for more than 50 percent of English words. For example, if the child doesn't recognize the word "knight," he can be shown "*kn*own," "*kn*ew," and "*kn*ee" to discover the beginning sound and "l*ight*," "r*ight*," and "s*ight*" to decode the ending sound. This eliminates talk about long vowels and silent letters. Research indicates that even reading teachers have difficulty passing the phonics tests they give their students.[2]

5. Each child has four reading levels: Frustration Level (child misses more than five words per hundred); Instructional Level (child misses less than five words per hundred); Independent Level (child reads easily without help); and Listening Level (child can comprehend in listening usually three to six years higher than his instructional level).

A child has the right to be taught at his Instructional Level, as determined by testing. Most children cannot learn to read if they are instructed on their Frustration Level. Parents with children who cannot read their school books can request an evaluation of their children's level. In a typical classroom, there may be a range of six instructional reading levels or more. With only one to three reading groups per class, there's a good chance that your child is not reaching his reading potential through school instruction. Each child has an Independent, Listening, and Instructional Level. A child in fourth grade could read his school books at fourth grade Instructional Level, read Dr. Seuss books to his little brother at his Independent Level, and listen to a *Tale of Two Cities* on tape and have his parents read to him *Superfudge* and *Tales of a Fourth Grade Nothing*.

Reading to Your Child

1. The *Read-Aloud Handbook* by Jim Trelease (see Part Five, "Recommended Reading") is an excellent guide for parents.

2. Young children want the same story read over and over again. The Magical Child (ages four to seven) enjoys fairy tales, and during the Concrete Logical stage (ages seven to eleven) biographies are excellent to read.

3. "Talking Books" produced by the U.S. Government are available for any child with reading disabilities.[3] Some parents fear that listening to tapes will somehow supplant the reading process, but many parents cannot spend sufficient time reading aloud to their children. Children who hear stories on tape have the chance to improve far beyond their current reading level, and (except for very auditory children who may prefer tapes) they automatically change over to books eventually.

Listening to Your Child Read Aloud

1. Encourage your child to read aloud to you. Some children need the reinforcement of their own auditory feedback in order to comprehend what they read.

2. In order to maintain continuity and increase comprehension, scan the reading selection and teach your child any new or difficult words ahead of time. If the child misses other words while reading, don't make him sound them out. It is too frustrating and the child

loses the flow of the story. Instead, fill in the words and let him continue reading.

3. To help an auditory child picture what he reads, have him read alternate paragraphs in different voices such as high or low or different characters' voices.

4. If a child dislikes reading and refuses to read, say, "You read a page, and I'll read a page," or alternate reading every other paragraph or every other word. Children love this!

5. Reading aloud in front of a group of students is too embarrassing for most children. Reading to a partner, on the other hand, is enjoyable. Encourage your child to have one or more reading partners—for example, a close friend or a favorite relative.

6. When a child is struggling for the meaning of a passage, read softly with him and provide intonation and expression.

7. Let the child follow with his finger; it can improve visual tracking.

8. Help an older child form positive beliefs about himself as a reader, especially if he has had negative experiences reading aloud. Create opportunities for him to read to you (a recipe, a cartoon, the words written on their favorite record album) where you can share his natural enthusiasm.

Getting Your Child to Read to Himself

1. To help a child read silently, point to one sentence and say, "Try saying this quietly inside your head. Now what kind of reading voice do you hear inside your head? Is it your own voice, or is it like mine or your teacher's?" Hearing this inner voice will help your child improve his ability to concentrate.

2. Provide a quiet time where each family member reads silently and then discusses what he reads. Read one of your child's school books during this time; your interest may well spark his interest!

Helping Your Child to Comprehend

1. Teach your child to think ahead by having him predict possible outcomes; for instance, you can ask, "What do you think is going to happen to that character?" "How will this story end?" This helps the brain look for patterns.

2. Preview the book with your child first; this increases reading comprehension and speed, and helps the child find mental hooks on which to hang new ideas.

3. Play a game of missing letters and missing words. Leaving *letters* out increases word decoding ability; leaving *words* out increases comprehension ability. In one of the best methods of teaching reading, the Cloze method, one word is left out and the child uses context to fill it in. The Cloze method is used in the Sunburst computer program *M-ss-ng L-nks* (see Part Five, "Recommended Materials," Computer Programs). Children fill in missing letters and words to reconstruct passages from literature. It's both ch-ll-ng-ng a-d f-n!

Motivating Your Child to Read

1. Limit TV. The question we ask children is "How much TV do you watch and how many books do you read?"

2. Be alert to opportunities when you and your child can read together—while traveling in the car, waiting in a line, or relaxing after dinner.

3. Keep a list of the books your child reads, entitled "Books I Have Read This Year." Review the list with your child. Put the list on the wall of your child's bedroom.

4. Whet your child's appetite by reading series of books, such as *The Hobbit Trilogy*, *The Narnia Chronicles*, *Paddington Bear*, *Encyclopedia Brown*, *The Great Brain*. Sometimes a child gets comfortable with a character and then the book ends. The familiar settings and characters in a series provide momentum for the child.

Spelling

Spelling (in English) is a visual, not an auditory, skill. Internal visual learners are the most accurate spellers. One twelve-year-old auditory girl, who was a poor English speller, did very well in Spanish because in that language she could sound out the words. Auditory learners tend to have more difficulty spelling because they tune in to how a word sounds.

The best way to learn how to spell English words is by patterns (bright, light, made, fade), not rules. The best way to remember patterns is to tap visual, not auditory, *memory.* "Spell it the way it sounds," therefore, is not a helpful message. In English, there is not a one-to-one relationship between letters and sounds. There are twenty-four different spellings of the phoneme /A/: for example, "ai" (straight), "ei" (eight), and "ay" (day). Visual parents may require extra patience when their auditory child has trouble spelling.

Kinesthetic children (unless they get a picture in their minds first) are often the worst spellers. With one very kinesthetic seven-year-old girl, we spelled out the words on her back and on her arm, and she spelled the words in the air with her finger. That was her way of creating visual memory.

The idea that spelling is, first, visual and, secondly, kinesthetic, was discovered by educator Robert Dilts and has revolutionized the possibilities for spelling instruction; it makes most spelling books obsolete.[4]

Here's what doesn't work with spelling: boring spelling books; writing words over and over again (though we still see this practice with many children); looking up a word in the dictionary, especially for young children; and penalizing a child in other subjects because he's a poor speller.

It is unacceptable for a child to lose points on a history or science exam because he's a poor speller. This teaches the child to give up. Robert failed every subject because his school counted five points per misspelled word. Without the spelling corrections, he would have had a ninety-five in history. We were able to get the teachers to give him grades without counting spelling. They agreed to grade his spelling separately from his knowledge in a subject area, so he got an A in history and a D minus for spelling in history. He needed to improve spelling, but not to be penalized in the process.

Teaching Your Child to Spell

1. Improve your child's spelling self-image. Poor spellers may have many negative beliefs about their abilities; they see themselves as poor learners in general. Work on these beliefs *before* teaching them to spell. Help your child put spelling in perspective by reassuring him that it has nothing to do with whether or not he is a good person.

2. Color code on large paper the patterns in your child's spelling words; for example, in the words "rough," "tough," and "enough" make the "ough" red. Help him find these patterns in newspaper articles, on cereal boxes, and in comic strips.

3. Part of spelling is knowing if a word looks right. Give the child credit for recognizing that it "looks funny." He does this by learning patterns. For example, he knows that four consonants won't appear together in English. When Faith taught, she asked children to underline words they were unsure of, write two or three other possible spellings, and put a check by the one spelling they thought was right. Often they checked the correctly spelled word.

4. Look for patterns of misspellings. Spelling "loud" as "lowed," for example, is an auditory spelling error and the child needs to learn to visualize the word. If there is no relationship between how a child spells the word and the correct spelling, he may need to go back and learn patterns.

5. Teach your child to store correctly spelled words in the upper left of the visual field. When a child doesn't know how to spell, you can watch his eyes searching all over for the word. He doesn't know where to store the word or where to find it. Hold the words up to the left for right handers and up to the right for left handers.

6. Computer spell checkers have become for writers what calculators are for mathematicians. They give immediate feedback and are effective spelling teachers.

7. You can design your own spelling program like this: using 3-x-5-inch index cards, write the words in your child's favorite color on the card. Hold the card up to the left or up to the right (as illustrated in number 5) and have the child practice imaging the word. Then, take the card away and have him see it in his mind's eye. A good test of whether he sees it is whether he can spell it backward.

8. Your child's school spelling list can be programmed into many of our recommended spelling computer programs, such as Behavioral Engineering's *Spelling Strategy*, which employs visual learning techniques (see Part Five, "Recommended Materials," Computer Programs).

Vocabulary

"The average child learns at the rate of 5,000 words per year, or about 13 per day."[5] Formal instruction is not the primary source for most of the words your child learns. He learns words from three sources: conversation, experiences, and reading and being read to. Encourage your child to learn from all three sources.

While learning decoding (sounding out words), the child can listen and speak far ahead of his reading vocabulary. He understands more when he is read to than when reading on his own. Take into account that girls are more verbal at an earlier age than boys and tend to score higher on vocabulary and reading.

What doesn't work are study-skills books suggesting vocabulary rehearsal on cards, without a set of mental strategies. Avoid multiple-choice vocabulary tests; they don't tell you whether the child really knows the word.

Teaching Vocabulary to Your Child

1. Use multiple processes to help your child learn the meaning of words. To learn the word "supercilious": a) Say, "Picture a man eating his supper on the ceiling because he thinks he's superior to everybody." b) Read this sentence, "His supercilious manner made the people he worked with feel inferior." c) From the dictionary learn the pronunciation, part of speech, definition of the word. Discover that the prefix "super" means "over," that "cilium" means "eyelid," and "ous" means "full of"—referring to a facial expression with raised eyelids such as "full of pride." d) Know that the Latin "cilium" means eyelid.[6]

2. A right-brained child may know everything about the word but have it stuck "on the tip of his tongue." Use memory techniques, such as reciting the alphabet ("Does it start with A, B, C, D . . ."), to unstick word memory.

3. Reading is the best way to increase vocabulary. Don't expect a child to increase vocabulary from a moderate amount of reading. Our recommendation: at least an hour a day for pleasure. If he's not doing that, read to him an hour a day, even if it's in twenty-minute segments. If the child says, "I don't want to be read to,"

change the place, mode, time, or almost anything so the experience is pleasurable.

4. Dictionaries have their place in learning vocabulary, especially when a child hears a word in conversation and any other time when he's curious about words. However, never have an elementary-school child stop and look up a word in a dictionary while reading. This interrupts the flow and takes words out of context. Instead, be a human dictionary: explain, act out, and draw a picture or tell a story to let the child guess the meaning of the word. When a child is in the seventh grade, buy him a dictionary that he can keep all the way through college. He puts a check mark by each word he looks up, then reviews that word again as he looks up other words.

5. For a young child, buy his favorite kind of notebook and encourage writing words and drawing illustrative pictures. Some families emphasize special sets of words, and form family vocabularies. For example, Ginny, age nine, knew the meanings of supercilious and surreptitious because she and her mother played with these words at home.

6. Conversational interaction is important. Be aware of the verbal level of your child's friends. If he doesn't tend to be very verbal, it might be good for him to have more verbal friends.

7. Cut down on TV. Advertising jingles and sit-com dialogue don't increase anyone's vocabulary.

8. Play games with the sounds of words (for example, Pig Latin.) Tell stories to illustrate the meanings of words: "Once there were three houses that formed an equilateral triangle, so that the owner of each house could walk to the other two houses in about the same amount of time." Use context to define made-up words, as in "Once upon a time Johnny had a glook, and the glook wanted to go to the supermarket with him."

9. Help your child learn vocabulary through other subject areas. Preview the text beforehand looking at the new words in math, science, literature. Make a vocabulary list for each subject area, giving concrete examples and stories to illustrate the words.

10. Kinesthetic and visual children may have the most trouble with vocabulary. Auditory learners are more naturally attracted to words and word play. A trick we once used for a kinesthetic child having

trouble was to tell her, "Words are all around you. Words will stick to you. When you come back next week you are going to be stuck with all these words you've learned. Every time someone says a word it will stick to you. You will have to run and figure out what it is and maybe even look it up in the dictionary and then secretly write it down in your notebook and put it in your pocketbook." Train children of all learning styles to form visual images of words they want to remember.

11. Have your child tape-record himself and listen to his own words. Explain inflection, voice tone, and modulation of sound and their effects on vocabulary.

12. Three good resources are word-a-day calendars, junior thesauruses, and *Wordpower* by Edward de Bono, an illustrated dictionary of vital words.[7]

Foreign Languages

"I'm not Spanish, I don't like Spanish, and I'm never going to Spain. Why do I have to study Spanish?" complained one fourteen-year-old boy, whose mother accepted the challenge of sparking his interest in Spanish. She used what has become the acknowledged method of learning foreign languages—total immersion. She took in a Spanish exchange student, bought Spanish records and tapes and, finally, sent her child to Spain.

Mastery of a foreign language opens worldwide opportunities for children.

Teaching Foreign Languages to Your Child

1. Encourage your child to put in a double effort at the beginning of the school year so that he does not fall behind. If he becomes frustrated, he may never tackle that language again.

2. To be good in foreign languages, a child needs a highly developed auditory discrimination system that allows him to mimic a sound, match a sound, and reproduce a sound. In learning-style terms, to translate a word from English to French, he must go to auditory remember for the English word then over to auditory imagine for the French word. One way to promote auditory discrimination is

to play songs from different countries and have your child identify the language.

3. For a child with serious language and speech problems, foreign languages may demand more than his auditory skills can handle. If your child really wants to study the language, he will need a great deal of parental and teacher assistance: He'll need language labs, tapes, computer programs. Eddie, fifteen, had a speech impediment. He had great difficulty with French because his auditory discrimination was inadequate. We encouraged him to take Spanish instead which is closer to English phonetics. With his mother's help (she made tapes of the vocabulary words), he was able to do very well.

4. At the clinic we use "Superlearning," a program of music and languages.[8] While it does require a great deal of preparation, and some teens call the background music "yuppie music," it's a very powerful program that combines rhythm, culture, and positive affirmations. The positive affirmations are good for children with low self-concept; the music is ideal as a background for studying.

5. Find creative ways to help your child's school improve its foreign language resources. One Maryland school system, with the aid of a local wealthy businessman, sent two French teachers to France to collect magazines, books, and video- and audiotapes for the language lab.

6. Emphasize conversational use of the language and take the emphasis off grammar. "Mastery of the pluperfect subjunctive," notes Myriam Met, "is no longer believed to be critical to one's success in communicating in a foreign language."[9]

Handwriting

With visions of scribes in their heads, parents and teachers sometimes worship handwriting as the core of American education. They spend inordinate amounts of time trying to get a child to keep the letters sitting straight on the line. Parents and teachers have a "perfect vision" of what handwriting must look like and how the perfect writer must look when he's performing well—seated fairly straight, with the hand relaxed and floating smoothly over the page—a mold very few children fit. No wonder children are so self-conscious about their handwriting.

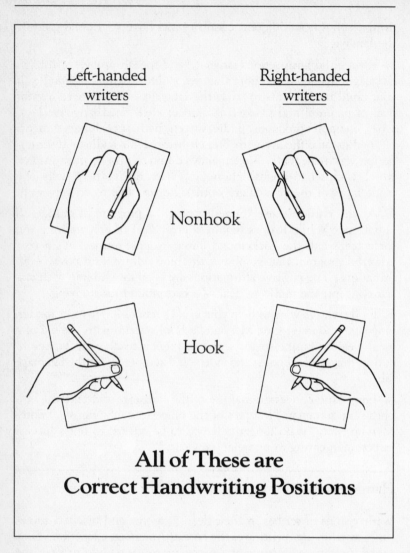

Left-handed
writers

Right-handed
writers

Nonhook

Hook

**All of These are
Correct Handwriting Positions**

We believe that handwriting is less important now because of the widespread use of the computer. Handwriting, however, becomes a problem when a child does poorly in other subjects because he can't translate thinking through his fingers fast enough to take down important material from the teacher.

Teaching Handwriting to Your Child

1. Plastic pencil grips are good for children who have trouble holding the pencil.

2. Have your child trace letters; it is an enjoyable activity that will increase his ability to form letters. The kinesthetic child can trace letters in the air or on sandpaper.

3. Tape examples of good handwriting to the child's desk. Handwriting is an imitative skill and a good model is important.

4. For a child to write well, he must be relaxed. Teach him to breathe in a slow and rhythmic manner.

5. Focus on the correct letters, not the incorrect ones, by saying, "I like the way you made that 'p.' "

6. Calligraphy is good for children ages nine to ten. Without knowing they are practicing handwriting, they get interested in how to form letters.

7. Let your child use the hand he wants to use and don't try to force left handers to follow right-handed techniques. We meet people every day in their forties and fifties who have trouble reading maps, and have other spatial problems, because they were left-handed but were forced to use their right hands as children.

8. If a child writes with a "hook," do not correct it. It's perfectly normal and it may be harmful to correct it. About 1 percent of the right-handed population has a right hook; that is, they turn their hand upside down when they write.[10] This is a sign of reversed left and right hemispheres of the brain: Language is more in the right hemisphere and pictures more in the left. Almost half of the left-handed population is similarly reversed. Left handers who write straight up and down are generally reversed; left handers who hook are generally not reversed.

9. Children can be taught how to type at a young age. Poor handwriters tend to be low in external visual or fine motor skills, in which case practicing handwriting is more punishing than helpful. Typing, building with Legos, and drawing will increase fine-motor coordination.

Math

Many parents find it particularly difficult to help children with their math homework; many adults are math-ignorant or believe they can't do well in math. We frequently hear, "I can't do my math, but neither can my mother," as if there were a genetic family problem in math. Bashing math, along with the third-grade teacher who "didn't teach me right," becomes a tradition in too many families. It needn't be.

Math is a right-brain visual-spatial skill that also uses the logical left brain. Algebra requires left-brain logical thinking and linguistic intelligence. Geometry uses both sides of the brain at the same time. Here's the secret to math: *See it in your head!*

Teaching Math to Your Child

1. Work on improving your child's (and perhaps your own) beliefs about math, a subject that gets more bad press than any other.

2. Use real-life examples of math in action, such as calculating the interest on $100 deposited in a savings account. For geometry, ask your child to search for triangles, right angles, trapezoids in the home. Give him a ruler to measure things.

3. Take the introduction of a new concept—division, multiplication, geometry—seriously the first time. Instead of dragging it out over many years, as happens far too often, have one bang-up introduction as if your life depended on it.

4. For children with poor internal visual skills, do division problems on graph paper with large squares. Make the numbers bigger; leave space around the problem. Do a gigantic division problem on the wall in your child's room. Use fluorescent paints to draw the multiplication tables on your driveway.

5. Calculators are good for the child who needs to speed up on concepts (for example, geometry) but is still stumbling on calculation.

6. Teach math to the kinesthetic child through jumping and moving. (There is no reason to sit still!) Count the number of jumps, claps, arm touches. While the child still needs to visualize to understand math, the movement may help create pictures.

7. Dreaded "word problems" need to be visualized, too. An intermediate step is to draw a picture of what is happening; for example, a man is running one mile in seven minutes and a train is traveling forty miles an hour. (Auditory learners don't have any less difficulty with these if they still have trouble visualizing.)

8. Math has to do with process. If the child is having problems, you need to say aloud, "First we do this, then we do this, then we calculate this." Ask your child to explain a division problem to an alien from another planet.

9. Guessing is important; it gives the child experience in mathematical thinking.

10. Help your child get a math "point of reference," a sense of estimation, so he realizes that 10 x 2 = 50 is wrong; in fact, it looks funny.

11. Replace parent drill sergeants with computer games; they are patient, emotionally neutral, and give quick feedback. Math homework is notoriously overassigned. The result: frustration, irritation, and cheating. In math, less is better, particularly of boring drills that do nothing to endear the child to the beauty of math.

12. Watch out for the Math Stumbling Blocks listed below. With care, they can all be overcome at home.

Math Stumbling Blocks

• *Number facts 10 through 20*; for example, 5 + 6 = 11. Number facts 1 through 10 can be counted on fingers, but 11 through 20 have to be visualized. (first and second grades)

• *Multiplication Tables* (third and fourth grades)

• *Fractions* (fourth and fifth grades)

• *Percentages* (sixth and seventh grades)

• *Pre-algebra* (sixth and seventh grades)

• *Algebra* (eighth and ninth grades)

• *Geometry* (ninth and tenth grades)

Science

A child is naturally curious about the scientific world. Unfortunately, the left-brain skills of students interested in science don't always match their curiosity. While a child may be interested in designing a frothing chemical mixture, he also needs to know how to use scientific measuring tools, develop and test hypotheses, and accurately report what he did.

We tell children that the scientific method is a description of how their brain works; they may run the method through their brain hundreds of times a day. When they choose a new friend, in a split second they develop a Hypothesis about that person based on Observation. As they get to know the friend more they gather Evidence through experiences and conversations to test the Validity of their Hypothesis. They put forth a Theory when they describe their friend to someone else.

Teaching Science to Your Child

1. Make sure the child has good notetaking and report-writing skills, but don't have him so caught up in skills that he misses the excitement of scientific discovery.

2. To understand science, a child must understand enumeration, classification, problem solving, comparison and contrast, and sequence.[11] Highlight numbers, classifications, problems/solutions, comparisons and sequences parts of the science book and teach them to your child. Your child also needs to understand hierarchy; for example, birds are more closely related to reptiles than to sponges.[12]

3. The left-brained auditory child who learns facts easily may be able to name all the bones in the body but may not know their location. Have him draw illustrations that show the relationship of the names to their places.

4. The right-brained visual internal child sees the whole skeleton, but mixes up the names. Children who can't easily remember the names of things may have trouble with science. Use memory techniques to form associations, and use mindmaps to make colorful displays of concepts. Play with the vocabulary in everyday conversation; for example, "Get those mitochondria moving faster."

5. Create songs or musical "raps" to help your child remember scientific concepts. A fifth-grade student of teacher Kathy Carroll in Washington, D.C. wrote this Respiratory Rap:

> Well, you breathe it out and you breathe it in.
> And the respiratory system is about to begin
> To the lungs, to the heart,
> And to the cell,
> The oxygen keeps your body well;
> Up up and out the nose,
> That's where the carbon dioxide goes.

History and Social Studies

A textbook, just-the-facts-ma'am approach to history is out. Learning to *think* about history is in. To demonstrate to her students the need for evaluating the source of information, one history teacher gave incorrect facts for a week. She hoped that someone would catch her contradicting the textbook, but no one did.

Dick Davala, a seventh-grade social studies teacher in Fairfax, Virginia, said he wanted to have his students write their own Constitution, but he didn't have time; his teaching had to be geared to the standardized test.

Sixteen-year-old Andrew spent his junior year in history preparing for the minimum competency exam. As he struggled to memorize the three branches of government, he was unaware that they were functioning less than twelve miles from his suburban Washington, D.C. home.

Research indicates that 90 percent of instruction in social studies is from textbooks.[13] The first step in teaching children to think about history is to reduce their dependence on textbooks and to create more hands-on experiences.

Teaching History and Social Studies to Your Child

1. At the beginning of the year, preview the history text with your child, and get a list of concepts to be covered. Start thinking of experiences to complement the lessons. Divide up the duties with other parents—one orders movies from National Geographic, one

gets materials from the U.S. Government, one is in charge of getting speakers. Rent videotapes recommended by your school.

2. Parents and children can learn much outside the history book through field trips, newspapers, et cetera. Catch history while it's happening. Talk about it at the dinner table. Relate current events to the past with questions such as "How are our current world leaders like the Medicis of Italy?

3. Help your child identify the history resources closest to him, particularly older relatives. Peter, who hated history, became intensely interested in the wars of this century when he interviewed his great-grandfather about World War One, his uncle about World War II, and his friend's older brother who had gone to Vietnam.

4. Connect new to old. Teacher Dick Davala notes, "Students always say, 'We don't want to learn the old junk,' and I say, 'You have to learn the old junk before you can understand the new junk.' " Davala compares students shot at the Boston Massacre with the students shot at Kent State.

5. Start assignments with the present and go backward. Notes Ernest Boyer, President of the Carnegie Foundation, "the larger issue is to help students discover that we are all products of the past and shapers of the future. . . . Start, not with the past, but with the present—and take leaps back."[14] For example, you can ask your child, "Starting with the space shuttle, and tracing backward, what contributed to its development?"

6. Encourage your child to move back and forth between the big picture and specific details. Make sure he doesn't get so involved in the minutiae of a battle that he doesn't see the entire war and how it fits into history.

7. Create a timeline and hang it around your child's room. Dick Davala has colonies on the ceiling, and pictures of the presidents, the *Mayflower*, Sputnik, and the space shuttle on the walls. The children are allowed to look at the timeline during tests for a reference point.

8. Use visual models to connect two things. Diagrams can be used to learn history.[15]

9. Use story telling to learn history. Read a chapter and say to your child, "You can use all the notes and books you want to make up

a story about what happened in World War One." He may say, "I really don't know what started it," and you can say, "Let's look in the book and see." Getting the facts from the book, the story might start, "Once upon a time there was an archduke. . . ." The idea is to make a mental movie of the historical happening, mixing fact and fantasy so your child can remember.

10. Have your child use a tape recorder and "ham it up." Tell the story of the bombing of Pearl Harbor in a radio reporter format. Have him play it for other family members.

11. History and social studies need not involve memorization to any great degree. However, when facts must be memorized, teach your child a memory technique.   ·

12. Schools have recently picked up on another one of Ernest Boyer's suggestions. In order to learn about "the commonalties of human experience," he suggests that all students engage in community service, to deal with "a sense of isolation and drift and anonymity."[16] Students can volunteer in nursing homes, homeless shelters, and child-care centers.

13. Stage debates and simulations in which students play world leaders and debate international issues.

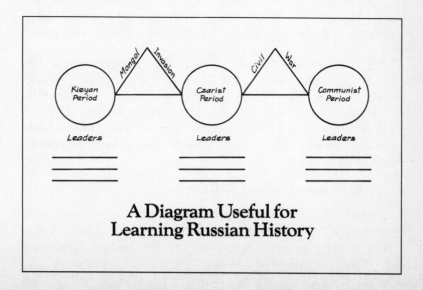

A Diagram Useful for Learning Russian History

14. Take students to hands-on museums, such as the Capital Children's Museum in Washington, D.C. and The Exploratorium in San Francisco.

15. Use music. Davala, also a disk jockey, brings in music from different historical periods. For example, the World War I song, "Over There," expresses a vibrant, gung-ho mood compared to the songs of the Vietnam War era, which were songs of protest and alienation.

Grammar

Of all the subjects taught in school, grammar has the fewest fans. Notes sixteen-year-old Jackie, "Just saying the word grammar makes my mouth go dry." Even educators have not given it much support and we have to admit that too many children get hung up in the scaffolding of the English language. While there is little evidence to suggest that knowledge of grammar per se improves writing, once a child understands grammar, he has an entrée to the world of language. Present grammar as a living dynamic of personal experiences rather than just a textbook experience.

The auditory child may like left-brain grammar rules or the impact of words, the visual child may like right-brain diagramming sentences, and the kinesthetic child may least identify with grammar.

There are three main things to remember about grammar, which children learn progressively: (1) There are parts of speech (noun, verb, adverb, and so on); (2) the parts of speech serve a function in a sentence (a noun is the subject of a sentence); and (3) these parts of speech occur in both simple (subject verb, subject verb object, et cetera) and complex (independent clauses, et cetera) sentence patterns.

Teaching Grammar to Your Children

1. Explain to children that in English words don't stay in their structural categories. For example, in the sentence "The man is a sailor," "man" functions as a noun. In "The sailor will man the ship," "man" functions as a verb.

At about the fourth-grade level, children begin to learn function and here confusion sets in; they may not realize that a word which used to be just the noun also serves the function of subject in the sentence. Teach the child that he's in a different ballpark; he's gone from nouns, adjectives, and adverbs to subjects, predicates, and direct objects.

2. Overview each part of grammar as the child gets to it. It helps children to know that grammar isn't endless.

3. Study a foreign language with your child and compare English grammar with the foreign language grammar. Many people say they first understood English grammar by studying a romance language, and especially Latin.

4. Use visual diagrams to help your child understand how the parts of speech are related to each other. Grammar has to do with relationships. The child needs to understand how a noun is related to a verb, to an adverb, to a participle. One teacher drew a large color chart to review the relationships of all the parts of speech.

5. "Sentence combining" is an excellent exercise: "The boy ran." and "The dog ran." combine to "The boy and dog ran." "He wanted to play." and "He had to do his homework." combine to "He wanted to play but he had to do his homework."

6. Diagramming of sentences is excellent for visual learning styles, but some children dislike it. We encourage schools to teach diagramming but to make it optional for each child.

7. Make a connection between grammar and literature, history, and current events. Ask your child to notice how Mark Twain uses adjectives or to find all the prepositional phrases in a newspaper story.

8. Label objects in the room (such as book, shelf, ceiling, window) to teach nouns to the Concrete Logical–stage child.

9. If your child is studying the parts of speech, you can play with language; for example, use adverbs at the dinner table. "Pass the butter," he said *eagerly* (adds the mother). "Where is the dessert?" he asked *expectantly*. "You are excused. Go *quickly*."

10. For punctuation, have your child make different sounds for a comma, a period, a semicolon, and quotation marks.

11. Teach passive and active voice with the following, all too familiar, example to the child: "Mother, while you were out the chocolate cake was eaten." vs. "I ate the chocolate cake." This uses the child's playful, naughty sense to give him an unforgettable model sentence to remember, and it usually results in one trial learning.

12. Teach your middle-school child to find the bare bones of sentence patterns in complex sentences: "The *boy*, who was running, *wrote* the *letter*." Tell them to find the *someone* who did *something* to or with *something*. Read the sentences in Tarzan and Jane language to get the feel of the bare bones sentence. (For example, John hit ball; Tom crashed car; Bill knocked can.)

13. Teach clauses and phrases by changing voice tonality and tempo to mark out the pattern being taught. For example, "The boy *who was chasing the bus in the morning, wearing a green shirt, followed by his dog*, is my brother." Read the clause in a high voice.

14. Teach your teenager the difference between verbs and verbals by showing verbs to be finite and verbals to be timeless. Verb: "He *swam* yesterday." Verbal: "*Swimming* is my favorite sport."

Homework Helpers

Music

Once, speaking to forty teachers at a seminar on new methods of learning, we made a suggestion that sharply divided the group: Encourage children to study with music in the background. The left brain, do-it-by-the-book group objected: Students would not listen attentively to the music and thus, would not be able to pick up measure, meter, and harmony nor appreciate the performance. Music, they said emphatically, is not to be mixed with anything.

The more right-brained group, on the other hand, was enthralled with the use of music everywhere. This group enjoyed a wider variety of music and made it a part of their daily lives.

Keep this in mind when you think about background music for homework. Some children will find music helpful while studying; others may find it a hindrance.

The first question we get at PTA meetings is "My child puts on earphones and listens to rock music. What can I do?" Our recommendation is to limit the amount of time a child spends listening to rock music, especially with earphones. (See Part Two, "Week 5: Concentration.") Children aren't entirely on the wrong track, however—the right kind of music can be a big Homework Helper.

Teaching Your Child About Music

1. Use baroque music. The best study music has no words, is in four-four timing, and has sixty beats per minute. These are the characteristics of the baroque classical music used in Superlearning, which has been shown to have a remarkable impact on deep concentration and memory.[1] In addition to listening to specific kinds of music, Superlearning involves relaxation with affirmations, mind calming, breathing to a beat, and using prerecorded tape, timed at eight-second cycles.

2. Allow your child to control the volume; some children may be extremely sensitive to volume. Piped music throughout the house is not helpful.

3. Use marching music or other cheerful music in the mornings to set the tone for the day. For parents not musically inclined, this might not sound like a good idea. Experiment with how your child responds.

4. Observe which components of music—words, rhythm, mood, pitch, tone, and so on—your child is attracted to and use these parts to teach her. If she picks up on rhythm and words, a rap may be appropriate for learning facts about the Constitution, for example.

5. Buy your child a cassette player. For Superlearning (see "Homework Hotspots," Foreign Languages), she'll need two—one for timing and one for music. Some children like to practice a speech on a tape recorder.

6. Use your child's favorite music to help her with speaking and listening. John, ten, had trouble with auditory discrimination; he couldn't understand words he heard. He talked rapidly and unintelligibly and he couldn't hear what others said; it all sounded like Chinese to him. He disliked standard auditory discrimination exercises that have directions like, "When I say *plub*, you say *plub*." We suggested that he listen to "Sgt. Pepper's Lonely Hearts Club Band," a song he loved, and write down the words. The extra elements of music—tone, pitch, volume—helped him distinguish the words. By doing this, he learned how to discriminate sounds through music and he was able to translate these skills to improving his speaking and listening abilities.

7. Use rhythm to help your child read. Sometimes a child is missing the "music" of reading, in which case reading is lifeless. Tap out music and provide sounds (*uh*, uh, *uh*, uh, uh, uh, *uh*, uh, uh, *uh*, uh, *uh*, uh) while your child reads the words, "The cow went down the hill to get a drink of water."

8. Use a drum to beat out the rhythm of multiplication tables and history facts. Ricky, fifteen, was always tapping out rhythms with his pencil on the table. We used this energy to beat out his spelling words, which he remembered beautifully.

9. To improve auditory memory and imagination, have your child imagine the sound of a snowflake, a volcano, leaves rustling, or the wind blowing. This is especially good before a creative-writing assignment.

10. Do movement to music followed by deep relaxation and guided imagery techniques to increase creativity. In the clinic, children move around with no particular pattern to Tomita's *Cosmos*, then we lie down with our eyes closed and listen to a guided imagery, DLM Teaching Resources' *Trip to a Star* (see Part Five, "Recommended Materials," Audiotapes). Children notice that colors are brighter afterwards and they feel refreshed.

11. Create a music portfolio, including a list of instruments the child has played, songs she sings (and ones she's made up), records she owns, her reaction to her first musical experiences, the first time she whistled, her favorite record, and the first time she heard a band.

Visual Arts

We ask every child who comes to our clinic with a homework problem to draw a picture of herself doing homework. While this picture is a good indication of how she feels about homework, the important part is this: The picture can be changed. We use art as both an evaluation of the present homework situation and as a way of showing the child the limitless capabilities of her own brain.

Teaching Your Child About the Visual Arts

1. For a very young child who won't even pick up a crayon, do what we call, "Scribble, Scribble." The child just scribbles with different colors across the pad, as hard as she can, following this important guideline: There is no wrong. At a later time, you can give art instruction.

2. Set up an art center in your home. Children tend to do art if it's readily available. Take a six-foot table and spread out all kinds of art media: poster boards, clay, colored markers. Get newsprint from the local newspaper and hang a mural so the child can write on the walls, a favorite activity of children. (Be careful about felt-tipped markers leaking through onto the wall.) One mother of four who was frustrated with the mess her four young boys made, fixed up an entire art room with white walls for the boys to draw on.

3. Art can be a way of determining your child's learning style. The internal visual child will see in her head the pictures she wants to draw. The external visual child may be very critical of what she draws. The auditory child will be less inclined to do art and may have to learn to appreciate it. The kinesthetic child likes textures (felt, velvet), smells, and 3-D models, and may be particular about having a fine-point (as opposed to a thick-point) pen. The very left-brained child may draw by formula, draw the same figure over and over, and dislike abstract art. The right-brained child will thrive on abstraction.

4. Compensate, if necessary, for the art your child *doesn't* get in school. Notes Howard Gardner, "If we omit the arts from the curriculum, we are in effect shortchanging the mind."[2] Help your child become confident in one particular art experience, such as drawing, sculpture, collages, et cetera.

5. While there are whole schools of thought that say parents must "Just observe," we suggest interactive art. Draw with your child, saying, "I'll draw the neck if you draw the legs." Ask your child to reflect on her own work in the same manner that she is asked to reflect on a poem by Emily Dickinson.

6. Grades are not recommended for evaluating art. Encourage your child to evaluate (noncritically) her own portfolio of art (that you keep over the years) so that she can note her improvement—"How

am I drawing legs differently than I used to?" The Prospect Archive in North Bennington, Vermont, the site of a collection of over 300,000 pieces of children's art, trains teachers and parents to evaluate children's art. They look at continuity, emotional quality, perspective, coherence, expressiveness, and artist's intention. ARTS PROPEL, a joint venture between Harvard Project Zero, Educational Testing Service, and the Pittsburgh Public Schools, funded by the Rockefeller Foundation, is searching for ways to evaluate children's art portfolios.

7. Help your child recognize motion, mood, personality, and the element of surprise in art. Ask, "What surprises you about your friend's picture?" Ask, "How does the artist make you feel about the person he painted?" The point of art is to help your child see things differently.

8. Let art seep into the uninteresting parts of an assignment. When Jay, a Magical Child who constantly daydreamed of dinosaurs and dragons, drew a cartoon series of the American Revolution (he called it "the American Resolution,") he quickly became very enthusiastic and wanted to study all of the battles.

The mother of a young boy who had a hard time doing history, social studies, and math, purchased an art easel and paints for the child and he was given permission to take notes using mindmaps.

9. Buy your child a slanted art easel for a study desk so she can study and draw at the same time or stand at the desk.

10. In Ohio, seventh-grade teachers use self-portraits combined with art history to help children understand how famous artists like Albrecht Durer got their ideas by looking in a mirror.[3]

11. We use activities from *Drawing on the Right Side of the Brain* by Betty Edwards (See Part Five, "Recommended Reading") with every child. One suggestion is to have your child draw with her nondominant hand; it will cause her to look at the world differently.

Movement

At our clinic, we do some kind of physical activity at least once every hour with every child. Often we teach a child juggling as a way of "waking up her brain." People are surprised to learn that juggling has something to do with homework, that the body and learning are intimately connected.

Of all the intelligences, kinesthetic intelligence is the most neglected in school. According to a recent study, "Six- to 9-year-olds weigh more and have more body fat than their counterparts of 20 years ago. . . . The average student probably spends no more than 2 or 3 minutes in moderate to vigorous exercise during a 34-minute physical education class."[4]

The lack of movement is especially detrimental to kinesthetic learners, who need physical activity to focus and direct their body's energy.

Teaching Your Child About Movement Activities

1. Plan movement activities during your child's study breaks; have her run, dance, jump, hop, use a punching bag, throw darts, play basketball.

2. Create an exercise space in the house; include a rebounder, juggling balls, rhythm sticks, encounter bats, or batakas (harmless foam bats that allow children and adults to release aggression and frustration).[5]

3. Dancing is a wonderful combination of art, music, and rhythm. As George Leonard notes, "If only one subject were to be required in school, it should be . . . some form of dance—from nursery school through a Ph.D."[6] Do a family dance before homework. Although one parent is usually a nondancer, the children will pull him or her in. If the parents begin to dance, the children begin to do their homework.

4. Increase your level of movement if you want your children to move more.

5. Set the tone of the day by playing ball with your child outdoors for a few minutes in the morning. Using tennis balls, play catch, double catch (each throws one ball to the other simultaneously), or quadruple catch (each throws two balls to the other simultaneously). Because these movements activate both sides of the brain at the same time, they are also excellent study-break activities.

6. Have your child throw a ball in the air and clap her hands as many times as possible before catching it. Start with one clap and

continue to twelve or fifteen or more, if possible. This improves motor coordination and timing.

7. Teach your child to use her kinesthetic (K) body to begin her homework (see Sidebar). Have her imagine that her K body is walking over and getting in her study chair. In a few minutes she will have the urge to sit in the chair and join her K body.

8. Show your child how to do breathing exercises to relax during homework and tests. (See Sidebar on Ninja Juggling.)

9. If your child is kinesthetic, you might purchase an art easel with adjustable legs to be used as her desk. This will allow her to stand

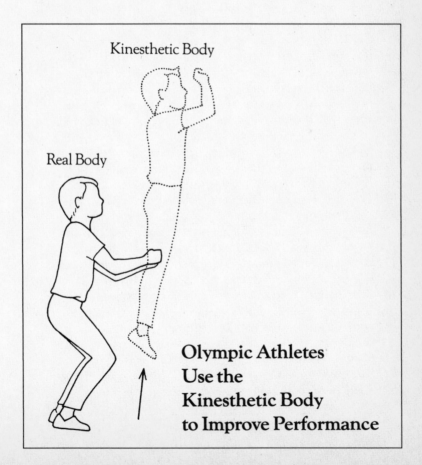

Kinesthetic Body

Real Body

Olympic Athletes Use the Kinesthetic Body to Improve Performance

Kinesthetic Body

Close your eyes and remember sitting in an elementary-school classroom. The teacher has asked a question to which you know the answer, and your arm shoots up. She doesn't call on you, so you stretch and wave your arm vigorously. Without moving your body, can you sense what that arm movement felt like? This "muscle memory" is what we mean when we speak of the kinesthetic body. When you access movement memory or when you imagine movement, you stimulate the motor cortex of your brain and the neurons fire—you can actually feel the imagined movement.

Think of your kinesthetic body as a kind of energy body which can step into and out of your real body. Olympic athletes use their kinesthetic bodies: When skiers imagine themselves going down the slope perfectly, they not only visualize it, they also sense the movement. Then their real bodies follow their imaginary bodies. Divers stand on the edge of the board with their eyes closed and feel their bodies diving perfectly; then their real bodies follow. Do this exercise to sense your own kinesthetic body:

Raise your right arm and really stretch it until you can feel your ribs expanding. Put your arm down, and then stretch again. Alternate several "real" stretches with an imaginary stretch by your kinesthetic body. Focus your attention on the imaginary stretch and really feel your ribs expanding. After several minutes, compare the two sides of your body. Most people find that one arm is heavier or one shoulder is higher, or there is a temperature difference between one arm and the other. Next, simply imagine—don't make a real movement—but imagine stretching your left arm several times. Now compare both arms. You may notice that simply by imagining movement, both arms are now fairly well balanced.[7]

as she does her homework, an alternative that many kinesthetic children enjoy.

10. Have your child move to learn concepts; movements help her code the information in more parts of the brain. For example, let her jump on the rebounder while reciting a poem or learning multiplication tables.

11. Have your child do rhythmic movements to music or to a metronome. There appears to be an important connection between body rhythm and reading.

Cross-Lateral Movement

Cross-Lateral Exercises

Any exercise that crosses the midline of the body is a cross-lateral. Cross-lateral movements are designed to increase right- and left-brain integration and to improve physical coordination. Since the right brain controls the left side of the body and the left brain the right side, when you move something on the right while moving something on the left, both sides of the brain are engaged and connections are made across the corpus callosum.

Crawling, walking, and running (left leg forward, right arm back) develop cross-lateral skills. When the left leg moves in one direction, the right arm moves in the other.

While jumping on a rebounder, lift your left heel up behind you and touch it with your right hand, bounce on both feet, then lift your right heel up behind you and touch it with your left hand. If your child is unable to do this movement, have her bounce, repeatedly lifting only her left heel. Use your voice to establish rhythm: "Bounce, touch, bounce, touch." Then add one movement at a time. Add touching her left heel with her right hand four times, then just bounce four times, and then have her touch her right heel with her left hand four times. "Bounce, touch, bounce, touch." Breaking the exercises down into small pieces allows your child to begin to develop coordination.

Ninja Juggling

We use beanbags for very young children and for children and adults who have difficulty catching a ball. Two pairs of rolled up socks also work well. At first, you may want to stand over a couch or bed or appoint another person as catcher, since bending over to pick up the balls interrupts the balanced state of mind that juggling promotes. If your child likes martial arts or is excited by adventure and science fiction, make her a Ninja juggler dedicated to the elimination of ignorance and "homework oppression" and to the development of concentration. Here's how:

1. Feel your feet planted firmly on the floor, so firmly that you can imagine roots growing out of your feet, into the earth. If you wanted to walk you would have to pull your feet up with great strength.

2. Hold your hands, palms up for catching the ball, a

little below your waist. (This lowers the shoulders and promotes deep breathing.)

3. Now, imagine taking your brain out of your head and putting it just beneath your belly button. This power center of your body is called the "Hara" in Japanese martial arts; putting your concentration there prevents the constant inner dialogue of unhelpful things we often say to ourselves when learning something new.

4. Take a deep breath. Imagine blue (or your favorite color) oxygen rising up through the soles of your feet, through your body, all the way to your brain. Imagine that the oxygen is collecting all tension and tiredness from your body. As it does so, it becomes somewhat dingy and gray. It rushes back out through your feet as you exhale and deposits the tension some distance from you. Breathe again, and blue oxygen surges up through your feet.

5. Start out with two balls and practice saying and doing, "Throw, throw, drop, drop."

6. Practice "Throw, throw, catch, catch." Auditory learners will say this out loud and use the words to remind them; visual learners may want to throw to the corners of an imaginary box, and kinesthetic learners may find that they catch the balls while you're telling them how. This may be enough for one day.

7. Add a third ball, which you throw up the middle, and say "throw, throw, throw, catch, catch, catch."

Computers

Computer learning programs are in many ways superior to human tutors. They have endless amounts of time, they are unlikely to say, "Son, you disappoint me"; they have the patience of a saint; they say nice things, such as "You're doing very well," even after an endless series of wrong answers; and they don't get bored. The microcomputer, with a parent's supervision and the right software, provides fascination, feedback, and flow. Children enjoy the power of blasting space invaders, the mystery of exploring enchanted castles, and the pure egocentric joy of seeing the computer respond with "That's dynamite, Laura." It is indeed gratifying to see a child with a short attention span happily immersed in a sentence-diagramming program. (All the programs mentioned here are listed in Part Five, "Recommended Materials.")

Teaching Your Child About Computers

1. A computer is not a passive instrument like a television. Without your active commitment, the child will be stuck, playing non-educational games or the computer will end up in the closet. To be effective as a home education tool, a computer takes at least as much planning as raising a new puppy. Expect frustration with hardware and software, and don't be surprised by squabbles between family members over who gets to use the computer.

2. Purchase a quality system with monitor, printer, and two disk drives if you are serious about making an investment in your child's education. We recommend Apple IIGS, Macintosh, IBM, or compatible systems. Educational software deserves hardware as sophisticated as that found in small businesses; do not buy entry-level hardware.

3. Buy software recommended by a review article or by a knowledgeable individual (rarely a salesperson), and favor best sellers.

4. Make educational computing a joint venture, especially with younger children. Sit at the computer with your child, allow the child to show you her accomplishments, and solve problems together in a friendly, competitive manner.

5. Begin each session with a typing tutorial program until your child learns to keep her eyes on the screen without wasting half her energy scanning the keyboard before each entry.

6. For the centerpiece of your software library, choose a best-selling word processor. Use it yourself, and encourage your child to use it daily for homework, letter writing, journals, or creative writing. Avoid word processors designed for children as well as "high-end" products for professional page layout.

7. Buy programs one at a time and allow your child to master and get the full benefits of each. If you come home with a large collection of programs, even good ones, there is a tendency for a child to run through them too quickly, without taking full advantage of each.

8. Select programs that are compatible with your child's learning style and that are geared to her interest and achievement levels. Preview the program at the store or elsewhere before buying.

9. Buy intuitive programs that require little or no reference to the manuals. Manuals, detailed instructions on the screen, and involved menus tend to discourage children.

10. Look for software that is interactive (you respond to it and it responds to you). Watch out for programs that merely put on the screen information that is more easily obtained from an encyclopedia. Avoid programs that present facts based on a question-and-answer format.

By the same token, don't underestimate your child when selecting software. Some computer programs have helped children advance through their developmental stages and have redefined what children can do. In The Learning Company's *Bumble Plot*, five-year-olds learn the x-y coordinate system.

11. Favor nonexpendable programs (programs a child will want to play more than once), such as *Magic Spells* by The Learning Company, or *Spellicopter* by DesignWare, which allow the child to have her own spelling words featured in the game each week.

12. Screen subject matter programs for completeness and quality of presentation. Be wary of "algebra" programs, for example, that are little more than a few book pages transferred to the screen. Good subject matter programs include Broderbund's *Calculus*, *Geometry*, and *Physics* for the Macintosh. These programs bring the subjects to life.

13. Avoid programming languages. In a misguided attempt at "computer literacy" many schools overemphasize learning BASIC or LOGO at the expense of teaching children how to use computers to do their work better. Schools, especially high schools, can make computer language instruction available to students, but few students really need it.

14. Add special-interest programs to your collection. Painting and drawing programs are fun and stimulate artistic expression in some children who are not inclined toward conventional artistic methods. Assignments can be enhanced with computer art, and computer music can add to a child's enjoyment. Look for programs that use sound effectively. Computers have been primarily visual, but sound chips can now be either built in or added on.

15. Use the computer as a diagnostic aid. See where your child's reasoning goes astray, note impulsiveness or a tendency to take thoughtless short cuts. Find hidden talents. Note her interest span in different activities.

16. Avoid "twitch response" games (for example, the child pushes one button to hit a rocket), which are fun but not educational (see "Week 5: Concentration"). Determine what skill your child is learning. Many stores carry popular, highly sensory programs, which may be good for teaching a child to aim but otherwise have little educational value. Given free choice, many children will go with the junk food of software.

17. Avoid computer toys. With few exceptions (Texas Instruments' popular *Speak & Spell*) these are not to be taken seriously as educational aids.

18. Avoid programs with tracking systems or passwords for classroom use. These impediments discourage use at home.

19. Look for reasoning games. *What's My Logic?* by Midwest Publications combines right brain/left brain thinking in a visual logical game.

Part Five

Recommended Materials

Computer Programs

Following is a selected list of the best computer programs for home educational use. All are used regularly by our therapists. All are available for Apple computers, many for IBM and compatibles. Only those indicated run only on the Macintosh. Average prices are in the $30 to $75 range.

These programs are, for the most part, not available in computer stores, where inventories of educational software are limited. But be careful when ordering software by mail. Computer companies merge and/or go out of business rather quickly. Fortunately, the telephone numbers, included for each company, tend to remain the same.

This is a sampling of programs each company offers. You may want to order the catalogues for full descriptions and prices. An updated list of programs by subject area may be purchased by writing to the National Learning Laboratory, Ltd., 8417 Bradley Boulevard, Bethesda, MD 20817.

ADDISON-WESLEY 2725 Sand Hill Road, Menlo Park, California 94025; (415) 854-0300
Mathematics Skills Software (Grades 2–7): Math basics are explained at each grade level in a thorough, easy-to-understand way.

Information Laboratory Software: Earth Science, Chemistry, Life Science (Grade 9–Adult): Valuable research tools that provide experience with using the computer as a data base.

BARRON'S EDUCATIONAL SERIES 250 Wireless Boulevard, Happauge, New York 11788; (516) 434-3311

Computer Study Program for the SAT (Grades 9–12): Provides thorough preparation for the SAT.

BEHAVIORAL ENGINEERING 230 Mt. Hermon Road., #207, Scotts Valley, California 95066; (408) 438-5649

Note: All programs from Behavioral Engineering are based on Neuro-Linguistic Programming (NLP), a communication model that shows how we use our senses—auditory, visual, and kinesthetic (tactile) —to store and process information in our brains. These programs can cause dramatic changes in abilities. *Math Gallery* (Grades 3–8): Arcade-style game in which the learner must "shoot" the math problems that have incorrect answers. *Math Strategy* (Grades 2–6): Uses the interplay between eye movement and memory to teach the best strategy for memorizing math facts; the child moves his eyes either *up left* or *up right* to access his visual memory as he "sees" math facts. *Spelling Strategy* (Grade 4–Adult): Teaches how to create visual images of words (an important step for poor spellers). *Spelling Gallery* (Grades 3–8): Arcade-style game in which the learner must "shoot" misspelled words in fast-moving lists. Player learns to reject misspellings and to choose correct spellings. *Composition Strategy* (Grade 4–Adult): Provides enjoyable strategies for improving creative writing. *Mind Master* (Grade 4–Adult): An advanced GSR (Galvanic Skin Response) biofeedback device that gives invaluable information about stress and stress reduction. *NLP Tools, Volume I and II* (Grade 8–Adult): Teaches and provides practice in reading eye movements and visual, auditory, and kinesthetic language patterns.

BERTA-MAX P.O. Box 31849, Seattle, Washington 98103; (206) 547-4056

Alpha Key (Preschool): As a voice repeats the letters of the alphabet, the young computer user locates keys on the keyboard. *Drill Math Facts Game* (Grades 3–8): Teaches basic math facts along with essential thinking skills such as sequential reasoning, deductive reasoning, and concentration; a valuable alternative/supplement to rote memorization. *Number Cruncher* (Grades 4–9): A nonthreatening introduction to algebraic functions; promotes systematic thinking. *The Reader* (K–College): A complete reading management system—the text is displayed at speeds from 20 to 2,500 words per minute; after each passage is read, five questions are asked to measure the reader's mastery.

BRITANNICA SOFTWARE 345 4th Street, San Francisco, California 94107; (800) 572-2272

Trap-A-Zoid (K–Grade 9): A creative way to learn basic geometry. *Math Maze* (K–Grade 6): Fosters strategic planning, creativity, and divergent thinking as it reinforces basic math facts. *Spellakazam* (K–Grade 6): Great for auditory learners; teaches the basic rules of vowels and consonants. *Spellagraph* (Grades 1–8): Spelling for visual learners. *Grammar Examiner* (Grades 7–12): Requires strategizing and offers a bridge for transferring grammatical skills to creative writing. *European Nations and Locations* (Grade 4–Adult): Teaches the geography and history of Europe. *States and Traits* (Grades 4–7): Teaches the geography and history of the United States. *Remember* (Grade 7–Adult): Develops memory skills; has disks for French, Spanish, chemistry, SAT vocabulary.

BRODERBUND SOFTWARE 17 Paul Drive, San Rafael, California 94903; (415) 492-3500

Calculus, Geometry, and *Physics* (Macintosh) (Grade 9–Adult): Graphics and motion are used to teach these three subjects to all kinds of learners, especially those who are visually oriented. The programs take advantage of Macintosh capabilities and contain more material than is available on less powerful computers. *Where in Europe is Carmen Sandiego?, Where in the USA is Carmen Sandiego?, Where in the World is Carmen Sandiego?* (Grade 3–Adult): Children learn geography through detective work. Parents may need to assist. The provided atlas is vital; guesses get nowhere! *Fantavision, Dazzle Draw, Animate* (Grade 2–Adult): Fosters visual creativity through the use of high-resolution graphics and seemingly unlimited menu variations.

CENTRAL PRODUCTS CORPORATION 2211 Norfolk, Suite 518, Houston, Texas 77098; (713) 529-1100

Power Math II (Macintosh) (Grade 10–College): Provides practice in solving equations and systems and evaluating expressions. Recommended as a home companion for the algebra student.

COMPU-TEACH 78 Olive Street, New Haven, Connecticut 06511; (800) 44-TEACH

Stepping Stones—Level II (Preschool–Grade 3): Provides practice in the basic skills of reading and math through a series of three games: Pictionary, Sentence Wizard, and Arithmetic: Addition. Animated graphics keep the child's interest.

CROSS EDUCATIONAL SOFTWARE 504 E. Kentucky, Ruston, Louisiana 71270; (318) 255-8921

Spell-A-Vision (K–Grade 6): Helps improve spelling and vocabulary; covers most decoding skills. Intriguing child-centered visuals.

DAVIDSON AND ASSOCIATES 3135 Kashiwa Street, Torrance, California 90505; (800) 556-6141

Math Blaster Plus (Grades 1–6): Arcade-style review and practice of math facts involving the four basic operations as well as fractions, decimals, and percents. ***Spell It*** (Grade 5–Adult): A four-part spelling program covering rules of spelling, syllabication, and context spelling. Also includes a word scramble game and an arcade-style game. ***Speed Reader II*** (Grade 5–Adult): Assists in sharpening perception through eye span and eye movement exercises. When used on a regular basis, this program can increase reading speed and efficiency. ***Read 'N Roll*** (Grades 3–6): Provides practice with four reading components: main ideas, facts, sequences, and inferences. A vocabulary "bowling" game is also available that uses words from the reading selections. ***Word Attack*** (Grade 4–Adult): A four-part vocabulary building program; personal word lists may be added. ***Word Attack Plus*** (Grade 4–Adult): An enhanced version of the above; wider range of menu options, better graphics and sound, larger vocabulary and spelling lists.

DESIGNWARE, INC. 185 Berry Street, Building Three, Suite 158, San Francisco, California 94107; (800) 572-7767

Spellicopter (K–College): Spelling becomes the key to an exciting mission—the learner, as a helicopter pilot, must unscramble a word missing from a sentence and return to the airport before the fuel runs out. ***Body Transparent*** (Grade 4–Adult): Teaches the location and function of body organs and bones.

DLM TEACHING RESOURCES One DLM Park, Allen, Texas 75002; (214) 248-6300

Number Farm (Preschool): Carefully sequenced activities use color, action, and nursery rhymes to teach children about numerals, number words, numerical order, counting skills, and beginning number concepts, such as greater than/less than. *Shape and Color Rodeo* (Preschool): Children can sharpen their eye-hand coordination and visual perception as they learn to discriminate shapes and colors. Teaches how colors are mixed to make new colors. *Spelling Mastery* (K–Grade 4): A flexible program that teaches spelling through a variety of techniques: spelling from memory, scrambled words, and sentence completion. Contains over 2,000 words. *Spelling Wiz* (K–Grade 12): Supplemental spelling program that focuses on 300 commonly misspelled words; uses animation, color, and a range of response options. *Language Carnival* (Grades 1–2): Builds language and thinking skills through the use of humor. Using jokes and riddles, the student compares and contrasts word relationships and explores the meaning of words and the reasons behind actions. *U.S. Atlas Action* (Grade 4–Adult): A myriad of map activities and games help the student learn important geographical facts about the United States, its regions, and individual states. Includes fifty-eight maps. *Sailing Through Story Problems* (Grades 4–12): Uses a pirate theme to provide practice in reading and solving mathematical word problems (often a troublesome area). The student accumulates gold coins and eventually becomes captain of a pirate ship while learning how to read maps and charts and work with money. *Decimal Discovery* (Grades 4–7): Games and activities with an oil-drilling theme help the student improve skills in comparing, adding, subtracting, multiplying, and dividing fractions.

EARTHWARE COMPUTER P.O. Box 30039, Eugene, Oregon 97403; (503) 344-3383

Volcanoes (Grade 7–Adult): Gives information about volcanoes as it teaches cooperation in dealing with natural hazards, decision making, budgeting, record keeping, and use of maps.

EDUCATIONAL ACTIVITIES, INC. P.O. Box 392, Freeport, New York 11520; (800) 645-3739

Geometry Alive (Grades 7–12): Three-part course covering the fundamentals of geometry, areas of triangles and quadrilaterals, and circles. Supplements classroom work. *Spelltronics* (K–Grade 6): An effective remedial spelling program. *Dragon Games* (Grades 3–6): Uses imaginative association to introduce early grammar. *Punctuation* (K–Grade 3): This "talking" program with reinforcing graphics is an excellent introduction to punctuation.

EDUCATIONAL SOFTWARE AND DESIGN P.O. Box 2801, Flagstaff, AZ 86003; (602) 526-9582

Black-Out (Grade 4–College): Excellent mental math exercise using a challenging and captivating format.

EDUCULTURE Suite 803-1, Dubuque Plaza, Dubuque, Iowa 52001; (800) 553-4858

Verbal Calisthenics (Grade 9–Adult): An interactive program that builds vocabulary through knowledge of word roots. Uses five different formats for learning each word (e.g., define, fill in the blank, use in context, unscramble a sentence). *English: Basic Mechanics* (Grades 7–12): One hundred lessons on five disks teach basic grammar and punctuation.

EDUWARE 185 Berry Street, San Francisco, California 94107; (415) 546-1937

Webster's Numbers (Preschool): Four exciting games that reinforce counting and visual-spatial skills. *Introduction to Counting* (Preschool): Teaches counting in multiple contexts with instant visual and musical rewards. *Decimals* (Grades 4–9): Finally—a program that makes decimals easy to learn! *Fractions* (Grades 4–9): An unforgettable demonstration of how to add, subtract, multiply, and divide fractions. *Compu-Read* (Grades 4–9): Uses the tachistoscope method (letters, words, or sentences are flashed on the screen) to improve reading speed, comprehension, and recall. Can be adapted to any learning speed. *SAT Word Attack Skills* and *PSAT/SAT Analogies* (Grades 9–12): Prepares students for the verbal section of the SAT by teaching word roots and prefixes/suffixes, and by providing practice in analogical thinking.

FIRST BYTE 3333 E. Spring Street, Suite 302, Long Beach, California 90806; (800) 245-4525

Note: This company publishes computer learning tools that "talk." No additional hardware or attachments are needed to use the speech component. *First Shapes* (Preschool): Innovative speech-enhanced software teaches basic shapes through five different activities. Builds creativity and memory. *Kidtalk* (K–Grade 9): Uses the "language experience" approach to reading and writing; has basic word-processing capabilities and a built-in voice/speech program.

FOCUS MEDIA 839 Stewart Avenue, Garden City, New York 11530; (516) 794-8900

The World (Grades 4–12): Imaginative method for developing geography skills. *The Heart Simulator* (Grades 6–12): Uses animated graphics to teach how the mammalian heart functions.

HOUGHTON MIFFLIN COMPANY (Educational Software Division) P.O. Box 683, Hanover, New Hampshire 03755; (603) 448-3838

Easy Graph II (K–Grade 6): A simple, straightforward approach to introductory graphing. "Walks" the user through an explanation of graphs (pictographs, bar graphs, line graphs, pie charts), and provides experience in creating one's own graphs. *Sound Ideas: Vowels* and *Consonants* (K–Grade 1): Two series of "talking" programs that reinforce classroom instruction for beginning readers. The Echo+ speech, music, and sound synthesizer makes it possible for these programs to talk. (Echo+ is a plug-in card with an unlimited robotic voice; made for the Apple II+ and IIe, it is available from Street Electronics, 1140 Mark Avenue, Carpinteria, California 93013.) *Note Card Maker* (Grade 7–College): Teaches how to prepare a bibliography and note cards for research papers. *Treasure Hunter* (Grades 4–9): Basic reference skills are learned as the student learns about famous explorers. Includes a reference manual. *Science Island* (Grade 4–Adult): Creates interest in science through the use of a reference manual that must be consulted in order to complete a computer adventure.

INFOCOM 55 Wheeler Street, Cambridge, Massachusetts 02138; (617) 492-6000

Planetfall/Enchanter/Seastalker (Grade 4–Adult): Three interactive fiction programs in which the player becomes the main character of the story. Improves decision making, creative thinking, memory, and following directions.

ISLAND SOFTWARE P.O. Box 300, Lake Grove, New York 11755; (516) 585-3755

Ribbons (Grade 4–Adult): Game for two players requiring skills of strategy and planning. *Mindstretchers and More Mindstretchers* (Grade 3–Adult): Develop and strengthen logical and sequential thinking, strategic planning, problem solving, and concentration. *Jigsaw* (Grade 3–Adult): Builds internal imagery and visual memory skills.

KAPSTROM 5952 Royal Lane, Suite 124, Dallas, Texas 75230; (214) 369-1718

Writing is Thinking (Grade 7–College): A creative, well-designed approach to improving writing skills and expression of ideas. Topics include: defining and narrowing your topic, outlining ideas, paragraphing, revising and editing. User must have basic knowledge of grammar.

KOALA TECHNOLOGIES 3100 Patrick Henry Drive, Santa Clara, California 95050; (800) KOA-BEAR

Koala Pad Touch Tablet allows the child to control input to the computer by moving his fingers across the pad, bypassing the complicated keyboard. The Koala Pad is an essential part of every Koala program. *Koalagrams Spelling I* (K–Grade 3): Beginning spellers must unscramble the name of a picture or an object before the Koala bear's honey runs out. *Koala Painter* (Preschool–Adult): Allows free expression of the imagination as it develops eye-hand coordination, creativity, and drawing ability.

THE LEARNING COMPANY 545 Middlefield Road, Suite 170, Menlo Park, California 94025; (800) 852-2255

Juggles' Rainbow (Preschool): A three-year-old can have an exciting computer experience with no instruction. Wherever the child touches the screen, it lights up in the form of a rainbow or butterfly. *Bumble Plot* (Preschool–Grade 3): Provides beginning experiences with the number line and grid. *Math Rabbit* (K–Grade 2): Uses a game format to teach number concepts, such as counting, adding, subtracting, whole numbers, more than, less than, same. Can be fine tuned to meet the needs of the learner by selecting various options: speed, range, math operations. Three different games on four levels. *Reader Rabbit* (Preschool–Grade 2): Lively, colorful graphics are used to help children improve letter and word recognition, memory skills, and vocabulary. Reading of basic words (consonant–vowel–consonant pattern) is also practiced. *Writer Rabbit* (Grades 2–4): Imaginative way to teach reading comprehension, grammar, and vocabulary—the parts of a sentence are taught through games, then the child creates his own amusing stories. Options allow for the control of time, speed, sound, and the number and kind of sentence parts to be used. *Magic Spells* (Grade 3–Adult): A creative, whole-word approach to spelling involving the unscrambling of words; the child can add his own spelling words to the programs.

M.E.C.C. (Minnesota Educational Computing Corporation) 3490 Lexington Avenue North, St. Paul, Minnesota 55126; (612) 481-3500

First Letter Fun (Preschool): The initial sounds of words are matched with the letters that make these sounds; pictures and musical notes reinforce correct responses. *Fraction Munchers* (Grades 4–12): Provides drill and practice with fractions including fraction types, equivalent fractions, comparing fractions, and fraction expressions. The student controls a creature on a grid as it "eats" designated numbers or fraction expressions. *Word Wizards* (Grades 1–6): Contains four games that improve spelling along with memory and concentration; allows for some originality. *Spellevator* (Grades 1–12): Provides practice in spelling words in an arcade-style format. Words are unscrambled and spelled from clues given by sentence context or word flash. *Word Munchers* (Grades 1–3): Fast-moving game that involves the recognition and matching of similar vowel sounds. *First-Letter Fun* (Preschool–Grade 3): The initial sounds of words are matched with the letters that make these sounds. *The Oregon Trail* (Grades 4–9): As the player journeys across the country he must make choices of what to bring—these choices will determine whether he makes it, is detained . . . or worse! Evokes the feeling of the Old West as it teaches planning, decision making, organization, and basic math. *Zoyon Patrol* (Grade 7–Adult): Develops problem solving, strategy and decision-making skills as the student locates and captures friendly fantasy creatures. Builds analytical thinking through gathering, sorting, and eliminating information. *Problem Solving Strategies* (Grade 6–Adult): Teaches trial and error, exhaustive listing, and problem simplification; varying levels of difficulty available. *Mind Puzzles* (Grades 6–Adult): Explores the problem-solving process through a "discovery" approach that involves following instructions and language encoding and decoding skills.

MIDWEST PUBLICATIONS P.O. Box 448, Dept. 5, Pacific Grove, California 93950; (800) 458-4849

What's My Logic? (Grade 4–Adult): Helps develop and sharpen analytical thinking skills for better academic performance and problem-solving skills.

MILLIKEN PUBLISHING COMPANY 1100 Research Boulevard, St. Louis, Missouri 63132; (800) 643-0008

Adventure Alpha (Grade 4–Adult): An interactive program using problem solving and decision making. Uses a variety of math skills to solve secret codes, puzzles, and riddles. Helps children overcome math anxiety. *Math Path Game* (Grade 4–Adult): A mind-boggling math experience that gives an inside look at the structure of math equations and formulas. *The Great Number Chase* (Grade 3–Adult): Popular arcade-style program that requires increasingly difficult mental math processing. *Pop 'R Spell* (Grades 3–6): Uses visual and logical skills to teach spelling and word recognition. *The Writing Workshop: Prewriting and Postwriting* (Grade 4–Adult): For parents who want a word processor, and also a process that teaches children to write. Uses brainstorming and branching (a technique similar to mindmapping) to stimulate ideas. Teaches descriptive and exposition writing. Free video. *Sentence Combining* (Grades 4–9): A new method of teaching sentence structure which emphasizes making sentences rather than analyzing them. *Lantern of D'Gamma* (Grades 4–12): An adventure game that requires creative thinking, internal-visual skills, and memory. *Secret Key* (Grades 4–6): An adventure game using minimal graphics but allowing internal imagery. Teaches problem solving and logic using writing and reading skills. *Discovery! Experiences with Scientific Reasoning* (Grade 4–Adult): Teaches problem solving through the use of scientific reasoning. Ten different problem "environments" plus a tutorial are included on six diskettes. Increasing problem complexity requires progressively higher level cognitive processes. *Tangrams Puzzler* (Grades 4–12): Improve visual perception, visual-spatial skills, logic, and creative thinking.

MINDSCAPE 3444 Dundee Road, Northbrook, Illinois 60062; (800) 221-9884

The Sea Voyagers (Grades 7–12): Gives valuable information about famous explorers. *Dinosaur Dig* (K–Grade 12): Provides historical, anatomical, and biological facts about dinosaurs. *America Coast to Coast* (Grades 4–8): U.S. geography is taught through five unique learning games. A keyboard overlay is included. ***Dr. Seuss: Fix Up the Mix-Up Puzzler*** (K–Grade 6): Pictures of Dr. Seuss characters are randomly scrambled into an endless variety of puzzles. Five levels of difficulty. ***Success with Algebra: Word Problem Series I, II, III, IV*** (Grade 7–Adult): Provides step-by-step instruction and practice in solving algebraic word problems. Uses a sequential process to help students overcome the tedium and anxiety often associated with algebra. ***Jumping Math Flash*** (Grades 1–4): Provides review and practice in the four basic math operations. The student must weave his way through fish swimming across the grid of numbers in order to locate the correct answer to a given problem. ***Developing Reading Power*** (Grades 3–6): Uses the Cloze technique (the child fills in missing words). Rockets soar to the moon to promote reading comprehension ability. ***Fantasy Land*** (Grades 2–6): Reading adventure that helps improve reading comprehension and inferential thinking as players sail their ships from island to island searching for wizards and, ultimately, the magic sword. ***Vocabulary Challenge*** (Grades 2–12): Uses a different approach to build vocabulary. The student is given a word and has to decide whether it is a complimentary or insulting term. An option to add own word list is provided. ***Crossword Magic*** (Grade 4–Adult): Allows the user to create a crossword puzzle using his own words or vocabulary lessons. ***Grammar Mechanics*** (Grades 4–9): Best when used with a group. Players earn prizes by correcting grammatical errors in a game format. ***Continents and Countries*** (Grades 6–12): Information about 142 countries can be accessed through various learning adventures. Includes a plastic keyboard overlay. ***Presidential Profiles*** (Grades 5–12): Information about each U.S. President can be obtained through three differently structured computer activities. Includes a plastic keyboard overlay. ***Understanding the United States Constitution*** (Grades 8–12): Useful as a supplement to classroom instruction. Contains ten sets of ten questions about the Constitution; may be used in either a "learning" or "testing" mode. ***Tonk in the Land of Buddy-Bots*** (K–Grade 3): An adventure game that teaches visual memory, strategizing, decision making, and concentration. ***Tuk Goes to Town*** (K–Grade 2): Develops early reading and vocabulary skills as the child directs "Tuk" on a trip through town; reinforces visual discrimination, memory, and concentration. ***Comparative Physiology Exploration*** (Grades 7–10): Develops scientific research skills through the study of vertebrates and the structure and function of organ systems. *Color Me* (Preschool–Grade 9): Stimulates creativity and imagination as the child "paints" using a variety of brush strokes and colors; needs Koala Pad (see KOALA TECHNOLOGIES) or joysticks to operate. *Magic Castle* (Grades 2–5): Students reach the top of the castle and earn the magic wand by correctly answering vocabulary questions hidden behind doors. *Mastertype's Figures and Formulas* (Grade 4–Adult): Provides experiences with math measurements and conversions. *Build a Book About You* (Preschool–Grade 3): Personal information about the child is used to fill in the blanks in the story, which is then printed out and placed in the accompanying binder with appropriate illustrations; excellent for developing self-esteem. *Mastertype's Writing Wizard* (Grade 4–College): One of the friendliest word processors on the market for children; masterful use of color, which entices children to edit, rewrite, and outline. *Pattern Maker* (Grade 4–Adult): Develops an artistic eye by teaching elements of composition, balance, positive and negative space, color; requires no art talent. *Songwriter* (K–Adult): Perfect for music-loving families—teaches rhythm, meter, and tempo and provides a player-piano scroll for composing and playing music. *Mastertype* (Grade 4–Adult): Uses an "invaders"-style video game to keep the user interested and attentive while learning to type.

NATIONAL LEARNING LABORATORY, LTD. 8417 Bradley Boulevard, Bethesda, Maryland 20817; (301) 365-7700

The National Learning Laboratory is a nonprofit educational, research, and training organization established in 1984 to disseminate information about the latest learning technologies. NLL's far-reaching goal is to raise global intelligence so that human beings can keep pace with the technology and living challenges of the twenty-first century. NLL specializes in up-to-date lists of computer programs and other learning materials by subject and grade. Lists are customized for the special needs of schools and all types of individual learning abilities. We generally use some form of needs assessment to make recommendations.

NORDIC SOFTWARE, INC. 3939 N. 48 Street, Lincoln, Nebraska 68504; (800) 228-0417

Lemonade Stand (Macintosh) (Grades 4–12): Simulates the operation of a small business. Requires consideration of several variables simultaneously: cost of lemonade, number of glasses to make, number and cost of signs, and the weather. Feedback is realistic and teaches consequences of decisions.

OPTIMUM RESOURCE, INC. 10 Station Place, Norfolk, Connecticut 06058; (203) 542-5553

Stickybear Programs (Preschool–Grade 1): A series of colorfully animated programs dealing with basic concepts and abilities, including eye-hand coordination, numbers, letters, shapes, opposites. *Exploring Tables and Graphs* (Grades 3–6): Highly interesting interactive programs that explain how to create and use tables and graphs. *Stickybear Math–2* (K–Grade 6): Provides drill in multiplication and division with levels ranging from simple multiplication to complex division using two-digit divisors and three-digit quotients. *Stickybear Spellgrabber* (K–Grade 4): Three colorful activities provide practice in spelling words either from a master disk or those entered by student. Especially captivating for the younger student, but adults and older students may secretly enjoy the format as well. *Stickybear Parts of Speech* (Grades 2–5): Provides practice in identifying the parts of speech through randomly generated word lists and sentences. Four levels of difficulty. *Stickybear Typing* (Preschool–Adult): Useful program for practicing typing; skills range from learning the keyboard to typing text.

ORANGE CHERRY SOFTWARE P.O. Box 390, Pound Ridge, New York 10576; (800) 672-6002

Mathworld Commander (Grades 2–8): Basic math operations are taught in this arcade-style drill and practice program. *Strange Encounters* (Grades 4–6) and *Voyages to the Future* (Grade 3–Adult): These programs enhance reading and logical thinking skills through the use of subject matter that many students find intriguing. *Prime Suspect Reading Adventure* (Grade 3–Adult): Uses deductive reasoning in a reading format. *Cloze Technique: Famous Fables* (Grades 2–5): Builds reading comprehension as the child "discovers" the missing words in passages presented from famous fables. *Introduction to Geography* (Grades 3–8): Introduces latitude, longitude, hemispheres, and other basic geographical concepts.

THE PROFESSOR 4913 NW 2nd Terrace, Pompano Beach, Florida 33064; (305) 427-5090

Concentration (Grades 1–6): Five levels of the traditional memory/concentration game in which the players try to remember and find matched pairs.

QED INFORMATION SCIENCES, INC. 170 Linden Street, P.O. Box 181, Dept. MW, Wellesley, Massachusetts 02181; (800) 343-4848

Typing Made Easy (Grade 4–Adult): A polished approach to typing that realistically measures speed and accuracy using a words-per-minute indicator.

QUEUE, INC. 562 Boston Avenue, Bridgeport, Connecticut 06610; (800) 232-2224

Beginning Algebra (Grades 7–10): Multimedia approach for developing algebra skills and problem-solving abilities; includes computer disks, audiotapes, worksheets, quizzes, and tests. *Mathwise* (Grades 7–12): Builds skills in number series, pattern recognition, and logic. *Wordwise* (Grades 7–12): A worthwhile supplement to vocabulary and spelling curricula. *Balance* (Grade 8–Adult): Process-oriented program that teaches the concepts and steps for solving algebraic equations. The user literally sees how to balance the two sides of an equation. *Guess My Rule* (Grade 6–Adult): A mathematics program in which the user collects information in order to guess an unknown rule. *Alice in Wonderland* and *Jack and the Beanstalk* (Grades 1–6): These two engrossing and delightful programs, based on the popular tales, teach planning ahead, memory, decision making, sequencing, and problem solving. *Geology in Action* (Grade 9–Adult): Allows the student to observe and experiment with processes that would naturally occur over thousands of years; illustrates rock formation, erosion, and faulting.

THE REGENTS/ALA COMPANY 2 Park Avenue, New York, New York 10016; (800) 822-8202

Word Alert (Grades 3–8): Contains three games—*Wordrace*, a fast-paced game which creates an understanding of verbal analogy; *Word Roulette*, a word recognition strategy game using grammatic closure; and *Clue-In*, a logic and word skills puzzler. Parents will enjoy playing these with their children!

SCHOLASTIC INC. P.O. Box 7502, 2931 E. McCarty Street, Jefferson City, Missouri 65102; (800) 541-5513

Turtle Tracks (Grades 4–8): Introduces students to computer programming and graphics; the user draws designs and composes melodies to accompany his artwork. *Logic Builders* (Grade 4–Adult): Builds spatial/perceptual skills at basic levels and logical/sequential thinking at higher levels.

THE SOFTWARE TOOLWORKS 1 Toolworks Plaza, 13557 Ventura Boulevard, Sherman Oaks, California 91423; (818) 907-6789

Mavis Beacon Teaches Typing (All ages): In our opinion, this is the best typing program. It has sequential, varied format; easy to follow on-screen instructions; and high-resolution graphics. The use of shadowed hands on the screen's keyboard helps the learner overcome the pitfall of looking down at the keys.

SPRINGBOARD 7808 Creekridge Circle, Minneapolis, Minnesota 55435; (800) 445-4780

Early Games (Preschool): Introduces a young child to the computer and teaches the alphabet, basic math, drawing, and visual discrimination. *Easy as ABC* (Preschool): Five fascinating games that appeal to the kinesthetic (movement) sense and provide visual-spatial experience. *Piece of Cake Math* (Grades 2–6): Uses a bakery to teach multiplication and division. Makes math appetizing! *Fraction Factory* (Grades 4–6): Colorful graphics and musical sounds make learning fractions an unforgettable experience.

SUNBURST COMMUNICATIONS 39 Washington Avenue, Pleasantville, New York 10570; (800) 431-1934

MATH: *Counters* (Preschool–K): Teaches counting through picture/number substitutions. *Getting Ready to Read and Add* (Preschool): Teaches shape discrimination and letter and number recognition using sound, color, and animation. *Tobbs Learns Algebra* (Grades 7–12): A new way of viewing algebra! *Green Globs and Graphing Equations* (Grades 9–12): A creative method for working with graphs and their equations; focuses on linear and quadratic graphs. *Interpreting Graphs* (Grades 7–12): Two programs that teach basic graphing. The student gains an understanding of functional relationships within graphs and then uses graphic information to trap on-screen bank robbers. **Number Quest** (Grades 3–9): Five programs that teach binary search strategies. Includes whole numbers, decimals, and fractions. **King's Rule** (Grade 4– Adult): Players try to discover numerical rules (equations) that allow them to work their way through the castle; the level of difficulty can be adjusted. **Pathfinder** (Grade 7–Adult): Another creative program for working with graphs. Students can create their own course or use provided information to construct one. **More Teasers from Tobbs** (Grade 5–Adult): Complex problems are solved through the use of fractions and decimals. **Balancing Bear** (K–Grade 4): A visual introduction to addition and inequalities. A bear is balancing a beam and the child must discover the way to make both sides equal.

READING: **Newbery Adventure: Charlotte's Web, Island of the Blue Dolphins, A Wrinkle in Time,** and **Mr. Popper's Penguins** (K–Grade 6): The Newbery Award–winning stories are used to teach reading comprehension. Children must be familiar with the stories in order to complete the adventures successfully. Graphic presentations of specific incidents in the stories trigger memory. **Tiger's Tale** (K–Grade 2): A series of interactive stories about the adventures of a cat named Tiger. The beginning reader uses a basic problem-solving approach to improve reading comprehension. **The Puzzler** (Grades 3–6): Contains five stories from which the student must predict, confirm, and integrate conclusions; helps increase concentration and attention.

VOCABULARY: **M-ss-ng L-nks** (Grade 3–Adult): A reading selection is given with letters or words missing (a variety of patterns are available) and the student must fill in the missing parts. Builds spelling, comprehension, vocabulary. **Word-A-Motion** (Grade 4– Adult): Reinforces concepts of synonyms, antonyms, categories, homophones, tense, and spelling patterns. User determines the relationship of one word to the next one in the sequence. **Wally's Word Works—Elementary, Junior High, and Senior High:** Three programs for children with language problems. Allows user to practice identifying basic parts of speech via a game format. **Odd One Out** (K–Grade 6): Teaches thinking skills to those who already have good math and reading skills.

LOGIC/PROBLEM SOLVING: **1, 2, 3, Sequence Me** (Preschool– Grade 3): The child must correctly sequence three parts of an event.

Teaches sequential reasoning and organization of information. *Color Keys* (K–Adult): Provides experience in scanning for clues, analyzing, and looking for a pattern or sequence (sometimes young children solve these games intuitively while their parents struggle over the logic involved!) *Enchanted Forest* (Grade 4–Adult): Logical thinking program with an adventure format. Problem-solving skills are reinforced. *Blockers and Finders* (Grade 1–Adult): Uses the thinking skills of conjecture and proof to locate the "blockers" that cause the "finders" to change direction on a grid; basic to complex levels. *Safari Search* (Grade 3–Adult): Inferential thinking is used to locate hidden "creatures" in a grid. Basic to complex levels help build scientific and mathematical thinking. *The Pond* (Grade 2–Adult): Builds logical thinking through strategizing. The student must generate and test a hypothesis in order to help a lost frog get out of a pond. *Puzzle Tanks* (Grade 3–Adult): Students are given two tanks of randomly set capacities and a storage tank; a target amount must be obtained through a series of transfers using numbers and logic. Basic to complex levels.

MEMORY/CONCENTRATION: *Memory Castle* (K–Grade 4): Uses left- and right-brain skills to teach memory. *Memory Building Blocks* (K–Grade 6): Develops visual association and sequential thinking skills. *Right Turn* (Grade 4–Adult): Develops internal visual abilities, like those used by architects and planners. *Algernon* (Grade 3–Adult): The student must visualize and program a series of steps to help Algernon find his way out of a maze.

VISUAL PERCEPTION: *The Super Factory* (Grade 3–Adult): Develops logical thinking through the visualization and building of three-dimensional cubes. Both hemispheres of the neo-cortex work together to solve these puzzles. *Building Perspective* (Grade 4–Adult): Builds spatial perception skills as student visualizes what buildings would look like when viewed from the top. *Plane View* (Grade 7–Adult): Improves visual perception and mental imagery. The user is challenged to identify a shape after seeing a "side view" of it.

Other Recommended Materials

This is a sampling of noncomputer materials that we use in our lab. We use audiotapes, videos, workbooks, and "hands-on" materials to teach thinking skills and study skills. These materials contain excellent techniques at many development levels and appeal to all learning styles.

Books and Skill Builders

CENTER FOR GUIDED DESIGN West Virginia University, Morgantown, West Virginia 26506; (304) 293-3445

Decision Making with Guided Design (Grade 7–Adult): Teaches the steps in decision making and how to apply them. The material provides a step-by-step guide to the process.

CHOICE POINT Institute for Human Evolution, Inc. 27 Congress Street, Salem, Massachusetts 01970; (617) 744-1262

A curriculum that teaches adolescents how to develop the skill of making choices.

CREATIVE PUBLICATIONS P.O. Box 10328, Palo Alto, California 94303

Tangramath (Grade 1–Adult): Teaches mathematical concepts along with how to divide space in the mind's eye. *Seeing Shapes* (Grade 5–Adult): Presents a variety of visual-spatial concepts including symmetry, rotation, and reflection.

DLM TEACHING RESOURCES One DLM Park, Allen, Texas 75002; (214) 248-6300

Design Cards for Small Parquetry I and II (K–Adult): Colorful blocks and pattern cards teach how to divide space in the mind's eye.

GROLIER ENTERPRISES Sherman Turnpike, Danbury, Connecticut 06816; (203) 797-3666

ValueTales Series: ValueTales are inspiring books about famous people. They are especially good for children ages four to nine.

MASTERY EDUCATION CORPORATION 85 Main Street, Watertown, Massachusetts 02172

Project Odyssey (Grades 4–12): Developed for use in Venezuela's Project Intelligence, the six volumes of this program can be used by groups or individuals. Covers a wide variety of general thinking skills, including observation, inference, induction, deduction, and creative thinking.

MIDWEST PUBLICATIONS P.O. Box 448, Pacific Grove, California 93950; (800) 458-4849

Building Thinking Skills: A variety of activities that develop visual and verbal thinking skills. *Mind Benders Warm-Up* (Grade 3–Adult): Simple to complex deductive problem solving (left brain). Develops attention to detail and internal auditory and visual perception skills. *Figural Analogies* (Grade 3–Adult): Works with analogous shapes, rotation, reflection (right brain, nonverbal skills). Those with low visual-spatial skills can draw upon internal auditory to help develop visual. *Figural Mind Benders* (Grade 6–Adult): Uses both right and left brains for pattern analysis and deduction to reach a solution.

NASSP-NAESP 84 Bowers Street, Newton, Massachusetts 02160; (617) 965-0048

This set of study skills books is a new generation in learning. There is no hint of the moralistic "you should," but presents rather the "here is how" and "try it" thinking skills. Recognizes learning styles and multiple intelligences: *Studies Skills Programs: Level B* (Grades 3–4), *Levels I* (Grades 5–7), *II* (Grades 8–10) and *III* (Grades 11–13); *Math Study Skills Program* (Grades 6–10); *Science Study Skills Program* (Grades 7–10); *GED Study Skills Program* (Adults).

PERGAMON PRESS, INC. Maxwell House, Fairview Park, Elmsford, New York 10523 (Packets), and Edward de Bono Resource Center, 56 Harrison Street, New Rochelle, New York 10801 (Workbooks).

CoRT Thinking, Pergamon Press, Maxwell House, Fairview Park, Elmsford, New York 10523; (914) 592-7700 (Grade 3–Adult): Based on the assumption that "intelligent" doesn't necessarily mean "good thinker." Individual skills sheets emphasize different approaches to "thinking through" situations laterally, for example, in broad terms rather than in the predetermined tracks of conventional logic.

UNIQUITIES Galt, California 95632; (209) 745-2111

Encounter Bats: Harmless foam bats that allow children and adults to release frustration and aggression.

ZEPHYR PRESS 430 S. Essex Lane, Tucson, Arizona 85711; (602) 745-9199

(K–Grade 8): Self-directed learning experiences for students; some instruction may be necessary. These booklets provide students with structured ways to become active participants in learning. The following skills are used: evaluating, classifying, comparing, imaging, researching, mapping and charting, creating, reporting, thinking, reacting, and exploring careers. Some of the packets available are: *American History Part I, Wassily Kandinsky, Futuristics, Science Fiction, Renaissance 1300–1600 A.D.*, and the *Complete Science Series*, which include *Marine Biology, Entomology, Paleontology, Volcanology, Ecology, Astronomy* and *Archeology.*

Videotapes

EDUCATIONAL ACTIVITIES, INC. P.O. Box 392, Freeport, New York 11520; (800) 645-3739

Learning Basic Skills; Music by Hap Palmer (Preschool–K): A fast-paced, lively tape. Whole-body movement to music helps young children learn their colors, letters, and numbers. *Singing Multiplication Tapes by Hap Palmer* (Grades 2–6): Adds a new dimension to the otherwise dreaded task of mastering the basic multiplication facts. Gives directions for playing active games while singing the facts.

LEARNING FORUM SUCCESS PRODUCTS (Super Camp) 225 Stevens Avenue, Suite 103, Solana Beach, California 92075; (619) 755-7065

Success Through Test Prep (Grade 7–Adult): This video is so full of useful information about how to prepare and take tests that it merits a number of viewings; helps the learner discover his best learning style. *Super Memory* (Grade 7–Adult): The best introduction we've seen to three memory techniques: loci, association, and narration. *Success Through Notetaking* (Grade 4–Adult): A clear, concise presentation and basic introduction to taking notes through the art of mindmapping. *Success Through Math* and *Success Through Algebra.*

MARSHALL UNIVERSITY c/o Virginia Plumley, Huntington, West Virginia 25701; (304) 523-0080

The Clinical Applications of Neurolinguistic Programming, Tape 2: Advanced level NLP tape. Richard Bandler, Cofounder of NLP, works with clients to remove "dread pictures."

NLP COMPREHENSIVE 2897 Valmont Road, Boulder, Colorado 80301; (303) 442-1102

New Choices Workshop, NLP Home Study: Excellent, brief introduction to basic concepts of NLP; includes a home study guide. *Future-Pacing:* An advanced NLP tape that teaches you how to tell your child something in a way that enables him to remember it; will also help you remember your "to do" list. *The Fast Phobia/ Trauma Cure:* Although this advanced NLP tape features adults, we have found that this technique also works with children who have phobias.

NORMAN BEERGER PRODUCTIONS 3217 S. Arville Street, Las Vegas, Nevada 89102-7612 and **Canyon Consort** Open Circle, Pier 5, San Francisco, CA 94111

The Grand Canyon, Natural States, Nani Kauai: These nature videos will provide a restful and enjoyable right-brain study background for students of all ages.

THE PACIFIC INSTITUTE 100 W. Harrison Plaza, Seattle, Washington 98119; (800) 826-7959

Becoming an Everyday Genius: Informative, family-oriented, "learning to learn" video series with Tony Buzan, internationally recognized expert on the human mind. Topics include study habits, brain function, mindmapping, communication, and memory improvement.

Audio Tapes

Parents:

GRINDER RESOURCE CENTER 110 Kenny Court, Santa Cruz, California 95065; (408) 476-6618

Prerequisite for Personal Genius by John and Judith Grinder: Advanced NLP training.

NATIONAL LEARNING LABORATORY, LTD. 8417 Bradley Boulevard, Bethesda, Maryland 20817; (301) 365-7700

Turning Homework Into Learning by Faith Clark: A good summary of how to help your child get organized for homework. *Parenting for Intelligence* by Cecil Clark: This tape is ideal for parents who want to improve their parenting skills and begin to unlock the intelligence of their children. Cecil presents his seven principles for intelligence; parents may find themselves expanding their own potential as they begin to model positive learning behavior for their children.

NIGHTINGALE-CONANT 7300 N. Lehigh Avenue, Chicago, Illinois 60648; (800) 323-5552

The Path of Least Resistance by Robert Fritz: Will clarify how to define your goals and how to make the choices that will get you there. *Choosing Your Own Greatness* by Dr. Wayne Dyer: Practical techniques for self-development and goal setting undergirded by an enthusiastic theoretical orientation. *Unlimited Power* by Anthony Robbins: A good explanation of NLP for beginners. Suggests ways for parents to break through feeling barriers with themselves and their children. *2005: A Child's Odyssey* by Denis Waitley: Topics discussed on this set of exceptional tapes include children's self-esteem, the reasons children use (or don't use) alcohol and drugs, and the damage done by excessive television viewing.

SYBERVISION 6606 Civic Terrace Avenue, Newark, California 94560; (800) 255-9666

Neuropsychology of Achievement: For teens and parents, the best tapes for applying recent brain/mind research to achieving goals. *Neuropsychology of Self-Discipline:* Be prepared to do some work. This is not a "listen in your car" experience. A step-by-step planning guide to create goals using visualization techniques.

Children:

CHIDREN'S BOOK AND MUSIC CENTER 2500 Santa Monica Boulevard, Santa Monica, California 90404; (213) 829-0215

Children's records, cassettes, and musical instruments.

DAWN PUBLICATIONS 14618 Tyler Foote Road, Nevada City, California 95959; (916) 292-3482

The Living Forest and *Flying with the Swans:* These tapes are creative visualizations of nature. Designed for children, but we recommend parents and children listen together.

DLM TEACHING RESOURCES 1 DLM Park, Allen, Texas 75002; (800) 527-4747

Peace, Harmony, and Awareness: The best tapes for training children to relax before homework; helps with study ritual. Includes fantasy experiences like *Trip to a Star* and *Trip to a Mountain.*

NIGHTINGALE-CONANT 7300 N. Lehigh Avenue, Chicago, Illinois 60648; (800) 323-5552

Power Memory, Techniques for Total Recall by Alan Butkowsky: Covers the latest and best techniques for improving memory (loci, chaining, et cetera) while providing interesting information about the brain. *Names & Faces* by Alan Butkowsky: Associative technique for remembering.

TROLL ASSOCIATES 100 Corporate Drive, Mahwah, New Jersey 07498; (800) 247-1053

Popular Troll Read-Along books with matching cassettes are excellent motivators for young readers. Titles include: *Amazing World of Dinosaurs* (Grades 1–3); *Harold and the Dinosaur Mystery* (Grades 1–3); *I Can Read About . . . Dinosaurs, . . . Fossils, . . . Prehistoric Animals* (K–Grade 2); *Dolphins and Porpoises* (Preschool–Grade 1); *What's Under the Ocean?* (Preschool–Grade 1); and *What Is a Reptile?* (Preschool–Grade 1).

Music and Tapes for Studying:

Certain forms of background music enhance and facilitate learning because they bring about relaxation and increased balance and integration between the left brain (logical, sequential hemisphere) and right brain (intuitive, artistic hemisphere). When both hemispheres are working together, it is possible to increase intelligence and improve concentration, memory, and creativity. There are many excellent music tapes available. Some of the tapes we use at our clinic are listed below.

ACCELERATED LEARNING SYSTEM, P.O. Box 140147, Dallas, Texas 75214

The Music Library: A set of twelve cassette tapes featuring classical music.

DELL PUBLISHING COMPANY, INC. *Superlearning* by Sheila Ostrander and Lynn Schroeder: This book contains an excellent list of appropriate baroque music.

THE GREATER SPIRAL P.O. Box 12515, Portland, Oregon 97212-0515

Crystal Meditations, Lightning on the Moon, and *Angels* by Don Campbell. *Lullabies from Around the World* by Steve Bergman.

THE INSTITUTE OF HUMAN DEVELOPMENT P.O. Box 1616, Ojai, California 93023

Becoming Efficient and Organized and *Peak Learning:* Two excellent subliminal tapes. ("Subliminal" tapes contain inaudible positive messages that help bring about new behaviors and habits.)

LEARNING FORUM SUCCESS PRODUCTS (Super Camp) 225 Stevens Avenue, Suite 103, Solana Beach, California 92075

Richard Del Maestro (Relax) and *Relax With the Classics, Volumes 1–4:* Study and relaxation music tapes.

MIND COMMUNICATION, INC. 945 Burton S.W., Grand Rapids, Michigan 49509

Better Vocabulary, Memory, Concentration, Effective Test Taking, Speaking and Writing with Confidence (All ages): Background music to be used to improve each of the skills listed above.

WINDHAM HILL RECORDS P.O. Box 9388, Stanford, California 94305

Autumn, December, Winter into Spring by George Winston; *Passage, It Takes a Year, Childhood and Memory* by William Ackerman; *Slow Circle, Turning: Turning Back* by Alex DeGrassi.

Organizations and Training

CAPITAL CHILDREN'S MUSEUM 800 3rd Street, N.E., Washington, D.C. 20002; (202) 543-8600

A "hands-on" museum. Ann Lewin, the museum's director, says that her mission is to "sow the seeds of intelligence and imagination in our youth, in whose hands our future lies."

DYNAMIC LEARNING CENTER P.O. Box 1112, Ben Lomond, California 95005; (408) 336-3452

Robert Dilts's advanced Neurolinguistic Programs and Training.

FOUNDATION FOR MIND RESEARCH P.O. Box 600, Pomona, New York 10970

Jean Houston, Director. Multisensory workshops that help participants discover and unlock more of their potential.

NATIONAL LEARNING LABORATORY, LTD. 8417 Bradley Boulevard, Bethesda, Maryland 20817; (301) 365-7700

Directors Cecil Clark and Faith Clark. A nonprofit educational, research and training organization established in 1984 to disseminate information about the latest learning technologies. NLL's far-reaching goal is to raise global intelligence so that human beings can keep pace with the technology and living challenges of the twenty-first century. Workshops in Homework, Learning Styles, and Beginning and Advanced NLP training. Programs for training educators in Learning Therapy.

NEW HORIZONS FOR LEARNING 4649 Sunnyside North, Seattle, Washington 98103; (206) 547-7936

An international network that disseminates the latest research in education.

NLP COMPREHENSIVE 2897 Valmont Road, Boulder, Colorado 80301; (303) 442-1102

Provides training by Connirae and Steve Andreas in Neuro-Linguistic Programming, especially in submodalities. *Human Excellence:* A videotape of advanced seminars given by John Grinder, one of the founders of NLP.

Recommended Reading

Andreas, Connirae and Steve Andreas. *Change Your Mind and Keep the Change.* Moab, Utah: Real People Press, 1987.

Armstrong, Thomas, Ph.D. *In Their Own Way.* Los Angeles, California: Jeremy P. Tarcher, 1987.

Bandler, Richard. *Using Your Brain for a Change.* Edited by Connirae and Steve Andreas. Moab, Utah: Real People Press, 1985.

———, and John Grinder. *The Structure of Magic I & II.* Palo Alto, California: Science and Behavior Books, 1976.

———, and Will MacDonald. *An Insider's Guide to Sub-Modalities.* Cupertino, California: Meta Publications, 1988.

Bragstad, Bernice Jensen, and Sharyn Mueller Stumpf. *A Guidebook for Teaching Study Skills and Motivation,* 2nd ed. Newton, Massachusetts: Allyn and Bacon, 1987.

Brandt, Ronald S., ed. *Content of the Curriculum, 1988 ASCD Yearbook.* Alexandria, Virginia: Association for Supervision and Curriculum Development, 1988.

Buzan, Tony. *Make the Most of Your Mind.* New York: E. P. Dutton, 1984.

———. *Use Your Perfect Memory.* New York: E. P. Dutton, 1984.

———. *The Brain User's Guide: A Handbook for Sorting Out Your Life.* New York: E. P. Dutton, 1983.

————. *Use Both Sides of Your Brain.* New York: E. P. Dutton, 1974.

Cameron-Bandler, Leslie; David Gordon; and Michael Lebeau. *The Emprint Method, A Guide to Reproducing Competence.* San Rafael, California: FuturePace, 1985.

Campbell, Don G. *Introduction to the Musical Brain.* St. Louis, Missouri: Magnamusic-Baton, 1983.

Cleveland, Bernard F., Ph.D. *Master Teaching Techniques.* Muskego, Wisconsin: The Connecting Link Press, 1986.

Cossey, Ruth; Jean Kerr Stenmark; and Virginia Thompson. *Family Math.* Berkeley: Regents, University of California, 1986.

Costa, Arthur, ed. *Developing Minds: A Resource Book for Teaching Thinking.* Alexandria, Virginia: Association for Supervision and Curriculum Development, 1985.

Csikszentmihalyi, Mihaly, and Isabella Selega Csikszentmihalyi, eds. *Optimal Experience: Psychological Studies of Flow in Consciousness.* New York: Cambridge University Press, 1988.

Culp, Stephanie. *How to Get Organized When You Don't Have the Time.* Cincinnati, Ohio: Writer's Digest Books, 1986.

de Bono, Edward. *Lateral Thinking.* New York: Harper and Row, 1970.

DeLozier, Judith, and John Grinder. *Turtles All The Way Down: Prerequisites to Personal Genius.* Bonny Doon, California: Grinder, DeLozier and Associates, 1987.

Devine, Thomas G. *Teaching Study Skills.* Newton, Massachusetts: Allyn and Bacon, 1987.

DiFrancesca, Sal, Ph.D. *Straight A's, How to Help Your Child Improve School Grades.* San Diego: Learning Process Center, 1985.

Dunn, Rita and Kenneth. *Teaching Students Through Their Individual Learning Styles: A Practical Approach.* Reston, Virginia: Reston Publishing Company, 1978.

Edwards, Betty. *Drawing On the Right Side of the Brain.* Los Angeles: J. P. Tarcher, 1979.

Elkind, David. *The Hurried Child.* Reading, Massachusetts: Addison-Wesley Publishing Company, 1981.

Ellis, David B. *Becoming a Master Student*. Rapid City, South Dakota: College Survival, 1985.

England, David A., and Joannis K. Flatley. *Homework—and Why*. Bloomington, Indiana: Phi Delta Kappa Educational Foundation, 1985.

EPIE Institute. *T.E.S.S. The Educational Software Selector*. Southampton, New York: Teachers College Press, 1986–87 Edition, 1988 Supplement.

Faber, Adele, and Elaine Mazlish. *How to Talk So Kids Will Listen and Listen So Kids Will Talk*. New York: Avon Books, 1982.

Feuerstein, Reuven. *Instrumental Enrichment: An Intervention Program for Cognitive Modifiability*. Baltimore: University Park Press, 1980.

Fiedler, Marilyn N. *More Psychophysical Frolic (Adaptations For Children of Energy Awareness Exercises by George Leonard and Others)*. Tucson: Zephyr Press, 1980.

Fritz, Robert. *The Path of Least Resistance*. Salem, Massachusetts: Stillpoint Publishing Company, 1984.

Gardner, Howard. *Frames of Mind*. New York: Basic Books, 1984.

Gazzaniga, Michael S. *The Social Brain*. New York: Basic Books, 1985.

Gelb, Michael. *Present Yourself!* Rolling Hills Estates, California: Jalmar Press, 1988.

Hart, Leslie A. *How the Brain Works*. New York: Basic Books, 1975.

Hayes, John R. *The Complete Problem Solver*. Hillsdale, New Jersey: Lawrence Erlbaum Associates, 1987.

Hendricks, Gay, and Thomas Roberts. *The Second Centering Book*. Englewood Cliffs, New Jersey: Prentice Hall, 1977.

Hirsch, E. D., Jr. *Cultural Literacy, What Every American Needs to Know*. Boston: Houghton Mifflin Company, 1987.

Jacobson, Sid. *Meta-cation, Prescriptions for Some Ailing Educational Processes, Neuro-Linguistic Programming*. Cupertino, California: Meta Publications, 1983.

———. *Meta-cation, Volume III, Powerful Applications for Strong*

Relief, Neuro-Linguistic Programming in Education. Cupertino, California: Meta Publications, 1986.

Jensen, Eric. *Student Success Secrets.* Hauppauge, New York: Barron's Educational Series, 1982.

Kail, Robert. *The Development of Memory in Children.* New York: W. H. Freeman and Company, 1984.

Keith, Timothy. *Homework.* West Lafayette, Indiana: Kappa Delta Pi, 1986.

LaConte, Ronald T., and Mary Anne Doyle. *Homework As a Learning Experience.* Washington, D.C.: National Education Association, 1986.

Lewis, Byron A., and R. Frank Pucelik. *Magic Demystified.* Lake Oswego, Oregon: Metamorphosis Press, 1982.

Link, Frances R., ed. *Essays on the Intellect.* Alexandria, Virginia: ASCD, 1985

Lipson, Eden Ross, ed. *The New York Times Parent's Guide to the Best Books for Children.* New York: Times Books, 1988.

Maker, Janet, and Minnette Lenier. *Keys to a Powerful Vocabulary.* Englewood Cliffs, New Jersey: Prentice Hall, 1988.

McCarthy, Bernice. *The 4MAT System.* Barrington, Illinois: EXCEL, 1987.

McKin, Robert H. *Experiences in Visual Thinking.* Belmont, California: Wadsworth, 1980.

Ornstein, Robert, and Richard F. Thompson. *The Amazing Brain.* Boston: Houghton Mifflin Company, 1984.

Ostrander, Sheila; Lynn Schroeder; with Nancy Ostrander. *Superlearning.* New York: Dell Publishing Company, 1979.

Packer, Alex J. *Bringing Up Parents.* Washington, D.C.: Acropolis Books, 1985.

Papert, Seymour. *Mindstorms: Children, Computers, and Powerful Ideas.* New York: Basic Books, 1980.

Pearce, Joseph Chilton. *Magical Child.* New York: E. P. Dutton, 1977.

————. *The Bond of Power.* New York: E. P. Dutton, 1981.

————. *Magical Child Matures*. New York: E. P. Dutton, 1985.

Perkins, David. *Knowledge As Design*. Hillsdale, New Jersey: Lawrence Erlbaum Associates, 1986.

————; Jack Lochhead; and John C. Bishop, eds. *Thinking, The Second International Congress*. Hillsdale, New Jersey: Lawrence Erlbaum Associates, 1987.

Ravitch, Diane, and Chester E. Finn, Jr. *What Do Our 17-Year-Olds Know?* New York: Harper and Row, 1987.

Restak, Richard. *The Brain—The Last Frontier*. New York: Warner Books, 1978.

Rico, Gabriele Lusser. *Writing the Natural Way: Using Right-Brain Techniques to Release Your Expressive Powers*. Los Angeles: J. P. Tarcher, 1983.

Robbins, Anthony. *Unlimited Power*. New York: Fawcett Columbine, 1986.

Samples, Bob; Cheryl Charles; and Dick Barnhart. *The Wholeschool Book*. Reading, Massachusetts: Addison-Wesley, 1977.

Stephens, Lillian S. *Developing Thinking Skills Through Real-Life Activities*. Newton, Massachusetts: Allyn and Bacon, 1983.

Sternberg, Robert. *Intelligence Applied: Understanding and Increasing Your Intellectual Skills*. Orlando, Florida: Harcourt Brace Jovanovich, 1986.

Trelease, Jim. *The Read-Aloud Handbook*. New York: Penguin Books, 1985.

Wahl, Mark. *A Mathematical Mystery Tour: Higher-Thinking Math Tasks*. Tucson: Zephyr Press, 1988.

Weiss, Helen Ginandes, and Martin S. Weiss. *Home Is a Learning Place: A Parent's Guide to Learning Disabilities*. Boston: Little, Brown and Company, 1976.

Winn, Marie. *The Plug-In Drug: Television, Children, and the Family*. New York: Penguin Books, 1985.

Zdenek, Marilee. *The Right-Brain Experience: An Intimate Program to Free the Powers of Your Imagination*. New York: McGraw-Hill Book Company, 1983.

Notes

Part One

Homework: Reframing an Old Subject

1. Frederic M. Levine and Kathleen Anesko, *Winning the Homework War* (New York: Prentice Hall, 1987), p. 177.

2. Herbert Walberg, Rosanne A. Paschal, and Thomas Weinstein, "Homework's Powerful Effects on Learning," *Educational Leadership*, April 1985, p. 79.

3. Levine and Anesko, loc. cit.

The Homework Brain

1. Richard Bandler, *Using Your Brain for a Change* edited by Connirae and Steve Andreas (Moab, Utah: Real People Press, 1985), p. 9.

2. For more information about Paul MacLean's research on the triune brain, read Paul MacLean, "The Triune Brain, Emotion, and Scientific Bias," in F. O. Schmidt, editor-in-chief, *The Neurosciences: Second Study Program* (New York: The Rockefeller University Press, 1970; Reprinted by the National Institutes of Health).

3. Joseph Chilton Pearce, *Magical Child Matures* (New York: E. P. Dutton, 1985), p. xix.

4. MacLean, op. cit., p. 339.

5. MacLean, loc. cit.

6. Robin Van Doren Beebe, "The Evolving Angel: Educating the Triune Brain," *Dromenon* 3:30. (This journal is no longer being published.)

7. MacLean, loc. cit.

8. Robert Ornstein and Richard Thompson, *The Amazing Brain* (Boston: Houghton Mifflin, 1984), p. 38.

9. Jerre Levey, "Children Think with Whole Brains: Myths and Reality," *Educational Leadership*, 40: 66–74.

10. For further information about choice systems, read Robert Fritz' *The Path of Least Resistance* (Salem, Massachusetts: Stillpoint Publishing Company, 1984).

Part Two

Week 2

1. Joseph Chilton Pearce, *Magical Child Matures* (New York: E. P. Dutton, 1985), p. 25. (This book is an excellent source for information about the developmental stages, triune brain, and bonding.)

2. Ibid., p. 19.

3. For more information about the seven intelligences, read Howard Gardner's *Frames of Mind* (New York: Basic Books, 1984).

4. Robert Sternberg, *Intelligence Applied* (Orlando, Florida: Harcourt Brace Jovanovich, 1986), p. 301.

5. Joseph M. Walters and Howard Gardner, "The Development and Education of Intelligences," edited by Francis R. Link, *Essays on the Intellect* (Alexandria, Virginia: ASCD, 1985), p. 16.

Week 3

1. Traditionally, among educators, the term "learning style" has referred to the external factors of learning. Dunn and Dunn, for example, at the Learning Style Network in New York, emphasize the learning environment with questions such as "Do you like to learn alone or with a group? What are your study preferences in terms of sound, classroom furniture, time of day, and temperature?" As pioneers of Learning Styles, they have done an excellent job of

making people aware of "outside the head" factors. But, be aware that if you mention "visual, auditory, kinesthetic" to teachers, most may think you are talking about lighting, seating, and so on, not internal brain processing.

2. Rita and Kenneth Dunn, *Teaching Students Through Their Individual Learning Styles: A Practical Approach* (Reston, Virginia: Reston Publishing Company, 1978), p. 13.

3. Richard Restak, *The Brain—The Last Frontier* (New York: Warner Books, 1978), p. 223.

4. Joseph Chilton Pearce, *Magical Child Matures* (New York: E. P. Dutton, 1985), p. 210.

5. Lawyers are almost always auditory. More than once when we've spoken at PTA meetings, we've asked how many parents read the encyclopedia as a child, and most of the people who raised their hands were lawyers. Encyclopedic information, as opposed to fiction and other kinds of narrations, is a very auditory kind of writing.

6. Joan Armstrong-Brisson, "Using NLP in the Elementary Classroom," *Anchor Point* 2:3.

Week 4

1. This exercise is based on Neuro-Linguistic Programming's Submodality Training. The following books contain more information about submodalities: Connirae and Steve Andreas, *Change Your Mind and Keep the Change* (Moab, Utah: Real People Press, 1987) and Richard Bandler, *Using Your Brain for a Change*, edited by Connirae and Steve Andreas (Moab, Utah: Real People Press, 1985).

2. This technique is called "Plus, Minus and Interesting" and is explained in CoRT materials. (See "Materials" section for address.)

3. This technique is adapted from a Neuro-Linguistic Programming seminar conducted by Connirae and Steve Andreas in Oakland, California, September 1986.

4. More information about this Neuro-Linguistic Programming technique can be found in the two books mentioned above by Connirae and Steve Andreas and Richard Bandler.

5. This "Success of Failure" technique was introduced by Leslie Cameron-Bandler in a Neuro-Linguistic Programming seminar held in San Francisco, California, in 1986.

Week 5

1. Joseph Chilton Pearce, *The Bond of Power* (New York: E. P. Dutton, 1981), p. 164.

2. Marie Winn, *The Plug-In Drug* (New York: Penguin Books, 1985), p. 4. Winn also notes that, "Preschoolers are the single largest television audience in America, spending a greater number of total hours and greater proportion of their working day watching television than any other age group. According to a 1983 Nielson report, children in the 2–5 age group, spend an average of 27.9 hours each week watching television while children in the 6–11 group spend 24.5 hours watching. Other surveys indicate even higher viewing times with figures up to 54 hours a week for preschool viewers."

3. We've known for a long time that visual training devices, such as computers and speed-reading machines, can train visual attention, but TV has the opposite effect.

4. Mihaly Csikszentmihalyi, "The Flow of Learning," *The Education Summit* (A conference held in Washington, D.C., June 25–29, 1988). This and other audiocassettes can be ordered from Sounds True, 1825 Pearl Street, Boulder, Colorado 80302; (303) 449-6229.

5. Csikszentmihalyi, loc. cit.

6. Pearce, op. cit., p. 162.

7. Mihaly Csikszentmihalyi and Reed Larson, *Being Adolescent: Conflict and Growth in the Teenage Years* (New York: Basic Books, 1984), p. 160.

8. Ibid., p. 161.

9. Peter Russell, *The Brain Book* (New York: Hawthorn Books, 1979), p. 96.

10. Gay Hendricks and Thomas Roberts, *The Second Centering Book* (Englewood Cliffs, New Jersey: Prentice-Hall, 1977), p. 6.

Week 6

1. Robert Kail, *The Development of Memory in Children* (New York: W. H. Freeman and Company, 1984), p. 25.

2. Carl Sagan, "The Persistence of Memory," *Cosmos* (KCET-TV, Program 11, 1982).

3. "Memory," *Newsweek,* September 29, 1986, p. 49.

4. John R. Hayes, *The Complete Problem Solver* (Hillsdale, New Jersey: Lawrence Erlbaum Associates, 1987), p. 102.

5. Thomas G. Devine, *Teaching Study Skills* (Newton, Massachusetts: Allyn and Bacon, 1987), p. 298.

6. Surgio Furgis, *Disney World Encyclopedias, Countries Volume* (Danbury, Conn.: Grolier, 1985). First published in Italy.

Part Three

Grades and Testing

1. Howard Gardner, "The School of the Future," *The Education Summit—June 25–29, 1988.* Conference audiotape available from Sounds True, 1825 Pearl Street, Boulder, Colorado 80302; (303) 449-6229.

2. Arthur Costa, "The School as Home for the Mind," *The Education Summit —June 25–29, 1988.* Conference audiotape available from Sounds True, 1825 Pearl Street, Boulder, Colorado 80302; (303) 449-6229.

3. Bernice Jensen Bragstad and Sharyn Mueller Stumpf, *A Guidebook for Teaching Study Skills and Motivation,* 2nd ed. (Newton, Massachusetts: Allyn and Bacon, 1987), pp. 289–90.

The Parent/Teacher Connection

1. Janice Wood, "School Based Homework Assistance Program." Paper presented at the Annual Meeting of the Florida Reading Association, Jacksonville, Florida, October 18–21, 1984.

Part Four

Homework Hotspot and Homework Helpers

1. William Allman, "Mindworks," *Science 86,* May 1986, p. 23.

2. David Perkins, "Mindware," *The Education Summit—June 25–29, 1988.* Conference audiotape available from Sounds True, 1825 Pearl Street, Boulder, Colorado 80302; (303) 449-6229.

Homework Hotspots

1. David Elkind, *The Hurried Child* (Reading, Massachusetts: Addison-Wesley, 1981), p. 33.

2. Faith Thompson, *Doctoral Thesis: Teachers' Knowledge of Selected Skills from the Florida Catalog of Reading Objectives* (Tallahassee: Florida State University, 1972), Chapter V.

3. For further information about talking books, contact the National Library Service for the Blind and Physically Handicapped, The Library of Congress, Washington, D.C. 20542; (202) 882-5500.

4. Robert Dilts, *Neuro-Linguistic Programming in Education* (Santa Cruz, California: Not Ltd., 1980), p. 13.

5. George A. Miller and Patricia M. Gildea, "A New Way to Teach Children Words," The Washington *Post,* August 30, 1987, C3.

6. Janet Maker and Minnette Lenier, *Keys to a Powerful Vocabulary* (Englewood Cliffs, New Jersey: Prentice Hall, 1988), pp. 3–4.

7. Edward de Bono, *Wordpower* (New York: Viking Penguin, 1979).

8. Sheila Ostrander and Lynn Schroeder, *Superlearning* (New York: Dell Publishing, 1979). pp. 6–7.

9. Myriam Met, "Tomorrow's Emphasis in Foreign Language: Proficiency," *Content of the Curriculum: 1988 ASCD Yearbook* (Alexandria, Virginia: ASCD, 1988), p. 96.

10. Richard Restak, *The Brain—The Last Frontier* (New York: Warner Books), pp. 218–19.

11. Bernice Jensen Bragstad and Sharyn Mueller Stumpf, *A Guidebook for Teaching Study Skills and Motivation,* 2nd ed. (Newton, Massachusetts: Allyn and Bacon, 1987), p. 177.

12. John R. Hayes, *The Complete Problem Solver,* (Hillsdale, New Jersey: Lawrence Erlbaum Associates, 1987), p. 123.

13. Paraphrased from Kevin O'Reilly, "Infusing Critical Thinking into U.S. History Courses," *Thinking Skills Newsletter,* Spring, 1988, p. 12. (This newsletter can be ordered from the Pennsylvania Department of Education, Harrisburg, Pennsylvania.)

14. Ernest Boyer, "On the High School Curriculum: A Conversation with Ernest Boyer," *Educational Leadership,* 46:6.

15. Vera Bej, "Teaching Thinking and Social Studies," *Thinking Skills Newsletter,* Summer 1988, p. 8.

16. Boyer, op. cit., p. 6.

Homework Helpers

1. For additional information about Superlearning, read Sheila Ostrander and Lynn Schroeder's book, *Superlearning* (New York: Dell Publishing, 1979).

2. Ron Brandt, "On Assessment in the Arts: A Conversation with Howard Gardner," *Educational Leadership*, December 1987/January 1988, p. 31.

3. Jerry Tollifson, "A Balanced Comprehensive Art Curriculum Makes Sense," *Educational Leadership*, December 1987/January 1988, p. 19.

4. "Our Children Are Fat, Not Fit," *Learning 88*, April 1988, p. 12.

5. Encounter bats can be ordered from Uniquities, Galt, California 95632; (209) 745-2111.

6. George Leonard, *The Ultimate Athlete* (New York: Avon Books, 1977), p. 238.

7. Jean Houston, *The Possible Human* (Los Angeles: J. P Tarcher, 1982), p. 18. (The complete kinesthetic body exercise can be found in this book.)

Index

About the Authors Cecil Clark, clinical psychologist, and Faith Clark, educator, opened the Human Development Clinic in suburban Washington, D.C., in 1975. The clinic is a unique professional practice combining psychotherapy, advanced educational technology, and learning style analysis. The Clarks and their staff, understanding that the major impediments to better learning and living are irrational beliefs, inappropriate emotions, and poor habits, form a trusting therapeutic bond with each adult, adolescent, or child client.

The learning style of each client is analyzed to find the underutilized strengths of that individual. This is more efficient and enjoyable than the negative focus on disabilities common in special education. Clients are usually eager to understand their own brain function and to learn how to use this knowledge to take control of their lives and learning. Motivation, organization, and self-confidence follow.

The clinic draws upon a large collection of computer applications and mind technologies to prescribe a development plan for each individual based on psychological testing and learning-style analysis. The client works with an individual therapist to master these techniques, first in the lab, then in life.

The National Learning Laboratory was incorporated in 1984 as a non-profit research and training supplement to the clinic. NLL offers training in Learning Therapy to professionals and gives courses in thinking and learning to all who are interested.

Before opening the clinic both Clarks were teachers. Faith earned a doctorate in education from Florida State University. Cecil is a graduate of Vanderbilt University with a doctorate in psychology. He has also been a researcher for a large public school system. He holds certificates from the Institute for Rational-Emotive Therapy in New York and from the Washington School of Psychiatry.

Each of the Clarks went through school with a major visual impairment, but they chose to find new ways to see and learn. This experience, along with their supportive parents, was the basis for the belief that they convey to their clients that the human mind is more powerful than any limitation that can be placed upon it by handicap or deprivation.

The Clarks believe that only one thing is more wholesome or more fun than exploring one's mental potential. And that is to make others aware of the infinite power and joy there is in learning about their own minds. When a mind is turned on to itself and cleared of neurotic loops and blind assumptions, then all knowledge and skills are eagerly mastered. Learning, that formerly required will power and suffering, now becomes absorbing and self-sustaining.

Marta Vogel is an independent journalist and author specializing in health and psychology. She is the coauthor with Diana Frank of *The Babymakers* (Carroll and Graf, 1988), a book about the legal, ethical and social problems of test-tube babies, artificial insemination, and surrogate mothers. She has written for numerous publications, including *Savvy, The Washington Post, Washington Woman, Regardie's, Runner's World, Creative Living, National Wildlife, Parents*, Time-Life Books, and the Gannett News Service. She has also taught at the Bernhardt Striegel Gymnasium in Memmingen, West Germany, at Texas Tech University, and at the University of Maryland.

BOOK MARK

The text of this book was composed in
the typeface Goudy Oldstyle
by Crane Typesetting, Inc.,
West Barnstable, Massachusetts

This book was printed
by R. R. Donnelley & Sons Company
Harrisonburg, Virginia

ILLUSTRATION BY JACKIE AHER

BOOK DESIGN
BY LAURIE JEWELL